WORKPLACE PRIVACY
REAL ANSWERS AND PRACTICAL SOLUTIONS
2nd Edition

Barbara S. Magill, Esq. and Worklaw Network

Edited by Burton J. Fishman, Esq.

Thompson Publishing Group, Inc.
1725 K St. NW, 7th Floor
Washington, DC 20006
202-872-4000 (Editorial Offices)
1-800-677-3789 (Customer Service
www.thompson.com

THOMPSON

Insight you trust.

⋔ THOMPSON

Thompson Publishing Group, Inc.

Thompson Publishing Group is a trusted name in authoritative analysis of laws, regulations and business practices that helps corporate, government and other professionals develop regulatory compliance strategies. Since 1972, thousands of professionals in business, government, law and academia have relied on Thompson Publishing Group for the most authoritative, timely and practical guidance available.

Thompson offers loose leaf services, books, specialty newsletters, audio conferences and online products in a number of subject and regulatory compliance areas. These Thompson products provide insightful analysis, practical guidance and real-world solutions to the challenges facing grants professionals today and beyond. More information about Thompson's product offerings is available at http://www.thompson.com.

To order any Thompson products or additional copies of this book, please contact us:

Call: 1-800-677-3789
Online: www.thompson.com
Fax: 1-800-999-5661
Email: service@thompson.com
Mail: Thompson Publishing Group
Subscription Service Center
PO Box 26185, Tampa, FL 33623-6185

Authors: Members of Worklaw Network
Barbara S. Magill, Esq.

Editor: Burton J. Fishman, Esq.

Desktop Publisher: Brock G. McClung

Cover design: Dan Zimmerman

Indexer: Kate Mertes

Acknowledgement: David M. Safon, Esq., now deceased, was the principal author of the first edition of this book

Workplace Privacy: Real Answers and Practical Solutions, 2nd Edition, is published by Thompson Publishing Group, Inc., 1725 K St. N.W., 7th Floor, Washington, DC 20006.

This publication is designed to be accurate and authoritative, but the publisher is not rendering legal, accounting or other professional services. If legal or other expert advice is desired, retain the services of an appropriate professional.

Printed in the United States

ISBN-10: 1-933807-05-9
ISBN-13: 978-1-933807-05-8

About This Book

Workplace Privacy examines one of the most difficult issues facing
you as employers, managers and human resource professionals today
— balancing the interests of your companies' need to know with your
employees' privacy rights. This balancing act cuts through a cross-section
of human resources and managerial endeavors: recruiting and hiring, conducting workplace investigations of alleged wrongdoing, controlling employee
behavior on and off site, and disclosing personnel, medical and other information
and records.

Electronic technologies such as the Internet, e-mail and network computers have given
employees more sophisticated methods of communicating and doing personal business
during work hours. They also have provided new ways to monitor employee behavior,
but at the same time saddled you with a host of new considerations and challenges with
regard to employee privacy rights, including protecting your workers from identify theft.

The right to privacy is one most American workers hold dear. It was recognized by the
U.S. Supreme Court as implicit in the U.S. Constitution and there are numerous federal
laws dealing with employee privacy. However, since 9/11, there are other laws that permit
intrusion into the workplace and require you to provide information that may have been
considered private in the past. More balancing is now required of you.

States also have adopted numerous constitutional provisions and statutes dealing with
employee privacy. *Workplace Privacy* emphasizes that it is imperative for you to understand
your state laws in addition to applicable federal laws. Failure to understand the nuances of
governing state laws can expose you to significant liability.

That's where the *"Real Answers and Practical Solutions"* come into play. Each problem discussed here includes both federal and state-by-state discussions, and features charts listing
state policies by issue for quick reference. The information was written by legal experts
and consultants, some of whom have an HR background. They are based on best practices
in the field and will help you avoid pitfalls and litigation, as well as improve the overall
management of your workforce.

What's Inside

Workplace Privacy is divided into six sections. Section I explains the overall legal framework and gives a brief description of the main federal laws that deal with workplace privacy. A quiz to test your knowledge of the numerous workplace privacy issues follows. The results may surprise you, as you find the answers by reading the referenced chapters.

Section II shows you how to conduct an effective recruitment and hiring process by maintaining a careful balance between obtaining as much information about an applicant as possible while adhering to the myriad of restrictions imposed by state and federal laws and respecting applicants' privacy rights.

Section III guides you through workplace investigations of alleged wrongdoing. It provides a thorough understanding of the sources of potential liability and shows how to conduct surveillance and searches of employee personal spaces without violating any laws. It also includes checklists on the investigation process in general and investigating sexual harassment in particular.

Section IV examines the limits to controlling employee behavior both on and off duty. Dating, smoking and nepotism are just some of the issues you face, especially as the "virtual office" blurs the division between workplace and personal space.

Section V deals with the electronic workplace and how to tell what your employees really are doing on those computers. It gives the pros and cons of monitoring and provides some sample policies to adapt for your workplace.

Section VI examines your rights and those of your employees to all of those personnel records you collect. Medical records especially are a potential minefield of liability under a number of laws. You will see how to reduce that liability.

Each section includes appropriate sample policies and at-a-glance checklists and charts. The appendices in the back of *Workplace Privacy* give guidelines on pre-employment inquiries and medical examinations, and provide Fair Credit Reporting Act and other forms. Indexes to both the court cases and the subjects covered in the book provide quick reference.

We think you will find this to be the easiest to understand and most complete book of its kind.

Our Guarantee

Please take a minute to review **Workplace Privacy.** You have our 30-day risk-free guarantee. We are confident that the book will become a trusted resource for your HR program. If you don't agree, just return the book to us with the enclosed invoice.

If we can be of any assistance, please do not hesitate to contact our customer service department at 1-800-677-3789.

About the Authors and Editor

Many of the law firms of the authors who contributed to the original edition of this book are members of the Worklaw Network, a coast-to-coast affiliation of independent law firms devoted to representing management in all facets of labor, employment and employee benefits law. The Worklaw Network can be reached at http://www.worklawnetwork.net.

David M. Safon, Esq., the principal author of the first edition of this work, died June 10, 2006, at the age of 43. A partner in the New York office of Ford & Harrison at the time of his death, he was a widely respected labor and employment lawyer with a knack for writing about complicated issues for human resource professionals.

Barbara S. Magill, Esq., is a senior managing editor at Thompson Publishing Group. She has written and edited numerous books on employment law, including the first edition of this book, and has particular expertise in the Americans With Disabilities Act, the Family and Medical Leave Act and the Uniformed Services Employment and Reemployment Rights Act. She served as an HR generalist prior to joining Thompson, with responsibility for benefits, equal employment opportunity and the company's affirmative action plan. Before that she was in private law practice in Illinois.

Burton J. Fishman, Esq., is of counsel with Fortney & Scott, LLC, a Washington, D.C., law firm specializing in labor and employment law. A former U.S. Labor Department deputy solicitor, he is co-chairman of the American Bar Association's Federal Legislative Development Committee. He devotes his practice to developing the "law of the workplace," an interdisciplinary approach that offers employers counsel and representation on a broad range of matters growing out of government regulation of business. He has written more than 70 books and articles on employment law.

Table of Contents

About This Book...**.i**

    What's Inside ii

    Our Guarantee ii

About the Authors and Editor ....**iii**

SECTION I: The Legal Framework **1**

Federal Laws **5**

Test Your Knowledge Quiz **9**

SECTION II: Recruitment and Hiring **13**

Pre-employment Inquiries **15**

    Application Forms...15

    Interviews..16

    Checklist 20

Screening..**23**

    Background Checks 23

    Employment References 29

    Medical Examinations and Inquiries 32

    Lie Detectors 37

    Other Tests — Honesty, Personality.......................................40

SECTION III: Workplace Investigations.......................**43**

Sources of Potential Liability **45**

    Common Law Rights 46

    Causes of Action for Wrongful Discharge 54

    Special Considerations With Sexual and Other Harassment ...58

Surveillance and Searches **61**

    Tape-Recording Telephone Conversations 61

    Workplace Conversations 63

    Video Monitoring 63

    Opening U.S. Mail 64

    Searching Personal Spaces 64

    USA PATRIOT Act 65

Pointers on Workplace Investigations..**69**

    Investigations Process...69

    Investigating Sexual Harassment 73

SECTION IV: Controlling Employee Behavior On and Off Duty **75**

Employee Dating **77**

    No Fraternization Policy 81

Smoking **83**

    Protecting Rights of Smokers 84

Telephone Use **89**

    Hospital/Nursing Home Telephone Use...90

    Professional Office Personal Use of Office Equipment and Supplies............90

Workplace Appearance...**91**

    EEOC Position 91

    State Laws and Cases..93

    Fashioning Policy 94

    Personal Appearance...94

Nepotism and Favoritism **95**

    Nepotism..95

    Favoritism 98

Public Statements by Employees (Duty of Loyalty) **101**

SECTION V: The Electronic Workplace...**105**

Computer Monitoring...**107**

    Employee Privacy or Employer Property?...107

    Reasons for Monitoring...110

    ESI Preservation Rules 112

    Union Solicitation and Other Protected Concerted Activity 112

    Defamation and Copyright Infringement..116

    Trade Secrets and Confidential Information 117

    Legal Restrictions on Employer's Ability To Monitor.................................118

    Invasion of Privacy 121

Blogging and Instant Messaging **123**

    Instant Messaging...125

Sample Computer and Electronic Communications Systems Policies.....**127**

    Need for Written Policy...127

Contents of Policy 127

Policy 1 — Broad Computer and Electronic Communications Systems Policy 128

Policy 2 — E-Mail, Voice Mail and Internet Usage 130

Policy 3 — Computer Use 130

Policy 4 — E-Mail Use 131

Policy 5 — E-Mail Systems 132

Policy 6 — Sample Release 134

SECTION VI: Disclosure of Workplace Records **135**

Personnel Files **137**

Defining 'Personnel File' 138

Recordkeeping Requirements 141

Employee Requests for Access 142

Disclosure to Former Employees 144

Protecting Against Identity Theft 145

Requests by Government Agencies, Attorneys and Others....................................148

Helpful Hints in Responding to Government Inquiries 149

Business Concerns, or Just Because the Law Says You Can, Should You?.............150

Employee Access to Personnel Records 150

Medical Records **153**

What Are Medical Records? 155

HIPAA 155

State Laws 157

Employee Assistance Programs 162

**APPENDIX I: State and EEOC Guidance on Pre-employment
and Disability Inquiries** **163**

Guidelines for Pre-employment Inquiries 165

U.S. Equal Employment Opportunity Commission..167

ADA Enforcement Guidance: Pre-employment Disability-Related Questions
and Medical Examinations 167

Introduction...167

Background 167

The Statutory and Regulatory Framework...168

The Pre-offer Stage..169

The Post-offer Stage 177

Confidentiality 179

Footnotes to ADA Enforcement Guidance: Pre-employment Disability-Related
Questions and Medical Examinations 181

APPENDIX II: Federal Fair Credit Reporting Act Forms **183**

Sample Certification for User of Consumer Report...184

Sample Notification and Authorization for Release of Consumer Report 185

Sample Pre-adverse Action Letter...186

A Summary of Your Rights Under the Fair Credit Reporting Act (FCRA)......................187

Sample Adverse Action Letter...190

Sample Notification and Authorization for Release of Investigative Consumer Report...191

A Summary of Your Rights Under the California Investigative Consumer
Reporting Agencies Act 192

Index..**193**

List of Sample Policies

No Fraternization...**70**

Hospital/Nursing Home Telephone Use.............................**77**

Professional Office Personal Use of Office Equipment and Supplies.........**78**

Personal Appearance **81**

Broad Computer and Electronic Communications Systems Policy **106**

E-mail, Voice Mail and Internet Usage.............................**107**

Computer Use **108**

E-mail Use...**109**

E-mail Systems..**110**

Sample Release **112**

Employee Access to Personnel Records...........................**124**

List of Figures

Fig. 4-1   Positions and/or Employers for Which Background Checks Are Required

Fig. 5-1   States That Recognize Private Employees' Rights to Privacy

Fig. 5-2   False Light Invasion of Privacy

Fig. 5-3   Privileges From Defamation Claims

Fig. 5-4   State At-Will and Wrongful Discharge Doctrines

Fig. 7-1   Pointers on Investigations Process

Fig. 8-1   State Statutes Addressing Employee Dating and Courts Upholding No Fraternization Policy

Fig. 12-1   States With Laws Prohibiting Discrimination on Basis of Marital Status

Fig. 17-1   Unofficial Personnel Files

Fig. 17-2   Federal Requirements for Employee Records

Fig. 17-3   State Personnel File Access Statutes

Fig. 18-1   Constitutional Right to Privacy

Fig. 18-2   HIPAA Privacy Terms

Fig. 18-3   State Medical Records Laws

SECTION I:
The Legal Framework

The technological capabilities now available in virtually every office in the United States provide greater opportunities for surveillance and intrusion into employees' conduct than ever before. Fortunately, neither employers nor legislators believe those capabilities should be used to pry into people's private lives. Indeed, the trend in the law is to use those technological capabilities not for snooping, but to protect sensitive personal data from thieves, hackers and opportunists.

In the workplace, technological advances and devices enable employees to shop, chat, blog, game and view almost without end. At the same time, employers have the capability to monitor many more aspects of their employees' workday, from the time of their arrival to the rate of production, even if they are using the company's computers for unauthorized activities. Looming over all of this are the twin fears of misuse of company equipment and of the loss of sensitive information, either through inadvertence, carelessness or theft. Indeed, the new world of workplace privacy is concerned as much with protecting employees and protecting information as it is with protecting privacy.

The legal landscape reflects this changing world. Everyone is far more aware today of the availability of electronic data, including personal data, and of the fragility of the means available to protect it and to protect those who need it and use it.

Over the past 20 years, the workplace has become much more regulated and the rights of employees have been given increased legal protections. In the federal arena alone, the Americans With Disabilities Act of 1990, the Civil Rights Act of 1991, the Family and Medical Leave Act of 1993, the Older Workers' Benefits Protection Act, the Worker Adjustment and Retraining Notification Act (also known as WARN, or the Plant Closing Law), the Consolidated Omnibus Budget Reconciliation Act (or COBRA), the Health Insurance Portability and Accountability Act, Fair and Accurate Credit Transaction Act of 2003, and the Uniformed Services Employment and Reemployment Rights Act, just to name a few, have been enacted.

Although these laws often impose duties and obligations on employers and employees, they are, for the most part, important landmarks in expanding employee rights. Some of these laws, particularly the ADA, HIPPA and credit transaction act, include significant protections for employee personal information, particularly with respect to health and financial credit.

By the same token, as their responsibilities have increased, employers have become both more wary and more diligent about protecting sensitive information and policing the ways the information could be lost, stolen or misused. In the wake of 9/11, the federal government's powers to gain access to certain employee information has increased. Moreover, increased enforcement of certain immigration laws has put employers in the middle of the country's most challenging social and political debates.

It is no surprise, in this context, that workplace privacy issues have arisen with increasing frequency and have attracted the attention of courts and legislators on both the federal and state levels.

Like defensive driving, an employer's most effective tool in dealing with contemporary workplace privacy is the ability to become aware of the range of responsibilities now placed at the employer's door and the means by which those obligations can be met. Once aware of the potential issues, the employer often can take steps to eliminate, or at least minimize, the risk of loss and of liability.

As a threshold matter, an employer should have a basic understanding of the legal framework of the expanded world of workplace privacy. What laws exist in this area? How are they enforced? What information must be protected? What information can be protected? What procedures and practices should be used? Where can a victimized employer or an aggrieved employee go for redress? Does any government agency play a role?

For public employees, the U.S. Constitution protects certain privacy rights against state or federal government action. The Fourth Amendment's right against unreasonable searches and seizures often is cited when public employer searches of employee offices are challenged. In 1987, for example, the U.S. Supreme Court in *O'Connor v. Ortega* (480 U.S. 709) ruled that the appropriate inquiry when a state hospital searched its employee's office, desk and file cabinet was whether the workplace environment created a "reasonable expectation of privacy" for the employee.

For employees of private companies, any such protections are more likely to be found in the state law, particularly the common law — a body of law based on judicial decisions that has developed over time and, indeed, continues to develop. In some jurisdictions, employee rights to privacy are found to be explicit or implied in a particular state's constitution; other times, a common law right to privacy is premised on the state's public policy — fundamental notions of due process and fairness.

Even within the framework of these laws, employers often need to intrude on their employees' privacy both to protect proprietary and sensitive personal information, to protect against potential liability for such things as sexual harassment and trademark infringement, and even to monitor for abuse of company policies regarding the appropriate use of the Internet. It is always advisable to have a policy in place beforehand so employees know what to expect. The checklist below provides a guide to follow before adopting a privacy policy or even determining whether one is needed.

If You Contemplate Adopting a Privacy Policy

Before determining what, if any, policies and procedures to adopt that restrict employee privacy rights, an employer should consider the following:

✓ **Determine business justification.** Employee privacy rights vary among different industries and job duties as well as between public and private employer. Decide what the business reason is for your action.

✓ **Review federal law.** Review the federal laws applicable to your industry and the job duties of the affected employees to ensure compliance. Don't forget to consider any applicable constitutional issues.

✓ **Review state and local laws.** Many employee privacy rights are derived from state laws. Review both state and local laws to determine if they impose more or different restrictions on employers than the federal laws do.

If the decision is to have a policy that in some way would restrict privacy rights in the workplace, the following procedures should be followed:

✓ **Draft a written policy.** A written policy should clearly explain the procedures you plan to implement. The policy should be reviewed by upper management and a legal advisor.

✓ **Communicate the policy.** Distribute the policy to current employees and update your employee handbook as necessary. Make sure all new employees receive and review the policy.

✓ **Obtain acknowledgement/consent.** Require employees to review and sign a form acknowledging that they have received and understood your policy.

Federal Laws

1

While most employee privacy rights are rooted in state law, both statutory and judicial, there are a number of federal laws that have an impact on privacy in the workplace. Some of these are employment discrimination laws, some are based on consumer rights and others on labor union rights. Consider the following federal laws:

- *Title VII of the Civil Rights Act of 1964* (42 U.S.C. §2000e *et seq.*) prohibits discrimination against employees and job applicants on the basis of race, color, religion, gender or national origin, including limitations on the questions that can be asked of applicants.

- *The Age Discrimination in Employment Act of 1967 (ADEA)* (29 U.S.C. §621 *et seq.*) prohibits discrimination against employees and job applicants aged 40 and older, including limitations on pre-employment inquiries.

- *The Fair Credit Reporting Act (FCRA)* (15 U.S.C. §1681 *et seq.*) governs credit and criminal background checks by consumer reporting agencies.

- *The Fair and Accurate Credit Transactions Act (FACT Act)* (Pub. L. No. 108-159, Dec. 4, 2003) amends the Fair Credit Reporting Act by requiring any person who maintains or otherwise possesses consumer information or any compilation of consumer information derived from consumer reports for a business purpose to properly dispose of it.

- *The Employee Polygraph Protection Act of 1988* (29 U.S.C. §2001 *et seq.*) limits the use by private employers of lie detector tests either as employment screening devices or during the course of workplace investigations.

- *The Drug-Free Workplace Act of 1988* (41 U.S.C. §701-§707) requires recipients of federal contracts and grants — private employers included — to adopt programs designed to reduce the workplace use of illegal drugs.

- *The National Labor Relations Act (NLRA)* (29 U.S.C. §151-§169) protects the rights of employees to support or not to support labor organizations and to engage in "protected concerted activity" for their "mutual aid or protection," including restrictions on what may be asked of job applicants regarding union membership and on the permissible responses of employers to collective action by employees, whether or not represented by a union.

- *The Americans With Disabilities Act of 1990 (ADA)* (42 U.S.C. §12111 *et seq.*) protects the rights of qualified individuals with disabilities, including limitations on the information that can be requested of protected individuals and confidentiality requirements for information generated through medical inquiries and examinations.

- *The Family and Medical Leave Act of 1993 (FMLA)* (29 U.S.C. §2601 *et seq.*) entitles covered individuals to 12 weeks of unpaid leave from work for the birth or adoption of a child or for the employee's or a family member's serious health condition and includes limitations on the information that can be required of employees seeking protected leave.

- *The Omnibus Crime Control and Safe Streets Act* (18 U.S.C. §2510 *et seq.*) prohibits wiretapping (including telephone monitoring by employers, depending on the circumstances) and other forms of electronic surveillance, with certain exceptions, by those not involved in law enforcement.

- *The Immigration Reform and Control Act (IRCA)* (8 U.S.C. §1324a and b) prohibits national origin and citizenship discrimination against individuals properly authorized to work in the United States, including mandating strict compliance with Form I-9 and preventing "documentation abuse" by employers seeking to screen out aliens through unnecessarily intrusive inquiries and burdensome documentation requirements.

- *The Health Insurance Portability and Accountability Act (HIPAA)* (Pub. L. 104-191, Aug. 21, 1996) as implemented by the Department of Health and Human Services regulations (45 C.F.R. §164.500 *et seq.*) governs the use and disclosure of employee health information. While the rules are not technically aimed at employers, those that administer health plans or employ a health plan provider must comply with the act's privacy requirements. Employers that come under the rules may release protected health information only if the covered individual authorizes in writing its use or disclosure.

- *The Homeland Security Act* (Pub. L. No. 107-296, Nov. 25, 2002) extends the good faith defenses of the Electronic Communication Privacy Act of 1986 to Internet service providers (and employers) so that the contents of electronic communications may be disclosed when they, in good faith, believe an emergency involving danger of death or serious injury to others requires immediate disclosure.

- *The Uniting and Strengthening America by Providing Appropriate Tools Required to Intercept and Obstruct Terrorism Act (USA PATRIOT Act)* (Pub. L. No. 107-56, Oct. 26, 2001) requires employers to provide private information about their employees to law enforcement authorities in more ways than before the law was passed. It permits some intrusion by the federal government into electronic communications, including those available from Internet service providers. Employers may be ordered to keep the law enforcement monitoring of e-mail, voice mail or other electronic communications secret from individuals under surveillance.

This list is by no means all-inclusive, even as to federal law alone. It also does not include the many state laws that cover some of the same areas as the laws listed as well as topics such as protections for off-duty legal activities, religious observances, the confidentiality of genetic information and prohibitions on the use of applicant screening devices such as voice stress analyzers and fingerprinting.

What is clear is that employers must be attuned to all the laws of the workplace, no matter their source. Focusing exclusively on the federal laws now in existence will not suffice, just as ignoring those laws in favor of laws in the state(s) in which a company does business can prove disastrous.

Equally important is keeping current on the laws affecting privacy and their development. While discrimination laws have made great strides in the years since Title VII first appeared, efforts to address privacy concerns are still in their relative infancy. Employers can, and should, expect much to happen in the immediate future.

Test Your Knowledge Quiz

2

Before going further, it may be wise to assess your knowledge of employer/employee rights and obligations vis-à-vis workplace privacy. Privacy issues, perhaps more than most in the employment area, often hold surprises, even for the seasoned human resources professional. Misconceptions are common; employers often are certain of the answers, only to find they are wrong on the law.

So, take a few moments and, with pencil in hand, test yourself with this sampling. Is the statement TRUE or FALSE in your state? Do you know why? Are you sure? *(References are provided to the chapters of this book in which the topics are discussed.)*

- An employer may remind a job applicant to bring a driver's license and Social Security card to an interview. *(Chapter 3)*

    (T) ☐   (F) ☐

- An employer may terminate an employee who is arrested for a crime that could affect its business, e.g., theft. *(Chapters 3 and 4)*

    (T) ☐   (F) ☐

- Random drug tests by private employers are unlawful unless authorized by the U.S. Department of Transportation. *(Chapter 4)*

    (T) ☐   (F) ☐

- If the employer intends to conduct a criminal background check on an applicant through use of an outside agency, it must include written authorization to do so on the job application form. *(Chapter 4)*

    (T) ☐   (F) ☐

- A company can be liable for defamation damages if it tells a prospective employer that its former employee is "not eligible for rehire." *(Chapter 4)*

    (T) ☐   (F) ☐

- Lie detector tests may be given to employees who have been accused of sexual harassment. *(Chapter 4)*

  (T) ❑   (F) ☑

- When an employer uses a third party to investigate workplace misconduct, it does not have to notify the target of the investigation. *(Chapter 4)*

  (T) ☑   (F) ❑

- An employer may include the results of medical examinations and inquiries in the personnel file as long as they are kept in a separate folder or envelope. *(Chapters 4, 16 and 17)*

  (T) ☑   (F) ❑

- An employer can be held liable for sexual harassment even when the complaining employee insists on confidentiality and asks that the employer take no action. *(Chapter 5)*

  (T) ☑   (F) ❑

- Statements made by managers about employees are absolutely protected from defamation claims as long as they are not made to anyone outside the company. *(Chapter 5)*

  (T) ❑   (F) ☑

- A supervisor who gives an employee a false reason for termination is only liable for defamation if the supervisor "publishes" the defamatory statement to others. *(Chapter 5)*

  (T) ❑   (F) ☑

- An employee is entitled to have an attorney present at a search of his or her locker or desk. *(Chapter 6)*

  (T) ❑   (F) ☑

- An employee may lawfully tape-record his or her conversations with a supervisor without that supervisor's knowledge. *(Chapter 6)*

  (T) ❑   (F) ☑

- Employees may be videotaped without their knowledge or consent as long as there is no sound component to the taping. *(Chapter 6)*

  (T) ☑   (F) ❑

- An employer may search an employee's locker without his or her knowledge or consent, even without any reasonable suspicion of wrongdoing by the employee. *(Chapter 6)*

  (T) ☑   (F) ❑

- A bargaining unit employee has the right to have a union representative present at a workplace search. *(Chapter 6)*

  (T) ☑   (F) ❑

- An employer may enforce a policy stating that, for security reasons, it will open all U.S. mail delivered to the company, even if addressed to an employee. *(Chapter 6)*

  (T) ❑   (F) ☑

- An employee's electronic workplace communications can be monitored by a law enforcement agency without notice. *(Chapter 6)*

  (T) ☑   (F) ❑

- A company may prohibit employee dating. *(Chapter 8)*

  (T) ☑   (F) ❑

- An employer must provide its employees with at least two breaks, one in the morning and one in the afternoon, within which to smoke. *(Chapter 9)*

  (T) ☑   (F) ❑

- An employer may not prohibit personal use of the telephone by an employee who can establish a compelling reason for making a call during working hours. *(Chapter 10)*

  (T) ❑   (F) ☑

- An employer can enforce a strict dress code in the workplace, including a prohibition on body piercing and tattoos. *(Chapter 11)*

  (T) ☑   (F) ❑

- Despite laws regarding sexual harassment, a supervisor is permitted to give someone he is dating the best assignments. *(Chapter 12)*

  (T) ❑   (F) ☑

- An employee may be fired for disloyal statements made while off duty. *(Chapter 13)*

  (T) ❑   (F) ☑

- A company may prohibit solicitations by a labor union made to employees through their workplace e-mail. *(Chapter 14)*

  (T) ❑   (F) ☑

- Employer-owned instant messaging equipment does not have the same employee privacy/employer property issues as computers. *(Chapter 15)*

  (T) ❑   (F) ☑

- A labor union has the right to see a bargaining unit employee's personnel file. *(Chapter 17)*

  (T) ☐   (F) ☑

- Employees generally have a legal right to see their personnel files. *(Chapter 17)*

  (T) ☑   (F) ☐

- Some states restrict an employer's use of its employees' Social Security numbers. *(Chapter 17)*

  (T) ☑   (F) ☐

- An employer must provide a former employee's attorney with a copy of the personnel file, if requested, prior to a hearing regarding unemployment insurance benefits. *(Chapter 17)*

  (T) ☑   (F) ☐

- Employers are not affected by HIPAA privacy rules because they apply only to health plans, not employers. *(Chapter 18)*

  (T) ☐   (F) ☑

If you are not quite sure of your answers, you are not alone. Many experts, attorneys included, also are uncomfortable with betting on their workplace privacy knowledge, particularly when a wrong answer can mean significant liability — sometimes, even personal liability.

So, read on. When you are through with the book, take the test again.

Above all, be sure to consult with an attorney or other skilled consultant before making real life decisions to ascertain the current law in your state.

SECTION II:
Recruitment and Hiring

An employer's first opportunity to attract and retain productive employees and avoid liability comes at the earliest stage of the employment relationship — the recruitment process. Some employers may view the recruitment of employees as an unpleasant, costly burden, but the value of an effective recruitment process should not be minimized.

If done properly, not only will the process achieve its bottom-line goal of filling the open position, but the employer will locate a valuable asset: a qualified, motivated employee. On the other hand, an unsuccessful recruitment process is not merely one that fails to find a qualified applicant, but one that results instead in the acquisition of a potential liability — an employee who causes damage, or simply proves to be litigious.

Conducting an effective recruitment process requires maintaining a careful balance between obtaining as much information about an applicant as possible, while adhering to the myriad of restrictions imposed by state and federal laws, and respecting the applicant's privacy interests.

The key to remember is: focus on the job you are trying to fill and the skills necessary to perform well the essential functions of that job. If the information being sought is not necessary to judge the applicant's competence for performing the job, do not ask the question.

Chapter 3 focuses on pre-employment inquiries. State and federal fair employment practice laws prohibit discrimination on the basis of race, gender, national origin, religion, age and disability, among other things. Asking some questions on application forms or during job interviews can raise issues with regard to these protected classes. The chapter includes a helpful checklist to prepare for the interview process.

Chapter 4 discusses the screening process and the types of background checks that are and are not permitted under various state and federal laws. It also discusses what medical information may and may not be obtained and the types of pre-employment testing that are permitted.

Pre-employment Inquiries

An employer uses the recruitment process to its best advantage by taking care to fashion job applications and conduct interviews to weed out undesirable candidates and introduce ideal candidates to the company. Employers cannot afford to ignore, however, the fact that they risk litigation each time they seek information about a candidate's identifying characteristics, personal life, employment history and other matters that could be privileged or could create the appearance of discrimination.

Application Forms

The first opportunity to gather information and begin sifting through potential hires is the employment application. But it is even more than that. The application can be an important document in an employment-related lawsuit. The questions and information contained in it could become the basis of a wrongful discharge or failure-to-hire discrimination claim, or, if used properly, it could provide a defense for an employer faced with those claims. Regrettably, numerous unwitting employers have been subjected to charges that the employment applications they used contained unlawful questions.

The Equal Employment Opportunity Commission (EEOC) has identified three basic questions an employer should consider when determining whether a particular question should be included on an employment application:

1. Does this question tend to have a disproportionate effect in screening out minorities or females?

2. Is the requested information necessary to judge this individual's competence for performing the job?

3. Are there alternative nondiscriminatory ways to secure the necessary information?

Following these basic guidelines and avoiding the pitfalls discussed below in the Interviews section can help ensure an employment application does not inadvertently demonstrate a discriminatory intent or provide evidence of discrimination.

Most states, in addition to the myriad of federal employment and labor laws, have their own laws and regulations concerning the types of questions and information employers may and may not ask on employment applications. Each employer should consult and comply with the rules applicable to it and prudent employers should regularly review their employment applications and modify them, as necessary. A number of states also offer written guidelines on pre-employment inquiries that can be obtained by calling the state's fair employment practices agency. (See Appendix I for an example of New York's guidelines on pre-employment inquiries.)

Information To Include

Employers should be concerned not only with which questions should be omitted from their employment applications, but also with what information to include in the document. Although employment applications will vary among industries and particular employers, most employers should consider including at least the following:

- **an Equal Opportunity Statement;**
- **notice of any pre-employment testing requirements;**
- **applicant name and address;**
- **position applied for and wage/salary desired;**
- **availability for work;**
- **prior employment with employer;**
- **education;**
- **work experience;**
- **references;**
- **reference check authorization;**
- **disclaimer of any employment contracts; and**
- **notice that incomplete, inaccurate or false responses could result in rejection of the application or termination.**

Interviews

An effective and legally sound interview process has many benefits. In addition to allowing a company to gather vital information to make sound personnel decisions, it may be the first chance the company gets to begin fostering loyalty.

An effective interview process involves two essential components. First, employers must establish a formal procedure for interviewing and evaluating candidates, with an emphasis on job skills rather than just an applicant's personality. Second, interviewers should be trained in conducting effective and lawful interviews. Specifically, employers should instruct their interviewers to focus on transferable characteristics and avoid the unintended influence of information and stereotypes unrelated to the qualifications necessary for the job.

For legal reasons, interviewers must avoid certain questions and limit inquiries to that information for which the employer has a legitimate business concern. Specifically, interviewers should avoid questions about race, color, religion, national origin, gender, marital or family status, age, physical attributes or disabilities and other issues not related to an applicant's ability to perform job duties. Asking these types of questions can lead to liability under both state and federal laws prohibiting discrimination, including Title VII of the Civil Rights Act of 1964, the Immigration Reform and Control Act of 1986, the Age Discrimination in Employment Act of 1967, the Americans With Disabilities Act of 1990, the Rehabilitation Act of 1973, and, for federal contractors and grant recipients, Executive Orders 11246 and 11141.

In addition to avoiding direct questions regarding these protected characteristics, the fair employment laws of numerous states prohibit employers from asking questions that may lead indirectly to disclosure of information that could not be obtained directly, for example, asking an applicant to provide any prior married name, which in effect asks whether an individual has been divorced.

The **Kansas** Act Against Discrimination is an example of such a state law. It prohibits pre-employment inquiries that express, directly or indirectly, any limitation, specification or discrimination as to race, religion, color, gender, disability, national origin or ancestry, or that express any intent to do so unless based on a bona fide occupational qualification (K.S.A. §44-1009(3)(1999 Supp.)). The Kansas administrative regulations provide examples of the kinds of inquiries that can lead, indirectly, to requesting prohibited information (K.A.R. §21-30-17), including:

- **inquiring into the birthplace of an applicant, the applicant's spouse or parent or any other close relative;**

- **requiring an applicant to submit a birth certificate, naturalization or baptismal record with an application;**

- **requiring or suggesting that the applicant submit a photograph with the application or at any time before he or she is hired;**

- **asking the name and address of any relative of the applicant other than the applicant's spouse or children; and**

- **inquiring into an applicant's membership in organizations, the name or character of which could indicate the race, religion, color, national origin or ancestry of the applicant.**

Normally, impermissible questions may be asked primarily in two situations. First, the questions generally may be asked if an employer is required to meet affirmative action plan goals and can demonstrate the information was collected solely for that purpose and maintained in a manner designed to keep it from decisionmakers. Second, though more difficult to prove, the employer can ask about protected characteristics if related to a bona fide occupational qualification (BFOQ). However, jobs will be closely and carefully analyzed and it is the exception that a protected characteristic qualifies as a BFOQ. Employers should consult legal counsel before relying on this exception.

Subjects To Avoid

The key to avoiding unlawful inquiries in interviews is to limit questions to those that will provide information regarding the applicant's ability to do the job. As a general rule, employers should avoid inquiries related to the following subjects:

Age or date of birth: Age-based inquiries may violate the federal Age Discrimination in Employment Act (ADEA) and state laws that prohibit discrimination against persons aged 40 and over or, for some states, even younger individuals (New York's protections begin at age 18, for example). In addition to direct inquiries, even indirect inquiries such as the date an individual graduated from high school generally are impermissible.

On the other hand, age inquiries generally are permitted to ensure a person is old enough to work in the job being filled (e.g., "Are you at least 18 years old?"), or when the job requires a driver's license or is of a type for which age-based distinctions are lawful such as hazardous work or piloting an airplane.

Availability for work on Saturday and Sunday: Asking this question may discourage an applicant whose religion prohibits Saturday or Sunday work. If a question regarding weekend work is asked, the interviewer should indicate that reasonable efforts are made to accommodate religious beliefs and/or practices. Employers are not required to make an accommodation if doing so would create an undue hardship on the business, though most government agencies will closely scrutinize an employer's proof of undue hardship and require more than just mere inconvenience.

Whether arrested or convicted: Many state laws prohibit inquiries into a person's past arrest or conviction records. In addition, the EEOC has ruled that, since minorities have suffered proportionately more arrests than others, even if an employer does not actually consider arrest information, simply requesting it tends to discourage minority applicants and is therefore illegal. Convictions, however, generally may be the subject of inquiries if substantially related to the job.

Familial status: Employers should avoid asking questions regarding whether an applicant has children, their ages, child care arrangements or pregnancy. Although most employers who ask such questions are concerned with the potential for absenteeism and tardiness, these questions are typically asked only of women, making them appear discriminatory. Even if asked of both men and women, these questions still can be suspect. If an employer is concerned about regular work attendance, a better question might be, "Is there anything that would interfere with regular attendance at work?" Although an applicant might reveal protected information as a result of this question, it is much broader and designed to obtain non-protected information such as whether the applicant has access to reliable transportation.

In addition to the foregoing limitations, **Michigan** law expressly prohibits discrimination on the basis of familial status, which is defined to include discrimination on the basis of the ages of persons living with an applicant or employee. Thus, not only is inquiring into whether a person has children prohibited, but questions that concern stepchildren or others that reside in the same household also may be unlawful.

Citizenship and right to work: Questions regarding an applicant's citizenship or country of birth generally are unlawful and imply discrimination on the basis of national origin. The EEOC's "Guidelines on Discrimination Because of National Origin" contain the following statement: "Because discrimination on the basis of citizenship has the effect of discriminating on the basis of national origin, a lawfully immigrated alien who is domiciled or residing in this country may not be discriminated against on the basis of his citizenship," except pursuant to national security requirements required by federal statute or executive order.

Further, the Immigration Reform and Control Act of 1986, which also prohibits national origin discrimination by employers of at least four employees, requires all employers to verify the identity and eligibility to work of each person to be hired. The verification, Form I-9, is to be completed after hire and, in fact, the verification process may result in the disclosure of information that might otherwise provide the basis for a charge of discrimination (e.g., citizenship). Prior to employment, at the job interview and on the application, the employer may ask an applicant: "Are you authorized to work on a full-time basis for any U.S. employer?" Employment can be conditioned on the company's verification of the applicant's response to that question.

An employer is prohibited from requesting or even identifying which documents an employee may submit to prove his or her identity and work eligibility. The I-9 Form contains lists of qualifying documents and the employee must be permitted to choose from those lists the documents he or she will produce. Thus, asking an applicant or employee to bring a driver's license or Social Security card to an interview generally will be considered unlawful "documentation abuse."

Credit or garnishment record: These inquiries are almost always irrelevant to job performance. In addition, because census data indicates that minorities, on average, are poorer than whites, consideration of these factors may have a disparate impact on minorities. A **California** court has ruled that an employer violated Title VII of the 1964 Civil Rights Act by discharging an African-American employee because his wages had been garnished several times. The court based its decision on findings that persons of color suffer wage garnishments substantially more often than do whites and the wage garnishments do not affect a worker's ability to perform effectively (*Johnson v. Pike Corp. of America*, 322 F. Supp. 490 (C.D. Cal. 1971)). Other states' laws also may prohibit employers from discharging a worker because of a garnishment.

Disabilities and health history: Asking about an applicant's health or workers' compensation history generally is unlawful. Under the Americans With Disabilities Act (ADA), and many state laws that mirror the federal statute, any inquiry at the pre-employment stage that would require an applicant to disclose a disability is unlawful. Employers should avoid these questions, or medical examinations, before making a job offer. However, an employer is not prohibited from inquiring about an applicant's ability to perform certain job functions and, within limits, may conduct tests of all applicants to determine if they can perform essential job functions, with or without an accommodation. Employers should review EEOC's published guidelines on interviewing without running afoul of rules prohibiting improper medical and disability inquiries. (See Appendix I, EEOC *ADA Enforcement Guidance: Pre-employment Disability-Related Questions and Medical Examinations.*)

Height and weight: Height and weight requirements, if not related to the job and if they have the effect of excluding a disproportionate percentage of women or members of certain nationalities, are probably discriminatory. In addition, state or local laws may expressly prohibit discrimination on the basis of height or weight. **Michigan's** Elliot Larson Civil Rights Act is one example. In addition, the District of Columbia Human Rights Act makes it unlawful to refuse to hire an applicant based on his or her "personal appearance."

Language proficiency: Although some level of English skill may be necessary for many jobs, both the EEOC and the courts have interpreted Title VII as barring English-only policies on the job, unless the policy can be justified as a bona fide occupation qualification or by business necessity such as safety concerns that might arise in communications with customers and co-workers. In addition, inquiries regarding the applicant's ability to speak a foreign language, when not job-related, could be used as evidence of national origin discrimination.

Marital status: In many states, an employer may not discriminate against a person because he or she is married, single, divorced, separated or widowed. Asking an applicant to provide any prior married name essentially asks whether the applicant is widowed, divorced or separated. Further, by its nature, this question is only asked of women. Thus, the question generally is discriminatory and should be avoided.

The foregoing list is not exhaustive. The bottom line is that all questions on an application form or in an interview should be related to a specific, job-related purpose. In determining whether a question is potentially unlawful, an employer should consider why the information sought is necessary. For example, why is it important to know an applicant's age or whether the applicant speaks fluent English? If the answer does not provide job-related information relevant to determining a person's expected performance on the job, that is a good indication the question should not be asked. Questions that do not aid the employer in finding the most qualified applicant may call into question the employer's motive for asking.

Checklist

Focusing on those characteristics most closely related to the position and job performance, employers should consider these guidelines for conducting an effective interview:

1. **Before the Interview:**
   Review the position for which applicants are sought.
   - What are the characteristics of a successful candidate for this job?
   - What skills and abilities are desirable?
   - What kind of experience is needed?
   - What are the qualifications?

   Study the employment application.
   - Are the above characteristics included in the application?
   - Are the applicant's experiences easily transferable to the company and this position?

- What has the applicant done to distinguish him- or herself from other applicants?
- What information is needed that is not included on the application but that you may need to procure in the interview?

Construct an informal list of questions based on the information provided by the applicant.
- List the points that need clarification or further investigation.
- Select both exceptional accomplishments and deficiencies.

2. **The Interview**:

Inform the applicant about the job.
- Describe the company and the atmosphere and philosophies of the workplace.
- Describe the available position, the job duties and working conditions.
- Provide the applicant with information regarding pay, benefits and opportunities for advancement.

Gather information about the applicant.
- Ask open-ended questions (what, where, why, when and who). This gives the applicant the opportunity to talk.
- What are the applicant's achievements?
- What is the applicant's current job situation?
- What are the applicant's qualifications?
- What are the applicant's weaknesses?
- How motivated is this applicant?
- Why did the applicant leave previous employers?
- What are this applicant's job experiences? How has this applicant handled difficult problems in past jobs?
- Does the applicant have the ability to supervise and be supervised?
- Can this applicant work with a team? Does this applicant prefer team or individual work?
- Who is the applicant's most/least favorite supervisor and why?

3. **After the Interview**:
- Write down initial impressions of the applicant immediately.
- Note the objective factors that make this applicant a hire or a rejection.
- Determine who is to contact the applicant regarding the employment decision or further interviews.

Screening

Background Checks

Employers are becoming increasingly aware of the dangers of hiring a job applicant with an unwanted background, criminal record or falsified credentials. Pre-employment background screening often can alleviate some of these concerns. Not only can it help to promote a safe and profitable workplace by identifying potentially undesirable employees, reducing theft and avoiding wasted time and resources spent hiring and training the wrong employee, but it can protect employers from exposure to negligent hiring liability, wrongful termination lawsuits and the potential for sexual harassment and the creation of other forms of hostile work environments.

Conducting background checks, however, is not as easy as it once was for employers, particularly when the checking is to be conducted by an outside agency such as a Consumer Reporting Agency (CRA). The process is highly regulated at both the state and federal levels.

Criminal Records

When performing background checks, obtaining criminal records and arrest information can be a double-edged sword. On the one hand, an employer can avoid hiring applicants with prior criminal problems that can lead to problems on the job and demonstrate diligence in screening applicants in the defense of negligent hiring claims. On the other hand, an employer risks invading an employee's privacy, running afoul of state and local laws governing reliance on criminal and arrest records in personnel decisions and opening itself up to disparate treatment lawsuits. An employer's caution, therefore, must be two-fold. First, employers should check an employee's criminal record only when substantially related to the job. Second, an employer needs to make sure that its inquiries, whether made by itself or an agent (such as a CRA), do not violate state or local laws. In many cases, in fact, an employer will be held responsible for the unlawful acts of its agents in obtaining such information.

Many states have mandatory procedures for procuring criminal background information. **Arkansas, Georgia, Kansas** and **Ohio** require that an employer obtain the written consent of that applicant. In Oregon, an employer must notify the applicant that it is seeking criminal record information and provide to the state the manner in which this notice was given to the applicant before criminal record information may be provided. An employer who obtains criminal record information is bound to use such information only for the purpose for which it was obtained and is prohibited from disseminating it to outside sources.

Most states allow private employers to perform background checks on applicants and employees. However, many distinguish between arrest and conviction records, prohibiting employment decisions based on an applicant's history of arrests. Some jurisdictions such as the **District of Columbia** also allow criminal records to be expunged or sealed and prohibit employers from obtaining these records.

Some states even require that employers perform background checks on applicants for certain positions, usually involving child care or health care. Others limit the required inquiries to certain types of criminal offenses, such as sex crimes or violent crimes. Although employers should check their respective jurisdictions, the following chart (Fig. 4-1) lists the positions and/or employers for which background checks must be conducted in some states:

The following states have particularly restrictive or atypical laws and regulations:

- **Arkansas** — Arkansas has statutory provisions governing the circumstances under which criminal records may be made available. Criminal records will be provided, for example, when requested by a government agency, as required by law or when authorized by the subject in writing.

- **Colorado** — Employers who require applicants to disclose information about sealed arrest records are guilty of a misdemeanor.

- **Florida** — An employer is granted a statutory presumption that an employee was not negligently hired if the employer conducted a background investigation and the investigation did not reveal any information that reasonably demonstrated the unsuitability of the applicant for the particular work to be performed or for employment in general.

- **Georgia** — If an employer makes an unfavorable employment decision based on information obtained from a criminal records check, the employer must inform the applicant of all information pertinent to that decision.

- **Hawaii** — An employer may consider an individual's criminal conviction record only if that record bears a rational relationship to the position and such investigation must occur after a conditional offer of employment has been made.

- **Idaho** — A prospective employer may obtain copies of an applicant's criminal record by submitting a written request to the Idaho Department of Law Enforcement (Idaho Code §67-3008). The information contained in that record generally may not be further disseminated by the prospective employee without a signed release from the subject of the record.

- **Illinois** — Employers may consider an employee's arrest or criminal record to determine a bona fide qualification.

- **Kansas** — A prospective employer has the right to require a job applicant to sign a release allowing the employer access to the applicant's criminal record information. In addition, no employer shall be liable for any employment decision based on knowledge of criminal record information, provided that the information relied on reasonably relates to the applicant's or employee's trustworthiness, or the safety or well-being of the employer's employees or customers.

- **Maryland** — An employer can obtain criminal conviction information by petitioning the Secretary of Public Safety and Correctional Services and demonstrating a particular need for information that relates to the duties of the job.

- **Massachusetts** — Employers must be granted access by a state board to an individual's criminal records. Discrimination and adverse employment actions related to arrests without convictions, a first conviction for drunkenness, simple assault, speeding, minor traffic violation, affray or disturbance of the peace, or a conviction for a misdemeanor that occurred five or more years earlier are specifically prohibited.

- **Missouri** — Inquiries into criminal convictions are permitted only when the employer can establish that a conviction is substantially related to an applicant's ability to perform a specific job.

- **New Jersey** — Employers can obtain criminal records from the Superintendent of State Police, but only if the employee or job applicant signs the document requesting the records. Once obtained, the information may not be disseminated to unauthorized persons. In fact, the record must be destroyed immediately after its use. In addition, if the information will be used to disqualify a person from employment, the employer must provide the person with adequate notice to complete or challenge the accuracy of any information.

- **New York** — Employers can inquire about convictions, but employment cannot be denied solely on the basis of the conviction unless there is a "direct relationship" between the conviction and the employment sought, or employing the applicant poses an "unreasonable risk" to safety or property.

- **Wisconsin** — Wisconsin's Fair Employment Act specifically prohibits employment discrimination based on arrest or conviction. However, there are exceptions when the conviction and offense or circumstances of the offense are substantially related to the circumstances of the job. There are also exceptions based on the nature of the job such as security system installers and employees with access to prescription drugs.

Fig. 4-1 Positions and/or Employers for Which Background Checks Are Required	
Alabama	Persons who have supervisory or disciplinary power over a child or children.
Delaware	Home health care agencies, management companies and others who provide services on behalf of a home health agency.
Florida	Employees in positions of trust or responsibility.
Georgia	Persons supervising children.
Illinois	Employers devoting a major portion of time to providing recreational, social, educational or safety services to children.
Louisiana	Licensed ambulance personnel and unlicensed health care providers in nursing facilities, intermediate care facilities, adult residential care facilities or adult day care centers.
Maryland	Employees at designated child care facilities, including child care centers and homes, juvenile detention centers and public and private schools.
Mississippi	Employers providing care for children with certain disorders, the aged or infirm.
Nevada	Employees having supervision of, direct contact with or access to any records of children served by the employer.
New Mexico	Child care workers, teachers and certified school personnel.
Ohio	Employees in child day care, hospice care, education and child preschool programs.
Tennessee	Employees with the Department of Mental Health and Mental Retardation, teachers, employees at adult day care centers and alarm systems contractor employees.
Texas	Employees of nursing homes, custodial care homes, assisted living facilities, home health agencies, adult day care facilities and facilities that provide mental health services.
Virginia	Teachers and school board employees.

Credit Reports

Many employers check an applicant's or employee's credit history as part of the hiring or promotion process. In light of the EEOC's position that disqualifying an applicant based on debtor status could have a disparate impact on minority applicants, it is advisable to make sure obtaining a credit report is pursuant to "business necessity."

In addition, the federal Bankruptcy Act prohibits an employer from discriminating against an employee or applicant solely because the individual filed for bankruptcy (11 U.S.C. §525(b)). If a bankruptcy shows up in an applicant's credit history report, the employer should base its hiring decision on legitimate business reasons independent of the bankruptcy.

A number of states have their own laws concerning the use of credit reports in hiring and promotions. **California, Colorado, Maine** and **New York** have laws that mostly mirror the Fair Credit Reporting Act (discussed below) in relevant respects.

Some states have requirements that differ, sometimes slightly, from those imposed by federal law. For example, **Kansas** law contains restrictions on a consumer reporting agency providing obsolete information with regard to bankruptcy (14 years), suits or judgments (seven years or until the statute of limitations has run), paid tax liens (seven years), accounts placed for collection or charged to profit or loss (seven years) and records of arrest, indictment or conviction of a crime that from date of disposition, release or parole, antedate the report by more than seven years.

Missouri does not permit pre-employment inquiries into an applicant's credit record unless the employer can establish the inquiry is related to the duties the individual will be performing.

In **New Mexico**, employers seeking information about an applicant from a credit bureau must complete a "service contract" that certifies inquiries will be made only for the purpose of granting credit or a bona fide business transaction such as checking the qualifications of potential or current employees.

Fair Credit Reporting Act Requirements

The federal Fair Credit Reporting Act (FCRA) (15 U.S.C. §1681 *et seq.*) governs background checks when they are performed by outside agencies, rather than by the employer itself. The law sets out various requirements and rules for obtaining and using background reports, referred to as Consumer Reports. A Consumer Report usually includes criminal and civil records, driving records, civil lawsuits, reference checks and other information obtained by a Consumer Reporting Agency (CRA). The FCRA is designed to protect the privacy of the individuals whose information is gathered and included in the Consumer Report. (See Appendix II, Federal Fair Credit Reporting Act Forms.)

What is required?

The FCRA requires an employer to notify the CRA that it will follow the steps set forth in the statute. These employer assurances include the following:

- the employer will use the information solely for employment purposes;
- it will not use the information in violation of any federal or state equal opportunity law;
- the employer will obtain all the necessary disclosures and consents;
- it will give the appropriate notices in the event an adverse action is taken against an applicant based in whole or in part on the contents of the Consumer Report; and
- if an Investigative Consumer Report (a special, more intrusive type of consumer report) is requested, the employer will give the additional information required by law.

The FCRA further requires an employer to obtain a written Release and Disclosure from an applicant before obtaining a Consumer Report (FCRA §1681b and d). The employer must obtain two separate documents:

- a clear and conspicuous disclosure that a report may be requested; and
- written consent from the applicant.

Release and Disclosure forms are commonly provided by the CRA and samples are included in Appendix II. The Federal Trade Commission (FTC), charged with enforcing the FCRA, recently stated that the Release and Disclosure can be in the same document as long as the language ensures that the employee is made fully aware that a report is being requested. Still, to avoid clarity issues later, employers are well advised to use two separate forms as originally intended.

Special procedures are required when an employer requests that the CRA obtain employment references. No special procedure is necessary when the CRA is merely confirming factual information such as dates of employment or pay rates. However, if the employer requests that the CRA gather other information such as that concerning job performance, the report is considered an Investigative Consumer Report and additional procedures apply.

1. There must be disclosure to the candidate that an Investigative Consumer Report is being requested, with certain specified language, within three days of when the request is made.

2. The applicant must be put on notice of the right to ask for additional information regarding the nature of the investigation.

3. If the applicant makes a written request, the employer must respond within five days and provide the employee with a copy of a document titled "A Summary of Your Rights Under the Fair Credit Reporting Act (FCRA)," prepared by the FTC. (A sample of this document is included in Appendix II.)

The CRA may handle these requirements as a service to the employer.

Before adverse employment action is taken

Once all of the required disclosures and notices are complete, the employer is obligated to notify the applicant if it intends to take an adverse employment action based on the Consumer Report such as refusing to hire the applicant. Before taking the adverse action, the employer must provide the applicant with a copy of the report and with the FTC Summary notice.

The notice is designed to ensure the applicant has the opportunity to review the report and contest any incomplete or inaccurate information. As a practical matter, an employer will have invested a substantial amount of time, money and effort by this point in the recruitment process. It makes sense to allow an applicant to explain any unfavorable information before rejecting him or her for the position. Even if the Consumer Report was merely one factor among many in the employer's decision not to hire the applicant, these rights and procedures still apply. To be safe, an employer should adhere to these procedures even if it feels it would make the same employment decision regardless of the report.

After refusal to hire

The applicant has certain rights even after an adverse employment action. An employer who has decided not to hire an applicant must send the applicant a Notice of Adverse Action (a sample has been included in Appendix II) informing him or her that it has reached its final decision. Again, the employer must include a copy of the FTC's Summary notice. The law clearly requires that the notice be given both before and after the adverse employment action is taken, giving the applicant the maximum opportunity to correct any incomplete or inaccurate information that could hamper his or her chances of employment.

Remedies

Employers who fail to obtain an applicant's permission before requesting a Consumer Report or to provide pre-adverse action disclosures and adverse action notices to rejected applicants subject themselves to potentially serious legal consequences. The FCRA permits individuals to sue employers for damages in federal court and allows the recovery of punitive damages in the case of deliberate violations, court costs and reasonable legal fees. In addition, the FTC, other federal agencies and states may sue employers for noncompliance.

Post-9/11: FACT Act

The Fair Credit Reporting Act was amended in 2003 by the Fair and Accurate Credit Transaction Act, known as the "FACT Act." The amendment deals primarily with investigations of employee misconduct.

When employers use third parties to investigate workplace misconduct, they do not have to notify the targets of the investigation or obtain their consent. Excluded from "consumer reports" are communications made to employers in connection with investigations of:

1. suspected misconduct relating to employment; or

2. compliance with federal, state or local laws and regulations, the rules of a self-regulatory organization or any pre-existing, written employer policies.

Investigations of applicants during the hiring process remain subject to the FCRA's requirements and use of the same compliance forms as before the FACT Act. Credit information about both applicants and incumbent employees is also subject to FCRA requirements and forms.

Employment References

At first glance, requesting and providing employment references would seem to be a straightforward matter as well as a useful and necessary component of the employment process. Exchanging references provides a prospective employer with a candid evaluation of an applicant's qualifications and previous job performance. However, references can be a source of liability for the unwary employer, particularly on the basis of alleged defamation. Fear of liability has prompted many employers to implement a "no comment" or "name, rank and serial number" policy regarding former employees, providing only dates of employment and position held. Of course, this may prevent good employees from getting deserved recommendations and permit problem employees to move on to new jobs where they may continue to disrupt the workplace.

Many states have recognized that the flow of information regarding the performance and work history of employees is desirable and grant a qualified privilege to employers when giving references. The privilege is qualified in that, in most cases, it is lost if there is evidence the statement's author knew the statement to be untrue, there was a lack of good faith, or the information was considered confidential by a nondisclosure agreement or local, state or federal regulations.

Consider the following state laws regulating employee reference checks:

- **Alabama** — Although Alabama does not have a specific statute providing immunity from civil liability to employers who disclose information regarding former or current employees, the Alabama Supreme Court has noted that "any publication made between a previous employer and a prospective employer is protected by a conditional privilege" if made with common interest or because of a duty owed and if made without malice (*Gore v. Healthtex, Inc.*, 567 So.2d 1307 (Ala. 1990)).

- **Arkansas** — Arkansas requires written consent from a current or former employee for providing the following information: date and duration of employment, pay rate and wage history, job description and duties, last performance evaluation prior to the date of request, attendance information, results of drug or alcohol tests administered within one year prior to the request, threats of violence, harassing acts or threatening behavior, whether the employee was voluntarily or involuntarily separated from employment and the reasons for separation and whether the employee is eligible for rehire (Ark. Code Ann. §11-3-204(a)(1)(1987)). Obtaining this consent gives the employer qualified immunity as long as it is acting in good faith.

- **Connecticut** — An employer's response to a request for information is limited to verification of the employee's dates of employment, title, position and salary, unless the employer has procured a written authorization permitting further disclosure (Conn. Gen. Stat. §31-128f).

- **Idaho** — A qualified immunity is granted to an employer with respect to good faith employment references (Idaho Code §44-201(2)). The presumption of good faith created by the statute is rebuttable on a showing the employer acted with actual malice or a deliberate intent to mislead. Actual malice may be demonstrated by showing the employer had knowledge the information was false or acted with reckless disregard of whether it was false.

- **Kansas** — The Kansas legislature has provided for absolute immunity for an employer who discloses the following information about a current or former employee to a prospective employer: dates of employment, pay level, job description and duties and wage history (K.S.A. §44-119a(b)). In addition, "unless otherwise provided for by law," an employer may respond in writing to a written request concerning a current or former employee from a prospective employer and will enjoy absolute immunity from civil liability for disclosing the following information: (1) written employee evaluations that were conducted prior to the request; (2) whether the employee was voluntarily or involuntarily released from service; and (3) the reasons for the separation (K.S.A. §44-119a(c)).

- **Maine** — An employer who provides a reference is presumed to be acting in good faith, unless it can be shown it knowingly gave a false and deliberately misleading reference with malicious intent (26 M.R.S.A. §598).

- **Michigan** — The Bullard Plawecki Act (MCL §423.501(1)(c)) provides that employment references may be excluded from the personnel file (and hence not supplied to the employee on request) if the identity of the person making the reference would be disclosed.

- **Nevada** — An employer has limited immunity from civil action when, at the request of a current or former employee, it provides references to prospective employers (Nev. Rev. Stat. §41.755). The information must be limited to: (1) the ability of the employee to perform the job; (2) the diligence, skill or reliability with which the employee carried out his or her duties; and (3) any illegal or wrongful act committed by the employee. Immunity from liability is lost, if the employer, in disseminating the information, acts with malice, ill will or otherwise distributes information it knows to be false or misleading.

- **Rhode Island** — An employer is protected when it provides references, as long as they are fair and unbiased (R.I. Gen. Laws §28-6.4.-1). A presumption of good faith is established that can be rebutted by a showing that the information disclosed was knowingly false, deliberately misleading, disclosed for a malicious purpose, or violative of the current or former employee's civil rights under discrimination laws.

- **Tennessee** — A qualified immunity exists for employers that provide references on former employees (Tenn. Code Ann. §50-1-105). A presumption of good faith is established that can be rebutted by a showing that the information provided was knowingly false, deliberately misleading, disclosed for a malicious purpose, disclosed in reckless disregard of its falsity or defamatory nature, or violative of the current or former employee's civil rights under discrimination laws.

In addition, **Alabama, Arkansas, Utah, Virginia** and **Washington** have criminal statutes prohibiting blacklisting. In Utah, violations are considered a felony, with other states charging misdemeanor violations.

Even considering that some states provide statutory protections, it may be that the risk of a defamation claim outweighs any benefit to an employer from providing reference information.

The truth is, even a positive reference can subject an employer to liability. The **California** Supreme Court held that a school district could be liable for damages for giving a favorable recommendation, but omitting important negative information about the employee (*Randi W. v. Muroc Joint Unified School District,* 14 Cal. 4th 1066 (1997)).

The school board in *Randi W.* recommended the employee despite the fact he had been disciplined for sexually touching students and other sexual harassment and had resigned under the threat of sexual misconduct charges. When the plaintiff was sexually molested by the employee in his new position, she brought suit against his former employer, who had written glowing recommendation letters on his behalf, alleging that the failure to mention any misconduct in the recommendations constituted fraud and negligent misrepresentation. The court ruled that a former employer providing a recommendation owes a duty to protect future employers and third parties and cannot misrepresent the qualifications and character of a former employee when there is a substantial risk of physical injury.

Instead of instituting a policy of outright refusal to respond to reference requests, a company might take less drastic measures to minimize liability and still provide references to inquiring employers. A company might consider:

- instituting a written policy and procedure for giving references and including this policy in the employee handbook;

- ensuring all reference information is channeled through a central source to guard against inconsistencies and to make certain the information given is accurate and not contrary to company policy;

- clearly documenting who requested the information and for what purpose, who is giving the information, and exactly what information is being provided; and

- asking for a written release from the employee or former employee, particularly when the information requested goes beyond verification of dates of employment and job title.

Despite the potential roadblocks, an employer should not overlook the benefits of thoroughly checking an applicant's references. Doing so will help ensure a successful hire and decrease the risk of the employment relationship ending in a dismissal and/or litigation. Even verifying only basic information can be valuable to confirm an applicant did in fact work for a particular employer for a particular time period.

Some additional rules of thumb for reducing the risk of liability:

- Make sure the application form requests the applicant's permission to seek references from previous employers.

- If a reference check turns up any discrepancies, obtain explanations from the applicant and/or reference giver.

- A previous employer's reluctance to provide specific information or failure to return your calls can serve as a red-flag.

- Ask a former employer about the applicant's interactions with co-workers, management and customers, strengths and weaknesses and achievements.

Medical Examinations and Inquiries

Prior to 1991, many applications contained the straightforward question: "Are you disabled?" With passage of the Americans With Disabilities Act of 1990 (ADA), however, an employer's ability to inquire about an applicant's medical or disability history was severely limited and regulated (see Appendix I). Generally, the only acceptable pre-employment inquiries an employer may make are inquiries into the ability of an applicant to perform job-related functions. Not only are direct medical inquiries prohibited (e.g., "Do you have AIDS?"), but so are indirect inquiries (e.g., "Have you ever filed a claim for workers' compensation benefits?") or those likely to solicit medical or disability information (*e.g.*, "Are you a runner?").

Under the ADA, an employer may require a medical examination, but only after tendering an offer of employment. The examination may be performed before the applicant begins employment and the employer may condition employment on the results of the examination, provided all entering employees in the same job category are subjected to such an examination. Should an employer withdraw an offer of employment because the examination reveals the applicant does not satisfy certain employment criteria, it is necessary that:

- the exclusionary criteria do not tend to or actually screen out an individual with disabilities or a class of individuals with disabilities; and

- the criteria are job-related and consistent with business necessity.

As part of the employer's showing that an exclusionary criteria is job-related and consistent with business necessity, it must demonstrate that there is no reasonable accommodation that would enable the individual with the disability to perform the essential functions of the job.

As discussed in Chapter 18, information obtained in connection with medical examinations or inquiries must be maintained on separate forms and in separate medical files and treated as confidential medical records, except that:

- managers and supervisors may be informed concerning necessary restrictions to the work or duties of the employee and necessary accommodations;

- safety and first aid personnel may be informed, when appropriate, if the disability might require some emergency treatment; and

- government officials investigating compliance with the ADA must be provided relevant information on request.

In addition to the ADA, many states prohibit medical inquiries prior to a conditional job offer, with some states limiting even the scope of the inquiry. For example, unlike the ADA, the **District of Columbia, Illinois, Kansas, Maryland, Massachusetts** and **Nebraska** limit post-offer examinations to conditions that are job-related. In **California**, broad testing and inquiries are permitted, but only after express consent by the applicant to each test and/or inquiry.

Further, some states limit an employer's ability to test applicants and employees for AIDS/HIV. For example, **Vermont, Washington** and **Wisconsin** have laws expressly prohibiting employment decisions on the basis of an AIDS test or refusal to submit to such a test. Other states — **Connecticut, Illinois, Michigan** and **Ohio** — require the written consent of an applicant or employee before an AIDS test can be administered. **Florida** allows such a test only when justified by a bona fide occupational qualification.

Drugs/Alcohol

Employer awareness of drug and alcohol abuse can help alleviate a number of problems that can arise in the workplace: increased absenteeism, theft, violence, decreased productivity, safety concerns and poor employee morale. Although the true impact of substance abuse on the workplace is difficult to assess, it is widely accepted that employees under the influence are less productive and more likely to injure themselves or their co-workers. From a bottom-line, cost-of-doing business standpoint, such abuse cannot be ignored.

There is no doubt it greatly increases the incidence of health-related absences and workers' compensation and disability claims.

Faced with these realities, more and more employers are developing and implementing comprehensive drug-free workplace programs, including drug and alcohol testing. In fact, pre-employment drug testing has become almost commonplace as a screening tool. Nonetheless, employers administering and requiring these tests should proceed with caution.

Although the ADA prohibits pre-offer medical examinations, a test to determine whether an applicant is illegally using drugs is not considered a medical examination under the statute. Thus, when state and local law permit, an employer can require an applicant to take a drug test even before an offer of employment is made, provided the test is limited to accurately identifying only the illegal use of drugs.

Testing employees for alcohol abuse as opposed to illegal drug use raises additional concerns. The ADA treats alcohol differently, classifying alcoholism as a disability. Alcohol tests are considered medical examinations under the ADA and, as such, employers cannot subject applicants to these examinations until after a conditional offer of employment has been made.

Using the positive results of an alcohol test also requires some forethought. While an employer can refuse to hire an inebriated applicant, an offer of employment cannot be withdrawn merely because the applicant is an alcoholic. Employers thus should pay special attention to the applicant's behavior or other indications of actual impairment during an interview and any medical examination.

Other bases on which employees might challenge pre-employment drug or alcohol testing include:

- Title VII of the 1964 Civil Rights Act and other discrimination claims for disparate application of drug testing programs.

- The Fourth Amendment, and corresponding provisions of state constitutions, which may be applicable to prevent unreasonable searches and seizures when drug testing is implemented by public employers.

- The National Labor Relations Act, which requires that an employer bargain with its employees' union representative concerning any proposed implementation of a drug or alcohol testing program.

State Laws

Several jurisdictions have statutes governing drug and alcohol testing in the workplace. Employers are well-advised to become familiar with these requirements prior to implementing any new testing programs. The rules and regulations established by the states may limit pre-employment drug testing in the following ways:

- A state may limit the circumstances under which an employer can conduct a pre-employment drug or alcohol test. For example, **Louisiana** permits employers to conduct tests for certain purposes: (1) maintaining the safety of employees or the general public; or (2) maintaining productivity, quality of services or products, or security of property and information.

- A state such as **Rhode Island** may impose conditions on testing current employees that do not exist when testing applicants or before employment has begun. The Rhode Island law requires a reasonable suspicion and prohibits termination for a first positive test.

- Some states prohibit an employer from implementing a testing program without first having the program reviewed and approved by a state administrative agency. For example, **Maine** law requires approval by the Maine Department of Labor and certain detailed procedures must be followed.

- Employers may be required to notify applicants that they will be tested or to get written disclaimers from employees.

- Employers may be prohibited from determining an applicant's or employee's eligibility for employment based on a drug test unless the test meets certain requirements. For example, in **Connecticut** and **Nebraska** an employer must use a urinalysis drug test and confirm a positive result with a second test using another, more reliable methodology. In **Rhode Island**, a positive test using blood, urine or other bodily fluids or tissues must be confirmed by a federally certified laboratory using gas chromatography/mass spectrometry test, or other verification standard recognized as equally accurate. In **New Jersey**, mandatory random urine testing of current employees may be an invasion of privacy in violation of the state constitution unless the nature of the employee's job is such that the public's interest in safety outweighs the employee's right to privacy.

- Certain regulations have been adopted in **Rhode Island** to protect the privacy and modesty of applicants such as prohibiting the employer from any direct observation of an applicant's urine production. (See R.I. Gen. Laws §28-6.5-2(a)(2).)

- Most states mandate that the employer bear the costs of the test. **Montana** requires employers to pay the cost of a subsequent test if the employee requests one if the test is negative. If it is positive, the employee must pay.

- States such as **Idaho** and **Louisiana** demand that the results of the tests remain privileged and confidential.

Of course, state laws also may provide the bases for claims of defamation or invasion of privacy in connection with an employer's administration of a drug or alcohol testing program and failure to safeguard the test results from disclosure to those without a "need to know."

Genetic Testing

As employers gain increasing access to genetic information, the workplace has been included in the debates concerning the potential misuse of this information. The law is still developing in this area, so employers must stay abreast of the changing legislative and legal landscape to ensure compliance and that their interests are adequately represented in the policy discussions surrounding future proposed regulations.

Why the concern?

Employers might use genetic information to identify potential or current employees who are susceptible to workplace risks, whose genetic material is being adversely affected by exposure to workplace toxins, who may become prematurely unable to work and who are likely to incur substantial health care bills.

What laws govern?

The ADA is the most likely source of liability for potential discrimination in the workplace arising from genetic testing. The Equal Employment Opportunity Commission's (EEOC) compliance manual interprets the ADA as covering genetic information relating to illness, disease or other disorders. The EEOC reasons that a person denied employment on the basis of genetic testing may not actually be disabled but is protected by the law due to being perceived by the employer as having or being prone to have a disability.

A number of states also have addressed the issue of genetic testing with laws protecting applicants and employees from potential discrimination. **California** recently amended its Fair Employment and Housing Act to add a new category prohibiting discrimination based on genetic characteristics. The legislature amended the definition of "medical condition" to include any scientifically or medically identifiable gene or chromosome that is known to cause or increase the risk of causing a disease or disorder. **Delaware** likewise amended its Fair Employment law to prohibit discrimination on the basis of a genetic test.

Other states have enacted laws to prohibit discrimination against individuals with specific genetic traits or disorders. **Florida** (in addition to requiring an applicant's informed consent prior to testing) and **Louisiana** prohibit discrimination on the basis of the sickle-cell trait. **North Carolina** prohibits discrimination based on an applicant's possession of the hemoglobin trait. A **New Jersey** law prohibits discrimination in employment based on "genetic information" or an "atypical hereditary cellular or blood trait."

As of Oct. 1, 1999, **Nevada** law prohibits employers, employment agencies and labor unions from asking or encouraging prospective or current employees to submit to a genetic test, and from denying or altering the terms of employment due to any information contained in such a test (Nev. Rev. Stat §613.345). **Rhode Island** law (R.I. Gen. Laws §28-6.7-1(a)) is similar. A **New York** law prohibits employers from denying equal employment opportunities based on "unique genetic disorders."

Wisconsin takes an even more comprehensive approach, prohibiting employers from requiring employees or applicants to undergo genetic testing, using genetic information in making employment decisions and merely accessing an employee's genetic information. Under Wisconsin law, a genetic test is permissible if: (1) requested by the employee; (2) the employee provides written and informed consent; (3) the employee takes the test for investigation of a workers' compensation claim or determining the employee's susceptibility or level of exposure to potentially toxic chemicals or substances in the workplace; and (4) the employer does not terminate or take any other adverse action against the employee based on the test results. Similar laws have been enacted in **Connecticut, Illinois, Iowa, Kansas, Maine, Missouri, Nebraska, New Hampshire, New Mexico, New York, Oklahoma, Oregon, Rhode Island, Texas** and **Vermont**.

Lie Detectors

1988 Polygraph Law

The federal Employee Polygraph Protection Act of 1988 (EPPA) prohibits most private employers from using lie detector tests either for pre-employment screening or during the course of employment. With certain exceptions, an employer generally is prohibited from requiring or requesting any employee or job applicant to take a lie detector test. In addition, employers are forbidden from discharging, disciplining or discriminating against an employee or prospective employee for refusing to take a polygraph examination or exercising other rights under the act.

The legislation affects only commercial businesses. Local, state and federal governmental agencies (e.g., police departments) are not covered, nor are public agencies such as school systems or correctional institutions. The act further exempts certain private businesses such as:

- Some businesses under contract with the federal government (e.g., those involved in counter-intelligence work).

- Businesses whose primary purpose consists of providing armored car personnel, personnel involved in the design of security systems or security personnel in facilities that have a significant impact on the health or safety of any state (e.g., a nuclear or electric power plant, public water works or toxic waste disposal).

- Companies such as pharmaceutical firms that manufacturer, distribute or dispense controlled substances.

Not all lie detector tests are ruled out. Polygraph examinations may be permissible for current employees under limited circumstances. A covered employer may request that an employee take a polygraph examination if it has a reasonable suspicion — not merely a generalized suspicion — the employee has been involved in a workplace incident that resulted in specific economic loss or injury to the employer such as theft or embezzlement. Even when permitted, there are strict standards and detailed procedures that must be followed in conducting the test. These procedures cover all phases and aspects of the test, including ensuring the employee is afforded the opportunity to review all questions in advance and to consult with an attorney and prohibiting needlessly intrusive questions or questions about union and political affiliations and other forbidden subjects. Further, the examiner must be licensed and bonded or have professional liability coverage. Moreover, the act strictly limits the disclosure of information obtained during the test and prohibits use of the results as a basis for an adverse action absent independent corroborating evidence.

An employer that violates the EPPA is subject to court action brought by the secretary of Labor to restrain the violations and assess civil money penalties of up to $10,000 per violation. The employee or prospective employee also can bring a private action against the employer for legal and equitable relief, including employment, reinstatement, promotion and payment of lost wages and benefits.

State Laws

The EPPA does not preempt more restrictive state or local laws or collective bargaining agreements. Consider the following:

- **Alabama** — The state's Polygraph Examiner's Act (Ala. Code §34-25-32) requires a polygraph examiner to advise any subject that participation in the test is voluntary.

- **Florida** — Florida has no law prohibiting an employer from compelling an employee or prospective employee to submit to a lie detector test, but a state court has ruled a public employer violates a police officer's due process rights if it terminates the officer for refusing to submit to a lie detector test (*Farmer v. City of Fort Lauderdale*, 427 So.2d 187 (Fla. 1983)).

- **Idaho** — A qualified immunity is granted to an employer with respect to good faith employment references (Idaho Code §44-201(2)). The presumption of good faith created by the statute is rebuttable on a showing the employer acted with actual malice or a deliberate intent to mislead. Actual malice may be demonstrated by showing the employer had knowledge the information was false or acted with reckless disregard of whether it was false.

- **Illinois** — The Illinois Detection of Deception Examiners Act (225 I.L.C.S. §430) prohibits licensed examiners who administer pre-employment or periodic examinations from asking existing or prospective employees about: religious beliefs or affiliations; beliefs or opinions regarding racial matters; political beliefs or affiliations; beliefs, affiliations or lawful activities regarding unions; or sexual preferences or activities. Exceptions apply if a prohibited topic is directly related to employment.

- **Louisiana** — The Louisiana Polygraphist Act (La. R.S. §37:2831 *et seq.*) requires that polygraph examiners inform persons to be examined that participation in the examination is voluntary and that the examination shall not be the cause of or justification for termination of employment within the meaning of any law related to unemployment compensation. However, the Louisiana courts have refused to recognize a private right of action on behalf of employees for violations of the act (*Ballaron v. Equitable Shipyards, Inc.*, 521 So.2d 481 (La. Ct. App. 1988)).

- **Maine** — Maine's polygraph protection law (32 M.R.S.A. §7166) prohibits employers from administering lie detector tests during pre-employment screening, except for prospective law enforcement agency employees. The law also forbids employers from requiring, requesting or suggesting that existing employees take a polygraph examination as a condition of employment. Unlike the federal law, there is no "theft or embezzlement" exception. Violation of the law is a criminal offense.

- **Maryland** — Maryland law requires that all employment applications contain the following language in boldface, uppercase type:

UNDER MARYLAND LAW, AN EMPLOYER MAY NOT REQUIRE OR DEMAND, AS A CONDITION OF EMPLOYMENT, PROSPECTIVE EMPLOYMENT, OR CONTINUED EMPLOYMENT, THAT AN INDIVIDUAL SUBMIT TO OR TAKE A LIE DETECTOR OR SIMILAR TEST. AN EMPLOYER WHO VIOLATES THIS LAW IS GUILTY OF A MISDEMEANOR AND SUBJECT TO A FINE NOT TO EXCEED $100.

- The prohibition against lie detector tests applies to both public and private employers, but exempts law enforcement officers, state, county and municipal employees of law enforcement agencies, and correctional officers of detention facilities. The statute further provides an administrative process whereby the Commission of Labor and Industry is to investigate written complaints by job applicants or employees who allege violations of the statute (Md. Code Ann., Lab. and Empl. §3-702(a)-(h)).

- **Nebraska** — Employers cannot require that an applicant or current employee submit to a "truth and deception examination" unless the employment sought involves public law enforcement (Neb. Rev. Stat. §81-1928). A prospective employer may, however, ask an applicant to submit to a test if:

  1. no questions are asked about the individual's sexual practices, labor union, political or religious affiliations, or marital relationships;

  2. written and oral notice is provided to the individual that the test is voluntary and can be terminated at any time;

  3. the individual acknowledges in writing that the test is voluntary;

  4. the questions asked are job-related;

  5. prospective employees are not discriminatorily selected for testing;

  6. the test results are not the sole basis of termination; and

  7. the questions and answers are kept on file for one year.

Violators of this statute are guilty of a Class II misdemeanor.

- **New Jersey** — The New Jersey Lie Detector Statute (N.J. Stat. Ann. §2C:40A-1), with limited exceptions, prohibits employers from "influencing, requesting or requiring an employee or prospective employee to take or submit to a lie detector test as a condition of employment or continued condition of employment." Even an employee's voluntary consent to the test may not be sufficient to prevent employer liability. Violations of the law can subject the employer to criminal penalties, making it guilty of a disorderly person's offense.

- **New York** — New York law prohibits employers from requiring, requesting, suggesting or knowingly permitting an employee or applicant to submit to a voice stress analyzer test or from using the results (N.Y. Lab. Law §735).

- **Pennsylvania** — Pennsylvania law provides that an employer is guilty of a second degree misdemeanor if it requires as a condition of continued employment or obtaining employment submission to a polygraph or other form of lie detector test (18 Pa. C.S. §7321).

- **Tennessee** — The Tennessee Polygraph Examiners Act (Tenn. Code Ann. §62-27-101(d)) expressly prohibits an examiner from inquiring into the following areas during an examination: religious beliefs or affiliations; beliefs or opinions regarding racial matters; political beliefs or affiliations; beliefs or affiliations regarding unions; sexual preferences or activities; any disability covered under the ADA; or actions or activities that occurred more than five years preceding the date of the examination, except for felony convictions and violations of the Tennessee Drug Control Act. The law further requires that an examinee must consent to the examination and has the right to refuse to take the examination or to answer any questions. In addition, the employer may not take any personnel action based solely on the examination.

- **Utah** — An employer may not conduct a "deception examination by instrument" in any of the following ways: (1) without the physical presence of the subject; (2) in a surreptitious manner, when the subject is not aware of the examination; (3) by out-of-state examination through telephonic means to anyone in Utah; and (4) by Utah examiners through telephonic means (Utah Code Ann. §53-5-312). An applicant's or employee's refusal to submit to an examination may not serve as the basis for denying or terminating employment. Violators of this law are guilty of a Class B misdemeanor.

- **Vermont** — In Vermont, when circumstances permit the use of a polygraph examination (similar to the federal exceptions), the examiner may not ask any questions regarding the examinee's political, religious or labor union affiliations, sexual practices, social habits or marital relationship, unless the questions clearly relate to job performance (Vt. Stat. Ann. tit. 21, §494c(b)(1)(2) and (3)).

- **Washington** — A Washington statute (R.C.W. 18.83.010) prohibits private or public employers from requiring employees or applicants to take lie detector tests.

- **Wisconsin** — Wisconsin's Fair Employment Act (Wis. Stat. §111.37) distinguishes between polygraphs and lie detector tests. A lie detector test includes a polygraph, deceptograph, voice stress analyzer, psychological stress analyzer or other similar device that is used to render a diagnostic opinion about the honesty or dishonesty of a person. A polygraph is an instrument that records continuously, visually, permanently and simultaneously any changes in cardiovascular, respiratory and electrodermal patterns as minimum instrumental standards and is used or the results of which are used to render a diagnostic opinion about the honesty or dishonesty of an individual.

An employer cannot, directly or indirectly, require, request, suggest or cause an employee or prospective employee to take a lie detector test or discharge or refuse to hire an individual for refusing to submit to a lie detector test. An employer that has administered a lie detector test must post a notice prepared by the Department of Workforce Development.

However, an employer may ask an employee to submit to a polygraph test for the same reasons allowed under the federal statute. The employer is bound by an exhaustive and detailed list of requirements when the polygraph test is administered. An employer also can incur criminal liability under Wis. Stat. §942.06, which prohibits a person from disclosing that another person has taken a polygraph test or releasing the results of such test without the prior written consent of the test subject.

Other Tests — Honesty, Personality

Employers generally can use honesty and personality tests in determining whether applicants have the integrity and personality traits they consider reliable indicators of successful employees. In **Rhode Island**, however, "honesty tests" are included in the definition of "lie detector tests" (R.I. Gen. Laws §28-6.1-4), which employers are prohibited from requiring employees to take. Honesty tests, in particular, have been highly effective when lawful to weed out dishonest employees. However, these tests, if improperly written or administered, also can provide the basis for claimed violations of a number of federal and state employment laws, including Title VII of the 1964 Civil Rights Act, the ADA and the Age Discrimination in Employment Act. Employers must be careful that their tests do not inquire about any information that could be used to discriminate such as those inquiries discussed in the application and interview sections of this chapter.

In addition, the tests can result in disparate impact liability if they are found to exclude a disproportionate number of minorities or females. An employer must be prepared to show that the test was both valid and relevant to the particular job. Also, employers who subject only certain applicants to the test while exempting others, subject themselves to potential claims of discrimination. Some states' prohibitions on lie detector tests may be broadly construed to include written honesty tests. In addition, a test designed to determine a personality disorder may be considered a medical examination subject to the ADA and state disability statutes.

SECTION III:
Workplace Investigations

The success of an employer in managing its employee relations and steering clear, or at least minimizing, its exposure to workplace liability is very often traceable to its ability to conduct prompt, thorough investigations of employee misconduct. An employer that can spot the issues, pin down the facts and see the possibilities will be best prepared to deal with the disgruntled employee or overzealous plaintiff's lawyer.

For that employer, "due process" — or affording employees, the accused as well as the accuser, the opportunity to be heard — is not just something followed to satisfy employee expectations. It is something that inures to the company's benefit and can prove to be an indispensable tool in defending against subsequent claims, whether based on privacy or other concerns.

This section discusses the various federal and state laws that are potential sources of employer liability when conducting workplace investigations, including employees' right to privacy, employers' liability for negligent hiring, defamation and wrongful discharge (Chapter 5); the limits on electronic surveillance and searches of employee workspace and personal property, including the changes the USA PATRIOT Act have made (Chapter 6); and provides a handy checklist for conducting legal investigations at work (Chapter 7).

Sources of Potential Liability

5

As a threshold issue, even before determining how to approach the investigation of a workplace problem, an employer should be aware of the types of liability that can result from (1) the alleged conduct about to be investigated, (2) the investigation itself and (3) the failure to conduct a proper investigation.

Virtually all businesses today are familiar with the most common sources of workplace liability:

- federal, state and local laws regulating employment discrimination based on certain immutable characteristics (*e.g.*, race, gender, religion, national origin, citizenship, age and marital status);

- wage and hour laws governing hours of work, wages and other compensation and benefits, including minimum wage and overtime pay; and

- laws establishing employee rights to leaves of absence for disabilities, family issues and more.

In addition to these employment-related statutory rights, federal and state constitutions, statutes and court decisions give all Americans certain rights to privacy, both in and out of the workplace. These rights, which vary widely from state to state, set limits on employers' entitlement to obtain information. Not only the type of information but the way in which it is sought may be limited. Violating those limitations can result in substantial liability for an employer.

Certain individual privacy rights are derived from the U.S. Constitution and have been supported by both federal and state courts. Workplace privacy rights addressed by the federal Constitution apply only to public employees, however, because the rights may be invoked only when government action is involved. The Fourth Amendment's prohibition against unreasonable searches and seizures, for example, applies to action by governmental entities, not private employers.

Some state constitutions include private-sector employers in their granting of privacy rights. In **California**, for example, an employee can sue a private employer for violating the state constitution's rights to privacy.

A number of federal statutes protect various aspects of employee privacy (see Chapter 1), including: the Bankruptcy Code, which prohibits discrimination against employees who are or have been bankrupt or associated with someone who is bankrupt; the Employee Polygraph Protection Act of 1988, which restricts or prohibits the use of lie detector tests by certain employers; the Fair Credit Reporting Act, which regulates how credit information is obtained and used by employers and consumer reporting agencies; the Mail Tampering Act, which prohibits the diversion of another's mail; the National Labor Relations Act, which restricts employer surveillance activities during union organizing or when employees engage in protected concerted activity; the Omnibus Crime Control and Safe Streets Act of 1968, which regulates interceptions of wire, oral or electronic communications; and the Health Insurance Portability and Accountability Act of 1996, which restricts certain disclosures of identifiable health information.

Some states have enacted "mini-privacy acts" similar to the federal Privacy Act of 1974, which gives U.S. citizens and aliens who have been lawfully admitted for permanent residence some rights to control the government's use and disclosure of identifying information. The state laws give the same rights concerning identifying information obtained by state and local governments.

Many states also have enacted laws regulating wiretapping and electronic surveillance and polygraph examinations of employees, information in personnel files, off-duty activities, and pre-employment inquiries concerning criminal history, marital and family status.

Common Law Rights

In addition to constitutions and statutes, employees often have common law causes of action. These are court made, as opposed to legislature made, laws. They grow from the ever changing customs and traditions that make up public policy and are fast becoming the claims of choice for employees' lawyers.

Unlike most of the statutes, for which money damages frequently are capped and government action often is required before a claim can be pursued in court, common law actions may hold out the possibility of unlimited damage awards and personal liability for accused supervisors, amounting to increased leverage that can be used by employees to prompt early settlements.

Privacy

Despite the commonly held misconception by employees that their personal office space is as private as anything in their homes, not all jurisdictions recognize an employee's right to privacy in the workplace. Where it exists, such a right often is premised on some privacy entitlement stated in the state constitution or developed through judges' decisions over time.

The significance of whether this right exists cannot be overemphasized. Not only does it impact on whether an employer can be sued for violating an employee's workplace right to privacy, it can affect the ability of an employer to conduct workplace searches and even to deny employees the opportunity to see their personnel files.

It is important for employers to know whether the jurisdictions in which they do business recognize this right. The following jurisdictions (Fig. 5-1) recognize a private-sector employee's right to privacy, whether based on statutory or common law (employers should consult with knowledgeable legal counsel regarding the state of the law of their jurisdictions before conducting a workplace investigation):

Fig. 5-1 **States That Recognize Private Employees' Rights to Privacy**			
Alabama	Iowa	Montana	Rhode Island
Alaska	Louisiana	Nebraska	South Carolina
Arkansas	Maine	Nevada	Tennessee
California (by statute)	Maryland	New Hampshire	Texas
Florida	Massachusetts	North Carolina	Vermont
Hawaii	Michigan	Ohio	Wisconsin
Illinois	Mississippi		

Negligent Retention

In most state jurisdictions, an employer is charged with the duty to protect employees and others from injuries at the hands of employees who pose a "known risk of bodily harm to others." (See, e.g., *Haddock v. City of New York*, 75 N.Y.2d 478 (1990).) When the failure to do so can be shown to be the result of gross recklessness or malice, a company may even be found liable for punitive damages. Notable exceptions to this include **Alaska, Delaware, Kentucky, Montana, Oklahoma, South Carolina** and **Vermont** — but those states, despite no current law on the subject, still might hold an employer liable under appropriate circumstances.

This cause of action, which has been raised with regard to claims of negligent hiring as well, often arises in connection with events that typically are broadcast as headline news: the public school custodian who sexually abuses a student, and whose prior criminal record for sexual crimes was never discovered by the school prior to his hire; the retail clerk who assaults a customer with a baseball bat, and who, despite prior threatening behavior on the job, had been retained by the store after receiving just a warning.

(Note: The courts in **Ohio**, while recognizing a cause of action for negligent retention, thus far have limited their application of this doctrine in the workplace to cases involving claims of sexual harassment. In **California**, a public employee is not liable for an injury resulting from an act or omission that was the result of exercising his or her authority, even if that power was abused.)

How does this affect workplace investigations? Consider the following: A popular manager is accused of sexual harassment. A female clerk in his department claims he fondled her breasts, brushed up against her and, on a number of occasions, made lewd remarks. She also states she has been affected, both mentally and physically, by his "assaults." The clerk, however, does not want to make trouble and would like the human resources professional to keep her complaint confidential in the hope things will get better on their own.

Should human resources honor the clerk's request and keep the matter private? Does the clerk have a right to expect such privacy?

Suppose human resources agrees to do nothing, but six months later the manager rapes a different (or the same) female subordinate. Is there any potential liability, aside from personal injury, civil assault or sexual harassment claims? Certainly, a claim the company negligently retained the manager, without any investigation despite being placed on notice of his potentially harmful tendencies, is a real possibility. What is more, even if the company is spared such a lawsuit, the company may have to suffer through the public relations nightmare that is likely to occur. Even if the manager is vindicated after an investigation, those who read about the allegations on the front page of the local newspaper are unlikely to take note of the final result printed months later on page 26.

Defamation

Most states also recognize the right of employees and former employees to be free from defamatory statements arising out of the workplace. In those jurisdictions, an individual who has been defamed, whether in writing (libel) or orally (slander), can recover money damages. (See Fig. 5-2 for a discussion of false light invasion of privacy.)

What is required to constitute defamation? While the elements may vary somewhat by state, to prevail on a claim of defamation, a plaintiff generally is required to show:

- there was a defamatory statement — in broad terms, one that injures a person's standing in the community or reputation in business;
- the statement was published, that is, passed on in some manner to a third party; and
- the statement was false.

In employment matters, a negative statement about an employee and his or her work often is presumed to be defamatory. If the statement is false, the only issue is one of publication. In most states, only the alleged defamer can publish a defamatory statement. In those jurisdictions, if a supervisor falsely accuses an employee of dealing illegal drugs, for example, but tells no one else of the accusation, the employee has no actionable claim for defamation, even if the employee lets others know about the supervisor's statement.

Fig. 5-2
False Light Invasion of Privacy

Employers in **Nebraska** are subject to "false light invasion of privacy" claims, which are statements that reasonably may be viewed as placing another in a false light before the public. While broader than the more typical defamation cause of action, this doctrine would appear to cover defamation-type claims. It has been applied, for example, to a case alleging an employee's former employer distributed libelous material and made slanderous statements regarding the plaintiff's termination.

Iowa, like Nebraska, recognizes a cause of action for invasion of privacy under the false light theory. This claim requires a plaintiff to prove more than mere publication of the defamatory statement to a third party. Proof of publicity — communication to the public at large — must be offered.

Michigan and **Ohio** recognize false light invasion of privacy claims.

In **Florida,** the law prohibits the public disclosure of private facts as an invasion of privacy when the publicized matter would be highly offensive to a reasonable person and is not a legitimate public concern.

Compelled self-publication

A minority of states — including **Arkansas, Iowa, Texas** and **Vermont** — have recognized (or, in the case of Vermont, a federal court has opined that the state would recognize) a doctrine of "compelled self-publication." Under this doctrine, an employer can be held liable when it reasonably should have known the plaintiff-employee would feel compelled to repeat the defamatory statement later, such as in a subsequent job interview when a prospective employer asks about the reasons the employee left his or her prior job and the plaintiff-employee in fact does "publish" the statement to others.

In **Texas**, however, an action for compelled self-publication exists only when the defamed person's communication of the defamatory statement was made without knowledge of the statement's defamatory nature and the circumstances indicated that communication to a third party was likely.

Privileged statements

An employer's statements about an employee may be privileged — that is, either qualifiedly or absolutely immune from defamation claims, depending on the context and the jurisdiction.

Consider, for example, why companies are not regularly sued for negative statements made by supervisors to employees during performance evaluations. Is it because the criticized employees generally accept the fact that they are poor performers? Doubtful.

One reason is that, in many states, the employer enjoys a qualified privilege for statements made during the course and in furtherance of the employment relationship. That often includes a supervisor's explanation to an employee of the reasons for termination and statements made during an employee evaluation. To overcome the privilege, a plaintiff generally has to prove malice or actual ill will on the part of the company. (See, *e.g.,* *Shapiro v. Health Ins. Plan of Greater New York*, 7 N.Y.2d 56, 60-61 (1959).)

An absolute privilege generally is applied to statements made in connection with litigation or in answer to a government inquiry. The idea, in certain jurisdictions, is to encourage employers to be honest and thorough in their responses without having to fear claims of defamation in addition to the proceeding in which they currently are involved. Thus, statements made during a labor arbitration, in an answer to a complaint filed by the employee in court or to a state labor department inquiry in connection with a former employee's claim for unemployment insurance benefits generally are immune from defamation claims — even if they, in fact, are false and defamatory. Fig. 5-3 lists states that recognize privileged communications.

Fig. 5-3
Privileges From Defamation Claims

The following states recognize qualified and/or absolute privileges for employer statements in appropriate circumstances (the state law itself should be examined to determine its scope):

Alabama
A qualified privilege has been applied to communications between previous and prospective employers. Indeed, communications between employees that are in keeping with the scope of the employees' duties do not even constitute a "publication" for defamation purposes. A privilege has been applied to statements made to the government concerning unemployment insurance benefits, but the court did not clarify whether the privilege was qualified or absolute.

Alaska
A qualified privilege was found for an employer's written statements, placed in the personnel file, that the employee was emotionally unstable, in desperate need of help and on the verge of a breakdown.

Arkansas
Qualified privilege generally attaches to statements made by an employer in connection with matters affecting its business, including misconduct investigations.

California
Qualified privilege generally exists for statements made by managers during employee evaluations. The courts, however, seem increasingly willing to recognize defamation claims in egregious situations. For example, the courts have suggested defamation claims could be brought by employees whose terminations were based, at least in part, on defamatory statements by co-workers.

Colorado
Qualified privilege exists for internal employer communications when (1) the communication is made in an appropriate situation, such as in the course of an investigation; (2) the communication is restricted to those with a legitimate need to know; and (3) the communication has sufficient factual support to demonstrate it was not motivated by malice. Information provided by employers to government agencies investigating claims of discrimination also has been ruled privileged.

Fig. 5-3 (continued)
Privileges From Defamation Claims

Connecticut	Qualified privilege extends to statements made by an employer in managing its business, including statements made in connection with employee evaluations. The privilege, however, does not apply to statements made to employees, including managers and supervisors, who do not have a need to know the information. An absolute privilege applies to statements made in quasi-judicial proceedings, including unemployment insurance benefits proceedings and proceedings involving the State's Commission on Human Rights and Opportunities.
Florida	Qualified privilege exists for communications between employees.
Georgia	A conditional, or qualified, privilege attaches to statements made to prospective employers. A privilege also extends to negative statements made in connection with a performance evaluation or intra-corporate investigation.
Hawaii	Conditional privilege exists for comments regarding employees. Moreover, Hawaii recognizes a qualified immunity for job references, presuming the employer acted in good faith (Haw. Rev. Stat. §663-1.95). The presumption can be overcome by showing the information provided was either knowingly false or misleading.
Kentucky	An absolute privilege applies to statements made in response to government inquiries.
Idaho	A qualified privilege exists for statements made to one who shares a common interest or has a legitimate need to know.
Illinois	Employers generally are protected when providing employment references as long as the references are made in a good faith effort to provide truthful information (745 I.L.C.S. §46).
	Qualified privilege extends to employer/employee statements made in a legitimate business context. An absolute privilege attaches to statements made in the course of judicial or quasi-judicial proceedings.
Iowa	Employers generally are protected in providing employment references as long as the references are made in a good faith effort to provide truthful information (Iowa Code §91B.2).
	Qualified privilege applies to statements made by employers during good faith evaluations and investigations undertaken within the bounds of the employment relationship.
Louisiana	Intra-corporate communications generally are entitled to a qualified privilege, provided they are in the usual course of business and reasonably necessary to effect the communication of the privileged matter to those entitled to receive it. Also qualifiedly privileged are good faith statements by employers concerning job performance and other work-related matters, statements made during a workplace investigation and statements made to a state agency such as the state's Office of Employment Security.

Fig. 5-3 (continued)
Privileges From Defamation Claims

Maine	A conditional privilege appears to exist for intra-company statements concerning an employee incident, provided those statements are communicated only to company personnel with a need to know.
Maryland	Employers generally are protected when providing employment references as long as the references are made in good faith (Md. Code Ann., Crts and Jud. Proceedings §5-423).
Massachusetts	A conditional privilege attaches to communications reasonably necessary to serve the employer's legitimate interest in an employee's fitness to perform the job. This includes an employer's good faith response to an employment reference inquiry.
Michigan	Employers generally are protected in providing employer references (M.C.S. §423.452).
Mississippi	Qualified privilege exists for statements made concerning an employee's job deficiencies. Except when maliciously false, statements made by employers in response to employees' petitions for unemployment insurance benefits are privileged.
Missouri	Communications between officers of the same corporation, or between different offices of the same corporation, are not considered "published" for purposes of a defamation action.
Montana	Although little case law exists on the privilege issue, Mont. Code Ann. §27-1-804 appears to apply a qualified privilege for statements made by employers in furtherance of their legitimate workplace duties such as statements made during performance reviews, and an absolute privilege for statements made in litigation or in responding to government inquiries.
New Hampshire	A conditional privilege exists for statements by employers about employees when made in good faith, without an intent to defame, and to a person having a common interest in the subject.
New Jersey	Qualified privilege generally attaches to employer statements concerning employee job performance and to statements by co-employees about an employee's misconduct or poor performance. An absolute privilege applies to statements made in connection with judicial, legislative or administrative hearings
New York	Qualified privilege generally applies for statements made during a legitimate workplace investigation and in connection with employee evaluations or exit interviews. An absolute privilege attaches to statements made pursuant to a government inquiry or in connection with litigation (for example, in an answer to a complaint filed in court).

Fig. 5-3 (continued)
Privileges From Defamation Claims

North Carolina	Qualified privilege generally attaches to good faith statements made by employers in connection with their workplace interests such as statements made during misconduct investigations. An absolute privilege applies to statements made in judicial and quasi-judicial proceedings. There is a recent state law (N.C. Gen. Stat. §1-539.12) that provides immunity for employers who disclose information in a reference check. However, the immunity does not apply if the information is false or the employer reasonably should have known it was false.
Ohio	A specific law limits the exposure of employers in giving employment references. The law (O.R.C. §4113.71) generally shields an employer from liability for such statements unless it knew the information was false, had the intent to mislead and acted with malice.
Oregon	Qualified privilege generally exists for statements made to protect an employer's interests. An employer normally is privileged to provide information to its employees regarding a co-employee's termination provided it has reasonable grounds to believe the information is true. An absolute privilege generally applies to communications made during judicial or quasi-judicial (e.g., unemployment insurance) proceedings.
	Employers generally are protected when providing employment references (O.R.S. §30.178). Limitations on that protection are similar to those in the Ohio law described above.
Rhode Island	Employers are protected when providing employment references (R.I. Gen. Laws 28-6.4-1(e)). Limitations on that protection are similar to those in the Ohio law described above. A qualified privilege attaches to employer statements about employees made in good faith to supervisors or other employees, provided the employer reasonably believes the co-workers are entitled to be advised of the misconduct.
South Carolina	Qualified privilege generally attaches to statements made during legitimate workplace investigations.
Tennessee	Qualified privilege extends to employment references, as well as to the written contents of a personnel file accessible only by management. An absolute privilege exists for records submitted by an employer to the state's Department of Employment Security.
Texas	Qualified privilege generally protects statements made during the course of employee misconduct investigations.
Utah	Employers generally are protected when providing employment references (Utah Code Ann. §34-42-1). Limitations on that protection are similar to those in the Ohio law described above.
Virginia	Employers generally are not prohibited from providing prospective employers with truthful, job-related information regarding an employee's voluntary departure or, if discharged, the reasons for the termination.

> ### Fig. 5-3 (continued)
> ### Privileges From Defamation Claims
>
> | | |
> |---|---|
> | **Washington** | An intra-office statement concerning an employee's job performance generally enjoys a qualified privilege. An absolute privilege exists for statements made during judicial proceedings. |
> | **Wisconsin** | State law protects employers from liability for statements made in connection with employment references (Wis. Stat. §895.487). A "conditional privilege" generally attaches to statements made in connection with misconduct investigations. The privilege may be lost if abused, for example if the employer communicated the information with knowledge or reckless disregard of its falsity, for an unprivileged purpose or to a person who did not need to receive the information. |
> | **Wyoming** | Employers are protected when providing employment references (Wyo. Stat. §27-1-113). Limitations on that protection are similar to those in the Ohio law described above. |

Causes of Action for Wrongful Discharge

With some exceptions, states generally can be divided into those that apply the doctrine of employment-at-will and those that recognize causes of action for wrongful discharge. That does not mean the two doctrines are mutually exclusive, however. There are states that fall somewhere in the middle, and, of course, there are numerous variations among the states in applying the different doctrines.

Employment-at-Will

In its strictest terms, employment-at-will means the employment relationship may be terminated, by either the employer or the employee, at any time — whether or not there is cause for the termination. The only limitations on the employer's right to terminate an at-will employee are those that might exist in constitutional or statutory law, or in an employment contract.

New York provides a good example of a relatively strict employment-at-will state. Suppose an employee reports for work one morning and immediately is fired by the manager for wearing brown shoes. Is that permissible? Is it fair? Does fairness even matter? Does it matter whether the company has a policy against wearing brown shoes? Or whether the employee first received a warning? Suppose this is the first time an employee ever has been terminated for wearing brown shoes, and it never happens again? Suppose still that the employee is highly regarded and just recently received great praise in his or her job evaluation? Has the employer violated the law?

Though it may be surprising, it generally is not unlawful in a state like **New York** for a private employer to terminate an employee for wearing brown shoes — unless there is an employment agreement (including a union contract) that expressly limits the employer's otherwise unfettered right to terminate its employees such as with a requirement that discharges be for cause. In fact, even in strict employment-at-will states, New York included, the courts have become increasingly liberal in finding the existence of implied contracts in employee handbooks and written policies and procedures.

Of course, this does not mean an employer should terminate employees for arbitrary reasons, even if it lawfully can do so. Such a policy does not make good business sense because it can cause employee morale problems and make it difficult to recruit quality employees. Moreover, it would cause substantial proof problems if the terminated employee were able to file a claim of disparate treatment under a traditional discrimination statute — a claim, for example, that the employer's reason for the termination (brown shoes) is really a pretext for race (or sex or age or national origin) discrimination. Few jurors would believe the brown shoes rationale.

Wrongful Discharge

The jurisdictions that have departed from the at-will approach generally have adopted one, or a combination, of three rationales — "violations of public policy, ...; breach of an express or implied contract; [and/or] breach of the covenant of good faith and fair dealing." (St. Antoine, *A Seed Germinates: Unjust Discharge Reform Heads Towards Full Flower*, 67 Neb. L. Rev. 56, 58-59 (1988)).

Public policy is the community common sense and conscience. It is the accepted public opinion about what is right and fair. It would be against public policy to fire an employee who refused to participate in an illegal act, for example, or who reported to the proper authorities a violation of law. Some states find an exception to employment-at-will when an employer's discharge of an employee violates the public's idea of what is just.

In every employment relationship there is a contract. Usually the contract is implied — an unwritten agreement between the employer and employee that the employee will perform a particular job in return for a stated compensation. Sometimes employment contracts are express, written documents signed by both parties. Sometimes personnel manuals and written policies are found by courts to be part of the employment contract. The parties have a right to enforce employment contracts just as they would any other contract, although some states do not permit the enforcement of implied contracts to overcome the employment-at-will doctrine.

It is implied in business dealings that all parties will treat each other fairly and act in good faith. If it is obvious that the employer was unfair or acted with bad intent when it hired or discharged the employee, those states that recognize the common law covenant of good faith and fair dealing permit the employee to sue to enforce the implied agreement that the employer would be fair.

 In states with causes of action for wrongful discharge, or similar claims by other names, employers generally must have cause to terminate employees — and be able to prove that cause if the termination is challenged. Moreover, the cause may not be one that violates public policy, the employment contract, or the duty to act in good faith and deal fairly with the employee.

The following chart, Fig. 5-4, lists those jurisdictions that have adopted the at-will and wrongful discharge doctrines. Most of the jurisdictions identified as adhering to the doctrine of employment-at-will nonetheless recognize a cause of action for wrongful discharge if the termination violates some public policy — such as the discharge of an employee in retaliation for his or her cooperation in a government investigation, for asserting an established right (to be paid an earned wage, for example) or for other reasons. In view of that, as well as the fact that the application of each doctrine may vary among the jurisdictions, an employer would do well to consult with knowledgeable counsel regarding the law of its jurisdiction and any recent developments.

Jurisdictions	Employment-At-Will-	Wrongful Discharge	Jurisdictions	Employment-At-Will	Wrongful Discharge
Alabama	✓		Montana		✓
Alaska	✓		Nebraska	✓	
Arizona	✓		New Hampshire	✓	
Arkansas	✓		Nevada	✓	
California		✓	New Jersey	✓	
Colorado		✓	New Mexico	✓	
Connecticut	✓		New York	✓	
Delaware	✓		North Carolina	✓	
District of Columbia	✓		North Dakota	✓	
Florida	✓		Ohio	✓	
Georgia	✓		Oklahoma	✓	
Hawaii	✓		Oregon	✓	
Kentucky	✓		Pennsylvania	✓	
Idaho	✓		Rhode Island	✓	
Indiana	✓		South Carolina	✓	
Illinois	✓		South Dakota	✓	
Iowa	✓		Tennessee	✓	
Kansas	✓		Texas	✓	
Louisiana	✓		Utah	✓	
Maine	✓		Vermont	✓	
Maryland	✓		Virginia	✓	
Massachusetts	✓		Washington	✓	
Michigan	✓		West Virginia	✓	
Minnesota	✓		Wisconsin	✓	
Mississippi	✓		Wyoming	✓	
Missouri	✓			✓	

California

Employers with offices in **California**, a wrongful discharge state, should take note of a recent decision. In *Cotran v. Rollins Hudig Hall Intl, Inc.* (17 Cal. 4th 93 (1998)), the California Supreme Court ruled an employer legally may terminate an employee when it has a reasonable, good faith belief the employee engaged in terminable misconduct, even if that belief later turns out to be mistaken. Prior to this case, juries were entitled to decide whether an employee actually committed the act for which he or she was fired. Now, a jury must determine whether the employer's decision was based on a reasonable, good faith investigation. Consequently, the quality of an employer's investigation takes on even greater significance.

The *Coltran* case involved claims of sexual harassment (obscene telephone calls, exposing oneself) by two female employees against a senior vice president. In response to the complaints, the company, an insurance brokerage firm, promptly suspended the vice president — who claimed he had been falsely accused — and conducted a two-week investigation. The company obtained sworn statements from the accusers and telephone records showing the vice president had called both women at home. In addition, the company interviewed 21 employees, five of whom at the vice president's request. One, an employee who had worked with the vice president at a previous job, reported he had made obscene calls to her home during the time they worked for the prior employer. The vice president himself also was interviewed.

Based on its investigation, the employer determined it was more likely than not that the vice president had engaged in the harassing conduct and terminated his employment.

The vice president sued the company for wrongful termination, alleging he was fired in violation of an implied employment agreement requiring good cause for termination. At trial, he strenuously denied the charges and presented evidence he had consensual affairs with both accusers, asserting both falsely accused him of harassment because they were angry he had two-timed them.

At the close of evidence, the trial court instructed the jury to find in the vice president's favor if they believed his rendition of events, regardless of whether the company had a good faith belief at the time it terminated his employment that the vice president had engaged in misconduct. The jury believed the vice president and awarded him $1.78 million in damages.

The company appealed and the California Supreme Court reversed. The court found that good cause in the wrongful discharge context means "fair and honest reasons, regulated by good faith on the part of the employer, that are not trivial, arbitrary or capricious, unrelated to business needs or goals, or pretextual." Also, the court ruled that the employer need show only its conclusion that there was misconduct and the decision to terminate the employee was "reached honestly, after an appropriate investigation"; it is not required to provide irrefutable proof that the employee, in fact, engaged in the misconduct. The employer cannot simply rely on its subjective belief an employee committed misconduct, but it is sufficient for the employer to convince a jury it acted as a reasonable employer would have acted under similar circumstances.

The court ruled that evidence of a good faith investigation may include:

- fair notice to the accused of the nature of the alleged offense;

- fair opportunity for the accused to offer evidence in his or her defense;

- an adequate investigation of all reasonable sources of information;

- a guarantee of procedural due process that is appropriate under the circumstances, (e.g., progressive discipline);

- a reasoned conclusion supported by substantial evidence;

- a decision that is not arbitrary, (i.e., that is consistent with past practice and treatment of others); and

- a decision that is based on legitimate business needs.

Colorado

In **Colorado**, the cause of action for wrongful discharge is reserved for cases in which an employee is terminated for failing to perform an unlawful act or contrary to a recognized and identifiable public policy. In general, the public policy must be evidenced by a statute, regulation, code or established common law principle. Even when these conditions are satisfied, an employee may not bring a wrongful discharge claim if there is a federal or state statute that provides a comprehensive remedial scheme to deal with the employee's situation.

Montana

In 1987, **Montana** enacted the Wrongful Discharge From Employment Act (Mont. Code Ann. §39-2-901 *et seq.*). Among other things, the act provides that discharges are wrongful if: (1) in retaliation for the employee's refusal to violate public policy or for reporting a violation of public policy; (2) not for good cause, when the employee has completed the employer's probationary period (good cause being defined as "reasonable job-related grounds for dismissal based on failure to satisfactorily perform job duties, disruption of the employer's operation or other legitimate business reasons"); or (3) in violation of the express provisions of the employer's own written policy. Under the act, moreover, an employee is required to exhaust any written internal grievance procedures before filing an action for wrongful discharge.

Special Considerations With Sexual and Other Harassment

Employee allegations of harassment, particularly sexual harassment, must be handled with heightened sensitivity. As discussed in connection with negligent retention claims and the hypothetical set out in that section of this chapter, the uniquely private nature of sexual harassment issues, and the harm that can come, publicly and privately, to both the accuser and the accused, increase the potential for employer liability and the need for prompt, thorough investigations.

The privacy concerns in such cases often come not only from the accuser, who may ask that the employer keep the complaint strictly confidential, at least "for the time being," but also from the accused, the alleged harasser. One of the best known examples of the risks faced by employers is the case brought against Miller Brewing

Company by an employee who was terminated after his secretary accused him of sexual harassment. The employee had watched an episode of the then-popular sitcom *Seinfeld* in which the main character, Jerry Seinfeld, could not remember an ex-girlfriend's name, but knew it rhymed with a female body part. Her name, the viewer later learns, was Dolores, which rhymes with clitoris. The Miller employee told his secretary about the episode and, when she did not seem to get the joke, copied the "clitoris" page from the dictionary and gave it to her. The secretary complained she felt she was being abused and that, even before this incident, she had felt "uneasy" around her boss.

After a trial, the jury returned a verdict in favor of the alleged harasser — for more than $26 million. Though much of that award was in connection with claims unrelated to the sexual harassment issues in the case and a sizable portion of the remedy was set aside on appeal, the cost incurred by the company and the secretary in defending against the lawsuit cannot be ignored.

In apparent realization of the devastating effect sexual harassment accusations can have on an accused individual and others, certain jurisdictions have taken steps to protect employees from such false accusations and from disclosure of certain private facts.

In **California**, for example, heightened protection can be found for individuals' sexual privacy. In one case, a court denied a plaintiff's request for information about the alleged harasser's sexual relations with other female employees (*Boler v. Superior Court*, 201 Cal. App.3d 467 (1987)). California courts, moreover, frequently will deny plaintiffs' requests for the names, addresses and telephone numbers of female employees sought to ascertain whether other women were harassed by an accused manager. In recognition of the right of sexual privacy, companies have been forbidden by the courts from disclosing such information absent written consent from those co-employees.

See Chapter 7 for a checklist on investigating sexual harassment claims.

Surveillance and Searches

6

In undertaking workplace investigations, employers should be aware of applicable federal and state laws before conducting electronic surveillance of employees such as tape-recording employee telephone conversations, recording in-person workplace conversations or initiating video surveillance of employees. There also can be legal ramifications for employers searching employees' personal spaces such as lockers, desks or handbags and briefcases.

Tape-Recording Telephone Conversations

Tape-recording employee telephone conversations is done by numerous employers, lawfully or unlawfully. Indeed, in the 1980s, when the ability to tap into another's telephone conversation surreptitiously was far from what it is today, it was estimated that as many as 15 million employees worked in industries where employers monitored employees' telephones (Shepard, Duston and Russell, *Workplace Privacy* (BNA) (2d ed. 1989) at p. 221).

The ability of an employer to listen in on its employees' telephone conversations is governed by both federal and state law.

Federal Law

The federal Wiretapping Law — Title III of the Omnibus Crime Control and Safe Streets Act of 1968 (18 U.S.C. §2510 *et seq.*) — makes it a criminal offense generally for employers to "intentionally interrupt" any wire, oral or electronic communication. An employer who violates the law is subject to punitive damages. Even if no actual damage is proven, or if the intercepted communication is kept private and no harm otherwise results from the interception, the law provides for a minimum recovery of $100 for each day of violation or $10,000, whichever is greater.

In some respects, however, as far as the workplace is concerned the exceptions permitted under the statute may make the rule ineffectual. An employer, for example, may monitor employee telephone calls by use of an extension telephone "in the ordinary course of business." The precise meaning of that phrase has been the subject of court interpretation and may vary depending on the jurisdiction. Monitoring has been upheld, for example, when the purpose was to determine if confidential information was being conveyed and when it was done to protect employees from abusive telephone calls; in both cases, the employees were notified of the monitoring in advance. One court, however, found that the monitoring of an employee's sales calls with an extension telephone was improper, even though prior notification was given to the employee, because the employer failed to cease the monitoring once it was clear the telephone call was of a personal nature (*Watkins v. L.M. Berry Co.*, 704 F.2d 577 (11th Cir. 1983)).

A second exception in the law, the provider exception, essentially permits telephone companies and other providers of wire communication services to monitor calls for service or mechanical reasons.

The most commonly known and applied exception to the prohibition on monitoring is that permitting interception if at least one party to the conversation has consented to it. Thus, a supervisor's tape-recording of his or her meeting with an employee is not unlawful because the supervisor is the consenting party to the conversation, as long as state law also permits it. An important consideration, then, is what state law provides.

State Laws

With notable exceptions for states with detailed regulations concerning telephone and other electronic monitoring, most state laws permit employer interception of employee telephone calls, but may require either the consent of one or even all parties to the conversation. In many cases, violation of the law is a crime in the state, carrying with it criminal as well as civil penalties.

Consent of one party required: **Colorado; Delaware; District of Columbia; Georgia; Hawaii; Idaho; Iowa; Louisiana; Maine, Missouri; Nebraska; Nevada; New York; North Carolina; Ohio; Oregon; Rhode Island; Tennessee; Utah; Wisconsin**; and **Wyoming**.

Consent of all parties required: **California; Connecticut; Florida; Illinois; Maryland; Michigan; Montana; New Hampshire; Pennsylvania**; and **Washington**.

Other jurisdictions:

- **Alabama** — No statute on this topic. Monitoring may provide the basis for a cause of action for invasion of privacy when the plaintiff can show an intrusion into matters of a private nature and the intrusions would be objectionable to a reasonable person (*Bushby v. Truswal Systems Corp.*, 551 So.2d 322, 323 (Ala. 1989)).

- **Kentucky** — No statutory or case law on the topic.

- **Massachusetts** — The interception of wire or oral communications is prohibited, with an exception for office intercommunications systems "used in the ordinary course of business" (Mass. Code Ch. 272, §99). Such use can include eavesdropping on a conversation to identify a suspect's voice, and recording telemarketing calls and randomly sampling them to assure quality control.

- **Mississippi** — Only the state Bureau of Narcotics may "own, possess, install, operate or monitor an electronic, mechanical or other device" (Miss. Code Ann. §41-29-507(1)). "Electronic, mechanical or other device" is defined as "a device or apparatus primarily designed or used for the nonconsensual interception of wire, oral or other communications" (Miss. Code Ann. §41-29-501(f)).

- **New Jersey** — The New Jersey Wiretapping and Electronic Surveillance Control Act (N.J.S.A. §2A:156A-1 *et seq.*) prohibits employer tape-recording of employee telephone calls. Like the federal Wiretapping Act, there is an exception for "providers."

- **New Mexico** — No statutory or case law on the topic.

- **Oklahoma** — No statutory or case law on the topic.

- **South Carolina** — Pen registers or trap and trace devices may not be installed without a court order (S.C. Code Ann. §17-29-20). A bill recently was introduced in the South Carolina House which, if passed and enacted, would, among other things, prohibit intentionally intercepting or attempting to intercept wire or electronic communication.

- **Texas** — The monitoring issue generally is addressed through a common law action for tortious invasion of privacy and turns on whether the monitoring was unreasonable, unjustified or unwarranted. Whether an employee had a reasonable expectation of privacy is an important consideration.

- **Utah** — In addition to the one-party consent rule (see the list of states requiring such consent above), Utah's prohibition on monitoring does not apply to (1) overhearing messages through a regularly installed instrument on a telephone party line or on an extension, and (2) interception by the telephone company or subscriber incident to enforcement of regulations limiting the use of the facilities to normal operation and use (Utah Code Ann. §76-9-403).

- **Vermont** — No statutory or case law on the topic.

Workplace Conversations

The recording of in-person workplace conversations such as during meetings with employees generally follows the same laws and rules as telephone monitoring (i.e., one-party versus all-parties consent) — see above.

In **Oregon**, however, all participants in the conversation must be informed of the taping and consent to it when the parties are present, whereas telephone monitoring requires the consent of only one party.

Video Monitoring

In a large number of states, video surveillance of employees simply has not been addressed by the legislature and is governed by the same considerations that apply to cases alleging violation of a tort of invasion of privacy, which generally is whether the employee(s) had a reasonable expectation of privacy. In still other states such as **New Jersey** and **New York** the sound component of the taping or monitoring is the issue most highly regulated. Accordingly, videotaping or surveillance, without sound, may be permissible, even without notice to the employees (although the installation of cameras in highly private areas such as restrooms still may be prohibited).

Other jurisdictions:

- **Alaska** — The issue turns on whether the employee had a reasonable expectation of privacy.

- **California** — The law is evolving. In a 1999 case, the California Supreme Court held that an employee who lacks a complete expectation of privacy in a workplace conversation because it may be overheard by other workers, but not by the general public, still may recover for violation of the tort of invasion of privacy by intrusion based on the covert videotaping of that conversation (*Sanders v. American Broadcasting Co.*, 20 Cal.4th 907 (1999)).

- **Hawaii** — The state's Electronic Eavesdropping Law (H.R.S. §803-41 to §803-50) prohibits the surreptitious installation of electronic viewing devices in a "private place" *(State v. Lo*, 66 Haw. 653, 659-61; 675 P.2d 754 (1983)).

- **Massachusetts** and **New Hampshire** — A federal court has ruled, in the public-sector context, that video monitoring was not an invasion of privacy in the workplace when it was knowingly performed, revealed and disclosed to the employees, soundless and a rational means to a legitimate goal of the employer (*Vega-Rodriguez v. Puerto Rico Tel. Co.*, 110 F.3d 174 (1st Cir. 1997)). The rationale of this case is equally applicable to the private sector and might be applied in that context as well.

- **Utah** — Follows the same rules as with telephone monitoring (see above).

Opening U.S. Mail

There is little authority, in any jurisdiction, addressing an employer's right to open U.S. mail that is addressed to the employee but delivered to the workplace. Most jurisdictions that recognize an employee's common law right to privacy might well analyze the opening of mail in the same way they would consider other claimed violations of privacy rights. Thus, cases in those jurisdictions may turn on whether the employee has a reasonable expectation of privacy — in other words, a reasonable expectation that his or her mail will not be opened or read.

In **New York** and **Wisconsin**, it is unlawful to open or read a sealed letter or other sealed private communication without the consent of the sender or receiver. (N.Y. Penal Law §250.25; Wis. Stat. §942.05.) In **New York** it has been held, however, that this law was not intended to protect letters sent to employees of municipalities, because permitting employees to use the city as a personal mailing address would be an illegal use of public funds (*People v. Freedman*, 386 N.Y.S.2d 306 (1976)).

Searching Personal Spaces

In the nonunion workplace, an employer's ability to conduct a search — of employee lockers, desks or handbags and briefcases — generally depends on whether the jurisdiction recognizes an employee's right to privacy. The list in Chapter 5 indicates those states that do so. When a right to conduct a lawful search is recognized, a private employer generally must show the employee did not have a reasonable expectation of privacy for items placed in the receptacle searched.

This "reasonable expectation of privacy" standard generally is applied by arbitrators in cases involving union-represented employees as well.

How, then, can an employer reduce or eliminate the employee's expectation of privacy? Essentially, the employer needs to put employees on notice, directly or indirectly, that searches may be conducted, even randomly and without prior notification. This may be accomplished in a number of ways:

- Promulgate a clear, written policy.

- For employee lockers, desks and other receptacles, prohibit the employees' purchase of personal locks or, at least, require that employees provide the company with a key to the lock or notify the company of the combination.

- Have employees acknowledge, in writing, their receipt of any search policy and their understanding of the policy and the need for it. This might best be done at the outset of employment, in conjunction with the employees' orientation and receipt of an employee handbook, if any.

In states that do not recognize a common law right to privacy for employees such as **New York**, there generally is no prohibition on the ability of a private employer to search the workplace, even without notice to its employees. That is not to say an employer would be wise to conduct such a search, even if it lawfully can do so. After all, if employees learn of a surreptitious search, they may not be too happy, and that unhappiness may have an adverse effect on their performance or, perhaps, cause them to search out a union for protection from such intrusions into their perceived privacy.

An issue that often arises in the union setting with respect to searches is whether targeted employees have the right to the presence of a union representative — a so-called *Weingarten* right — at the time of the search. Simply put, a *Weingarten* right, which takes its name from a 1975 decision by the U.S. Supreme Court, is the right of a bargaining unit employee to have a union representative present, on his or her request, at an investigatory interview that he or she reasonably fears might lead to his or her discipline or discharge. It is not a right to legal counsel in the workplace, as no such right generally exists (*NLRB v. Weingarten*, 420 U.S. 251 (1975).

It has been held that there is no *Weingarten* right to union representation at an employer search of a locker, desk, handbag or briefcase because such searches do not constitute investigatory interviews. Nor is there such a right in connection with an employee lineup, shown to witnesses, even though the lineup is part of an investigation.

USA PATRIOT Act

Shortly after 9/11, the United and Strengthening America by Providing Appropriate Tools Required to Intercept and Obstruct Terrorism Act, commonly known as the USA PATRIOT Act, became law. The legislation made changes to national security authorities, criminal law, money laundering statutes, immigration law, victim assistance statutes and laws dealing with the federal government's surveillance and intelligence-gathering capabilities.

The PATRIOT Act also amended the federal wiretapping laws and the Electronic Communication Privacy Act, both as to interception of electronic communications and access to stored wire and electronic communications. The changes created new obligations and new rights for employers in monitoring employees' communications.

The law requires employers to provide private information about their employees to law enforcement authorities in more ways than before. Search warrants, subpoenas, governmental orders or requests can trigger the need to provide information about current or former employees.

The PATRIOT Act:

- Allows government investigators to use search warrants to obtain stored e-mail or voice-mail evidence related to an investigation of any criminal offense. Court wiretap orders are no longer required for access to stored voice-mails. Accordingly, employers are required to comply with search warrants for employee e-mail and voice-mail messages.

- Permits participation in "sneak and peek" searches and seizures without notice to the subject employee. The law authorizes this tactic when the interests of law enforcement are balanced with the privacy interests of the person under surveillance. When authorized, this permits law enforcement to obtain evidence of criminal activity and the employer (or other provider of the communication service) may be ordered to keep the monitoring of communications secret from the individual under surveillance.

- Provides access by the FBI to business records or other tangible items. This is permitted under the Foreign-Intelligence Surveillance Act. The scope of the FBI's authority permits it to not only obtain information concerning agents of foreign powers, but information about U.S. citizens as well. The FBI can obtain an order that the employer or other business record provider keep the record production secret.

- Permits wire and electronic communications in the workplace to be monitored by the government by use of "pen register" and "trap and trace" devices. If authorized, the government can use these devices to trace communications moved over telephone lines or the Internet.

Employers have new rights to pursue computer hackers under the "computer trespasser" exception in the law. A warrant is no longer required to intercept the contents of Internet communications sent by a computer trespasser. Employers may authorize law enforcement to intercept communications on company computer systems, which expedites the apprehension of the trespasser. Interception is limited to communications by the trespasser.

If an employer is sued by employees who are monitored, as long as the monitoring was the result of a government request or order, the "good faith" defense shields it from civil liability. The defense is lost if the employer exceeds the scope of the request or order, or if it discloses to an employee that the government asked for the monitoring or that monitoring has occurred.

No investigation of a U.S. citizen may be conducted solely on the basis of activities protected by the First Amendment to the Constitution.

Concerns for Employers

Because of the requirements imposed on Internet service providers (ISPs), employers now have some legitimate concerns for their own privacy. Proprietary or confidential business information may be accessed and disclosed by ISPs.

The PATRIOT Act permits some government intrusion into Internet-related communications that did not previously exist. It expands the ways electronic communications providers that serve the public may access and disclose the stored electronic communications of those who use their services. The exceptions allow ISPs to access or disclose the contents of communication in electronic storage:

- to an addressee or intended recipient of the communication;
- with the lawful consent of the originator or an addressee or intended recipient or the subscriber, in the case of a remote computing service; and
- when it is necessary to provide the service or protect the provider's property rights.

ISPs may also access or disclose the contents of communications to law enforcement in broader circumstances as well.

1. A provider that inadvertently obtains content of stored communications that appear to pertain to the commission of a crime may disclose the contents to law enforcement.

2. A service provider that reasonably believes there is an emergency involving immediate danger of death or serious injury to anyone may disclose the contents to law enforcement.

3. An ISP may disclose customer records, but not the content of communications, in other specified circumstances.

ISPs have a "good faith" defense shield against civil liability if they disclose the contents of electronic communications in the belief that an emergency involving danger of death or serious injury to someone requires immediate disclosure. This defense comes from the Homeland Security Act of 2002, which extended the good faith defenses of the Electronic Communication Privacy Act, Titles I and II, to ISPs.

Pointers on Workplace Investigations

7

There is no one blueprint or formula that can be applied to produce an effective investigation. The twists and turns of each investigation necessarily depend on the facts and circumstances at hand. That being said, there are rules of thumb that should be remembered to avoid common errors.

Investigations Process

Fig. 7-1
Pointers on Investigations Process
1. Keep an open mind.
2. Interview the accused to get his or her side of the story.
3. Focus on the Five W's — the Who, the What, the When, the Where and the Why.
4. Avoid loose lips litigation.
5. Be cognizant of potential liability, including privacy concerns.
6. Use a chronology.
7. Consider using suspension pending investigation.

1. Keep Open Mind

Everyone has a different favorite expression for this concept: do not rush to judgment; there are at least two sides to every story; or, act in haste, repent at leisure.

Too many times employers engage in results-oriented investigations. They enter the process believing they already know the answer. The end result often is an incomplete job with significant open issues and insufficient documentation.

The employer needs to ensure that all sides of an issue are examined, and all potential witnesses, including the accused employee, are afforded the opportunity to explain fully their sides of the story. This is not only because it is the right and fair thing to do, but because employees will gain respect for the process — even if things ultimately do not go their way — and because the government or an arbitrator or some other decisionmaker will assess the company's conduct in part by the thoroughness and care taken in the investigation.

Along these lines, the employer should:

- **Interview all employees and supervisors who are witnesses or potential witnesses to the alleged misconduct.** Employers have a tendency to stop short in their investigations, believing they have sufficient information to take action. If it turns out, however, that critical issues were not covered, it will be more difficult to learn the facts and gain the cooperation of witnesses as time passes.

- **Get signed statements when possible.** In the early stages of an investigation, before word gets around and employees begin to think about the ramifications of what has occurred, witnesses may be willing to sign statements setting out their versions of events. Generally, do not delay taking a statement just to make it perfect or more complete; supplemental statements always can be sought.

Consider, as well, taking "know nothing" affidavits — statements from witnesses who claim they do not know anything and did not see anything. Such statements will help to neutralize those witnesses should they later claim in a subsequent proceeding they have had a miraculous recovery of memory and can explain fully the facts that exculpate the aggrieved employee.

- **Avoid one-on-one interviews, if possible.** Many a lawsuit is premised on what a manager or supervisor allegedly said or did, behind closed doors, to the employee. While not always possible, the risk of the "he said — she said" lawsuit can be minimized if one-on-one interviews are avoided. Having another person such as a supervisor at the interview serves another useful purpose — someone who can document the meeting and the witness' statements.

2. Interview Accused To Get His or Her Side of Story

There are very few instances — perhaps a murder in the workplace witnessed by management — that justify a decision not to afford the accused an opportunity to weigh in on the issues at hand, to give his or her version of the events. Still, employers sometimes do not interview the accused employee, presuming they already know what he or she will say or, in some instances, wishing to avoid a confrontation.

The benefits of interviewing the accused are many: appealing to the employees' sense of fairness and the perceived need (even if not legally required) for due process; demonstrating that management is not afraid to consider all sides and all arguments; and, placating the accused by allowing him or her a "day in court."

Perhaps the greatest benefit is that of discovery. In litigation terms, discovery is that part of a lawsuit during which the lawyers gather facts and evidence from the opposition. Interrogatories, document requests and depositions are all devices of discovery. In a litigation, there generally is a lawyer representing the plaintiff or the accused who can help to shape his or her responses. At the outset of the company's investigation, however, the lawsuit probably has not yet been filed and the accused most often has not retained legal counsel. The story he or she gives at that stage is more likely to be the truth or, if a lie, not thoroughly considered and full of holes. At the very least, the company should use the investigation as an opportunity to pin down the accused and other witnesses, so that the stories that emerge later are not surprising. Better to know the accused's defenses, or claims against the company, at the outset, so that the remainder of the investigation can be tailored to collect the facts and documentation necessary to address them.

Moreover, when interviewing the accused, the employer should seek to obtain acknowledgements or admissions that might later form the basis for disciplinary action. If, for example, there is a question about whether the accused knew the company's policy against working unauthorized overtime hours, he or she could be asked, "You were aware, weren't you, that the company has a policy against working overtime hours without authorization?" rather than simply told the rule and told that he or she violated it.

3. Focus on Five Ws

Every good reporter learns the importance of the Five W's — the who, what, when, where and why — in investigating a newsworthy event. The employer should consider itself a reporter and follow those same guidelines.

Vague or conclusory responses by witnesses should not be accepted. Witnesses' statements should be as specific as possible even if that means having the witness draw a diagram of the incident or return with management to the "scene of the crime." This is probably a good practice, even if the manager is fully familiar with the physical surroundings in which the event allegedly occurred. The witness' ability to describe what occurred, in detail, may help management assess his or her credibility.

4. Avoid Loose Lips Litigation

What may have started as a relatively straightforward investigation — into an alleged violation of company policy, for example — may turn into something quite different if the investigator offends witnesses or the accused with ill-conceived statements. Such statements might even be viewed as evidence of the manager's discriminatory intent or sexually harassing behavior. ("Mary, a pretty girl like you shouldn't have a need to go to the beauty parlor on your lunch hour. What were you really doing between 12:30 p.m. and 1:00 p.m.?")

- **Engender cooperation, not hostility.** In other words, "you can catch more flies with honey than with vinegar." Often, management can get to the truth more easily if witnesses are treated with respect and asked for their assistance, rather then mercilessly cross-examined. ("Mary, we need to understand what happened here" versus "What are you hiding, Mary? We know you know something.")

- **Avoid personal attacks; conduct the interviews professionally.** Managers sometimes lose sight of the purpose of the meeting and mix in issues that, though important, may cloud the message being sent. ("Mary, not only were you absent 10 times in the past month, but when I saw you at your work station yesterday, you were obnoxious.")

- **Do not be defensive or apologetic**. Firm, yet fair, is the perception management generally should strive to create.

5. Be Cognizant of Potential Liability, Including Privacy Concerns

The liability issues and potential claims identified throughout Section III should be kept in mind during the planning stages and the entire course of any workplace investigation:

Invasion of Privacy: Know whether the jurisdiction recognizes such a claim; if so, consider whether privacy issues will be implicated in the investigation and whether the employees have reasonable expectations of privacy with regard to areas that may be searched or monitored.

Defamation: Involve others on a need-to-know basis; avoid the rumor mill to the extent possible.

Negligent Retention: Recognize the need to conduct an investigation and for the investigation to be prompt and thorough; take decisive action when warranted.

Wrongful Discharge: Understand whether the jurisdiction adheres to the employment-at-will doctrine, recognizes a cause of action for wrongful discharge, or falls somewhere in between; if an at-will jurisdiction, be mindful of recognized exceptions.

In all situations, consider whether the company should embark on a course of action merely because the law permits it to do so. What are the employee morale implications? Does it make good business sense? Will the company expose itself to claims of pretext? (Remember the "brown shoes" example in the discussion of at-will employment earlier in Chapter 5.)

6. Use Chronology

One of the most useful, yet underused, tools in conducting workplace investigations and making employment decisions is the chronology — a simple arrangement of the facts according to date. The chronology can be a living document, updated as the investigation proceeds and annotated with references to the sources of the facts listed (witnesses' statements, documents, company policies, etc.).

Why use a chronology?

- By its nature it organizes facts into a sequence that can be understood quickly by people who are unfamiliar with the situation as it developed but who need to review what was done. This is particularly helpful to higher management and counsel.

- It enables the company to compare different versions of the same event for consistency. Sometimes, something that is not obvious jumps out when put in the perspective of other events. Do dates, times and places — identified by witnesses and in documentation — match? Ask, "Could it have happened that way?" and "Does it make sense?"

- It may show patterns of conduct — for example, patterned absence.

- It will help identify possible weaknesses in the case for discipline or discharge. It may show, for example, the supervisor's failure to give a warning after serious misconduct or the staleness of a warning.

- It will help identify areas in need of further investigation.

- It provides the organization for the company's presentation in court or to a government agency or in arbitration.

7. Consider Using Suspension Pending Investigation

In certain situations such as those involving threats of violence or other dangers to the business (e.g., sabotage, embezzlement) employers should consider whether it is advisable to suspend the employee, generally without pay, pending the outcome of the investigation. That approach, in appropriate cases, may help to minimize the risk of a repetition of the misconduct, even during the investigations period, and any resulting liability for negligent retention, personal injury or other causes of action.

In the interest of employee morale, such suspensions should be kept short (and the investigation concluded quickly), and the employee should be paid for his or her time on suspension, if vindicated.

Investigating Sexual Harassment

In view of the heightened sensitivities on all sides with sexual harassment issues, consider some suggestions for planning and conducting workplace investigations:

1. Ensure there are special complaint procedures in place, including reporting options so that a potentially victimized employee need not submit a complaint of harassment to the alleged harasser himself or herself.

2. Assign the investigation to those sensitive to sexual harassment issues and trained in such investigations.

3. Include on the team an investigator of the same sex as the complainant.

4. Recognize the importance of ongoing assurance and notification to the accuser and the accused that the allegations, and explanations given in rebuttal, are being taken seriously and are part of an active and expeditious investigation.

5. Involve individuals only on a need-to-know basis (avoid the rumor mill to the extent possible).

6. Avoid promises of strict confidentiality, but assure the accuser and the accused the matter will be treated with sensitivity to its confidential nature. Remember, once on notice of possible sexual harassment, an employer cannot ignore it.

7. Avoid a formula approach — recognize that each investigation has its own nuances and peculiarities.

8. Ask the accusing employee his or her position as to what course of action he or she believes is appropriate. Document this and other discussions with all concerned.

9. Do not jump to conclusions; do not simply assume the evidence supports the accusation.

10. Be attuned to the need to bring in an outsider to conduct the investigation or a portion of it, when appropriate.

11. When harassment has been found to have ceased, there is still the need for an employer to complete the investigation and fashion an appropriate remedy.

SECTION IV:
Controlling Employee Behavior On and Off Duty

Although most employees understand that their employers can place restrictions on their conduct within reason, even as to how they dress, while they are "on the clock," many would object to any attempt by those employers to regulate how they act — what they say, whom they date, what activities they engage in — while on their own time. However, employers do have an interest in and *some* degree of control over off-duty activities, though the extent of that control has been the subject of state and local legislation designed to increase the protections afforded employees. Indeed, while employers have greater latitude to regulate on-the-job conduct by their employees, even that degree of control is not unlimited.

The reason an employer can reasonably be concerned about an employee's conduct is that the conduct, both on duty and off, can have an adverse effect on the employer's business: damage to the company's reputation, disclosure of sensitive information, health and safety concerns, strained relationships with clients or customers, poor employee morale and potential liability to third parties. Today these concerns are even more prevalent as the concept of the workplace has expanded.

It used to be that when an employee was physically out of the workplace, she or he was probably off-duty. With the continuing proliferation of "virtual office" working arrangements, increasingly mobile electronic devices and greater numbers of employees telecommuting on a regular basis, the definition of "workplace" has become blurred, and employers have increased cause for concern about employee behavior even off their premises.

Consider the following:

- Do employees owe any duty of loyalty to their employers? Can they make disparaging statements about their employers in public or on a personal blog without risking termination? What about free speech?

- Is it the employer's business if the employee is shown to be participating in inappropriate off-duty conduct on "You Tube"?

- Can an employer take any action against an employee convicted of a crime, such as domestic violence or viewing child pornography, that is unrelated to the job?

- Does an employer have a valid interest in an employee's outside activities at all? Does a meat-packer have to keep employing someone who is advocating vegetarianism on her own time?

- Can an employer prohibit employee dating? Does it matter whether one employee is a supervisor and one a subordinate?

- Is a company that prohibits telephone usage by employees acting lawfully? What if the employee has an emergency? Does that matter?

- Are "No Beards," "No Nose Rings," "No Cornrows," "No Hats" and "No Tattoos" appearance or grooming policies lawful for employers? Can they be enforced against only certain employees such as those on floors open to the public or to customers or on the floor where the CEO maintains his or her office? Does it matter if the employee claims a religious reason for certain clothing?

- Can an employer prohibit nepotism? Are there any limitations?

- Is favoritism unlawful? Does it matter whether the favoritism — giving the best assignments or the highest wage increases — is bestowed on the manager's golf buddy, boyfriend or girlfriend?

These and other issues are confronting today's employers daily and with good reason, because a wrong move can result in lawsuits, public relations nightmares and morale problems.

Employee Dating

8

Consider the following questions: Does a workplace relationship generally affect the working environment? What happens if and when it ends badly? What can be the result if the relationship that ended was between the department manager and an employee in that department? Any cause for concern by the employer?

Most employers agree there is cause for concern when employees date. Conflicts of interest; the ability of employees to remain objective; distractions and disruptions; the potential that a good employee will leave the company over a broken relationship; and, of course, the creation of fertile ground for a claim of sexual harassment are just some of the risks.

What is the answer? Is an absolute prohibition on employee dating such as a strict "no fraternization" policy lawful? If so, is it desirable? After all, depending on the location of the business and the size of the employer, the pool of potential dates in the community may be comprised mostly of employees who work for the same company.

The legality of a no dating policy and, when lawful, the extent of any limitations on an employer's right to prohibit dating, are essentially governed by state and local laws. There is no federal law on the subject. In fact, most states do not yet have laws that directly address the issue. Thus, it appears that, in many states, strict no fraternization policies generally are legal and enforceable.

Of course, even lawful policies can be ruled unlawful if administered in a discriminatory manner. The Ohio case of *Russel v. United Parcel Service* (673 N.E.2d 659 (Ohio App. 1996)) illustrates the point. In that case, a female supervisor was terminated after she admitted violating a company policy forbidding supervisors from romantic involvement with employees. The court found a primary issue to be whether the policy had been disparately enforced against females.

In states with laws or court decisions that, directly or indirectly, protect dating to some degree, it appears that even those laws and decisions generally draw the line at supervisor/subordinate dating, recognizing the increased potential for problems and conflicts that those relationships bring.

Some examples:

California — Effective Jan. 1, 2000, employers may not take adverse action against employees for lawful conduct occurring during nonworking hours away from the employer's premises (Cal. Lab. Code §96(k)). The extent to which this statute will be applied to employee dating remains to be seen.

However, as early as 1983, a California court upheld a company policy prohibiting fraternization between managers and their direct subordinates (*Crosier v. UPS*, 150 Cal. App. 3d 1132 (Cal. Ct. App. 1983)). The policy had been established to prevent problems of perceived or actual favoritism and sexual harassment. When a manager was fired after it was discovered he was involved in a romantic relationship with a subordinate, he sued, claiming his rights to privacy and association were denied. The court ruled the company's policy and the manager's termination were lawful, notwithstanding any privacy concerns, due to the overriding concern with keeping the workplace free from sexual harassment.

Colorado — An employer with more than 25 employees is prohibited from refusing to hire an applicant or terminating an employee because the applicant or employee is married to or plans to marry a current employee of the employer (C.R.S. §24-34-402). However, this rule does not apply if one spouse would exercise supervisory or disciplinary authority over the other, or if one spouse would audit or be entrusted with money received or handled by the other, or if one spouse has access to the employer's confidential information, including personnel and payroll records.

Louisiana — In the words of one Louisiana court: "Even during off-duty hours, an employee must meet the standards of conduct which an employer may reasonably expect of an employee in that position. Furthermore an employer may impose reasonable rules of off-duty conduct for its employee" (*Johnson v. Board of Commnrs. of the Port of New Orleans*, 348 So. 2d 1289, 1292 (La. App. 1977)).

Also, the termination of an employee who violated a company no fraternization policy has been upheld (*Smith v. Wal Mart Stores*, 891 F.2d 1157 (5th Cir. 1990)).

New York — New York's Legal Activities Law (N.Y. Lab. Law §201-d) prohibits an employer from failing to hire, discharging or otherwise discriminating against an applicant or employee because of that person's off-duty legal (1) political activities, (2) use of consumable products (e.g., cigarettes, alcohol), (3) membership in a labor union, and/or (4) recreational activities. To qualify for protection, the activity must occur outside working hours, off the employer's premises and without use of the employer's equipment or property.

While the parameters of the law are still being defined by the courts, there currently is a split of authority as to whether dating qualifies, and is therefore protected, as a recreational activity under the statute. According to one state court, dating is not protected and can be regulated by an employer: "Dating is entirely distinct from and, in fact, bears little resemblance to 'recreational activity'" (*State v. Wal Mart Stores Inc.*, 207 A.D. 2d 150 (3d Dept. 1995)). A federal court interpreting the statute, however, ruled that an employee's cohabitation with a former executive of the employer was a protected recreational activity (*Pasch v. Katz Media Corp.*, 10 IER Cases (BNA) 1574 (S.D.N.Y. 1995)).

Even if dating is, in fact, protected, an exception in the law still may enable New York employers to prohibit supervisor/subordinate relationships. Otherwise protected activity that creates a material conflict of interest related to the employer's trade secrets, proprietary information or other proprietary or business interests can be prohibited. Arguably, such a conflict exists when a manager dates an employee under his or her supervision.

South Carolina — An employer's no fraternization policy was upheld when a court found that a supervisor's refusal to end a relationship with a subordinate could constitute good cause for termination of the employment contract (*Young v. McKelvey*, 333 S.E. 2d 566 (S.C. 1985)).

Texas — While Texas law does not deal with issues of dating among employees in the private sector, for government employees the Texas State Constitution has been interpreted to implicitly create a "zone of privacy" on unwarranted governmental interference into individual autonomy. For the government to intrude into an employee's private life justifiably, it must be able to show that the intrusion was reasonably warranted for the achievement of a compelling governmental objective that can be achieved by no less intrusive, more reasonable means (*Texas State Employees Union v. Texas Dept. of Mental Health*, 746 S.W. 2d 203 (Tex. 1987)). In Texas, then, it would appear that public sector employers are not at liberty to dictate the terms of an employee's private life absent compelling circumstances.

Still, the Texas Supreme Court has determined that public employees do not have a privacy right to have an adulterous affair. The violation of an anti-cohabitation policy by a police officer having an affair with another officer's spouse was held to be reasonable grounds for an adverse employment action, even though the employee's behavior took place away from work and within the police officer's theoretical "zone of privacy" (*City of Sherman v. Henry*, 928 S.W. 2d 464 (Tex. 1996)).

The following chart (Fig. 8-1) shows the states that have statutes addressing employee dating, as well as those in which the courts have upheld some form of no fraternization policy.

| **Fig. 8-1** State Statutes Addressing Employee Dating and Courts Upholding No Fraternization Policy | | | | | |
Jurisdictions	Statutory Authority Regarding Employee Dating	Courts Have Upheld Anti-Fraternization Policy	Jurisdictions	Statutory Authority Regarding Employee Dating	Courts Have Upheld Anti-Fraternization Policy
Alabama			Montana		
Alaska			Nebraska		
Arizona			Nevada		
Arkansas			New Hampshire		
California	✓	✓	New Jersey		
Colorado	✓		New Mexico		
Connecticut			New York	✓	
Delaware			North Carolina		
District of Columbia			North Dakota		
Florida		✓	Ohio		✓
Georgia			Oklahoma		
Hawaii			Oregon		
Kentucky			Pennsylvania		
Idaho			Rhode Island		
Indiana			South Carolina		✓
Illinois		✓	South Dakota		
Iowa			Tennessee		
Kansas			Texas		✓
Louisiana		✓	Utah		
Maine			Vermont		
Maryland			Virginia		
Massachusetts			Washington		
Michigan			West Virginia		
Minnesota			Wisconsin		
Mississippi			Wyoming		
Missouri					

No Fraternization Policy

Before any policy on fraternization is implemented, it should be reviewed by knowledge-able professionals to ensure it complies with the law of the employer's jurisdiction. The example below may provide some guidance.

Sample Policy

No Fraternization

To maintain a productive and professional work environment, and to guard against the potential for workplace harassment or the creation of a conflict of interest, real or perceived, the Company has adopted a No Fraternization policy.

Supervisors are strictly forbidden from dating or otherwise pursuing a romantic re-lationship with any subordinate. In the event such a relationship is discovered by an employee, he or she must report it immediately to the General Manager or President of the Company. Violations of this policy, including any failure to report the existence of a relationship inconsistent with it, may result in demotion or discipline, up to and including termination.

Smoking

As tobacco companies increasingly came under attack in the media and in the courts during the 1990s, anti-smoking prohibitions spread to all corners of society, even to places where smoking had been widely accepted. Trains, buses and airplanes, as well as restaurants, began creating no smoking sections, and later even banning smoking altogether.

Workplaces were no different. Most public employers — whether at the federal, state or local government level — now are subject to laws restricting or prohibiting smoking in government office buildings. In addition, many states have promulgated statutes that require private employers to maintain some sort of smoking policy in the workplace. Many of these laws permit employers to prohibit smoking altogether on their premises. At lunch and break times in **New York,** for example, it is not unusual to see scores of employees gathered outside the entrances to office buildings, even in the dead of winter, to smoke.

Hawaii prohibits smoking in the workplace altogether (Haw. Rev. Stat. §328j, as does **North Dakota** (N.D. St. 23-12-16). **In the District of Columbia,** smoking is not only prohibited in all places of employment, but also in all public places (D.C. Code §7-742).

Other states are like New York and leave the decision of whether to completely ban smoking up to the employer. States where employers are required to develop smoking policies include the following:

Maine — The Workplace Smoking Act (22 M.R.S.A. §1580-A) requires every employer to establish a written smoking policy, which must be posted, and prohibit smoking except in designated areas.

Maryland — Smoking is prohibited in all enclosed workplaces. Employers may, under direction of the state statute, designate an area for smoking (Md. Regs. Code, title 9, §12.23.01 *et seq.*).

Missouri — Pursuant to Missouri's Indoor Clean Air Act (Mo. Rev. Stat. §191.767), it is unlawful for persons to smoke and/or for employers to permit smoking in public places, including workplaces, except in a designated smoking area that is no more than 30 percent of the public place. However, it is improper to discriminate against or otherwise disadvantage any employee with respect to terms and conditions of employment due to that individual's lawful use of tobacco products off company premises and during nonworking hours, unless that use interferes with his or her job performance or the overall operation of the business (Mo. Rev. Stat. §290.145). Religious organizations, church-operated institutions and not-for-profit health care organizations are exempt from this particular section.

New Jersey — The New Jersey Smoking Act (N.J. Stat. Ann. §26:3D-1 *et seq.*) requires employers with 50 or more employees to establish written rules and procedures governing smoking in designated areas of the workplace. The employer need not designate smoking areas, although if it does, nonsmoking areas are mandatory as the statute makes clear the right of nonsmokers to breathe clean air supersedes the right of smokers.

New York — The New York State Clean Indoor Air Act requires that employers adopt and implement written smoking policies (N.Y. Pub. Health L. §1399-n-x). These policies must include at least the following: (1) a smoke-free work area for nonsmoking employees; (2) a designated work area for smoking if those who work in that area agree; (3) a contiguous nonsmoking area in the employee lunch areas and lounges; (4) a prohibition on smoking in auditoriums, restrooms, elevators, gyms, hallways, employee medical facilities, office equipment common rooms, classrooms and company vehicles, unless all occupants agree to permit smoking; (5) a prohibition on smoking in conference rooms, unless all present consent; (6) a designated smoking room at the employer's option; and (7) a prominently posted policy with copies supplied on request.

Washington — Washington's Department of Labor and Industries has adopted a rule prohibiting smoking in indoor offices. This rule generally requires employers to ban smoking in public and private office work environments and requires that employee exposure to environmental tobacco be controlled. "Employers shall prohibit smoking in their office's entirely, or restrict smoking indoors to designated enclosed smoking rooms that satisfy the minimum requirements" (W.A.C. §296-800-24005).

Smokers, in fact, generally have found little protection from the law. Despite attempts by some to portray themselves as disabled (due to nicotine addiction) under the discrimination laws, most courts have thus far refused to extend to smokers the protections of disability rights laws such as the Americans With Disabilities Act.

Protecting Rights of Smokers

Some states have enacted laws that protect the rights of smokers under certain circumstances.

Colorado — Employers are prohibited from terminating employees for engaging in lawful activities off the employer's premises during nonworking hours, unless the employer's rule: (1) relates to a bona fide occupational requirement or is reasonably related to the activities and responsibilities of a particular employee or group of employees, as opposed to all employees; or (2) is necessary to avoid a conflict of interest or the appearance of a conflict of interest with any responsibilities to the employer (C.R.S. §24-34-402.5).

Connecticut — An employer in Connecticut may not require that an employee refrain from smoking or using tobacco products off the employer's premises (Conn. Gen. Stat. §31-40 *et seq.*).

District of Columbia — It is unlawful for an employer to discriminate against an applicant or employee because of that individual's use of tobacco products, except when permitted by District of Columbia or federal law, or when consistent with a bona fide occupational qualification (D.C. Code §7-746).

Kentucky — Employers are prohibited from discriminating because of an employee's smoking preference (K.A.R.S. §344.040).

Louisiana — Louisiana forbids employers from discriminating against smokers (or non-smokers) outside the course of their employment, as long as they comply with applicable laws and workplace policies concerning use of tobacco on the job (La. R.S. 23:966).

Maine — Under Maine's Smoker's Rights Act (26 M.R.S.A. §597), an employer may not discharge or discriminate against an employee because he or she smokes tobacco off-duty.

Mississippi — It is unlawful for an employer to require as a "condition of employment that any employee or applicant for employment abstains from smoking or use of tobacco products during nonworking hours, provided that the individual complies with the applicable laws or policies regulating smoking on the premises of the employer during working hours" (M.C.A. §71-7-33).

Montana — An employer is prohibited from discriminating against an employee for use of a lawful product during nonworking hours (Mont. Code Ann. §39-2-312). "Lawful product" means a product that is legally consumed, used or enjoyed and includes food, beverages and tobacco. This protection does not apply to the use of a lawful product that affects an individual's ability to perform job-related employment responsibilities or the safety of other employees or that conflicts with a bona fide occupational qualification that is reasonably related to an individual's employment.

Nevada — Employers are prohibited from discriminating against individuals based on their use of legal products on their own time and away from company premises. However, an employer has the right to regulate the use of tobacco products during working time and on company property. Further, the employer may dictate the use of tobacco products off company premises when the use of such products interferes with the employee's ability to fulfill his employment obligation, or otherwise affects the safety of co-workers (Nev. Rev. Stat. §613.333).

New Hampshire — Smoking in places open to public access, including the workplace is restricted and regulated (N.H. R.S.A. §155:64 *et seq.*). "Workplace" is defined as any enclosed space where four or more people work under any type of employment relationship. The act further requires that employers designate the entire workplace as non-smoking or establish "effectively segregated" areas where smoking is permitted. Further, employers are prohibited from requiring any covered employee or job applicant, as a condition of employment, to abstain from using tobacco products outside the course of employment as long as the employee complies with any workplace smoking policy (N.H. R.S.A. §275:37(a)).

New Jersey — The New Jersey Workers' Protection Act (N.J. Stat. Ann. §34:6B-1) prohibits employers from discriminating against job applicants based on their smoking habits, whether they are smokers or nonsmokers, unless there is a rational basis for the discrimination reasonably related to the employment. Violations can subject an employer to civil liability of up to $2,000 for a first violation and $5,000 for each additional violation.

New Mexico — Under the New Mexico Employee Privacy Act of 1991, it is unlawful for an employer to refuse to hire, or to discharge or otherwise disadvantage any individual based on whether the individual is a smoker or nonsmoker. However, the individual must still comply with applicable laws or policies regulating smoking on the premises of the employer during working hours. Further, employers may not require, as a condition of employment, that any employee or applicant abstain from smoking or using tobacco during nonworking hours. Employers may create a bona fide occupational requirement that is reasonably and rationally related to the employment activities and responsibilities of a particular employee without running afoul of the act.

New York — New York's Legal Activities Law (N.Y. Lab. Law §201-d) prohibits discrimination against an employee or applicant based on that individual's off-duty, off premises smoking. Indeed, much of the motivation for enacting this legislation came from a desire to protect the rights of smokers outside the workplace.

North Carolina — It is an unlawful employment practice for an employer with three or more employees to fail or refuse to hire a prospective employee, or otherwise discriminate against any employee because of the employee's use of lawful products if such use: (1) occurs off the premises of the employer during nonworking hours and does not adversely affect the employee's job performance; or (2) does not adversely affect the safety of other employees (N.C. Gen. Stat. §95-28.2).

North Dakota — Prohibits discrimination in hiring and/or firing for tobacco use (N.D. St. 23-12-16).

Oklahoma — Employees may not be disadvantaged with respect to compensation, conditions or privileges of employment because of their use or nonuse of tobacco products during nonworking hours. In addition, an employer cannot require an employee to abstain from smoking or using tobacco products during nonworking hours as a condition of employment. However, this does not apply when any restriction on smoking relates to a bona fide occupational requirement or when a collective bargaining agreement prohibits or allows off-duty use of tobacco products (Okla. Stat. tit. 40, §502).

Oregon — Any employer is prohibited from requiring, as a condition of employment, that any employee or prospective employee refrain from using lawful tobacco products during nonworking hours, except when the restriction relates to a bona fide occupational requirement, or if an applicable collective bargaining agreement prohibits off-duty use of tobacco products (O.R.S. §659.315).

Rhode Island — An employer may not prohibit off-duty smoking by its employees (R.I. Gen. Laws §23-20.7.1.-1).

South Carolina — Employers are prohibited from basing personnel actions on the use of tobacco products outside the workplace (S.C. Code Ann. §41-1-85).

Tennessee — The termination of an employee for smoking off-duty is prohibited (T.C.A. §50-1-304).

Virginia — Prohibits requiring state or local government employees to abstain from smoking as a condition of employment (Va. Code Ann. §2.2-2002; §15.2-1504).

Wisconsin — An employer may not refuse to hire, and cannot suspend, terminate or otherwise discriminate against an applicant or employee because of that person's use of a lawful product such as tobacco or alcohol, on his or her own time and off the employer's premises. This provision is inapplicable if the company is a nonprofit organization that primarily serves to discourage the general public from using a lawful product, if the individual is hired to be a firefighter, or if the use or nonuse of the lawful product:

- impairs the employee's ability to undertake the job-related responsibilities of employment;
- creates a conflict of interest or the appearance of a conflict of interest with the job-related responsibilities of employment;
- conflicts with a bona fide occupational qualification that is reasonably related to the job-related responsibilities of employment;
- violates the state statute governing the sale of cigarettes to and by individuals under the age of 18; or
- conflicts with any federal or state statute, rule or regulation (Wis. Stat. §111.35).

Wyoming — Wyoming law prohibits employers from requiring as a condition of employment that any employee or applicant use or refrain from using tobacco products outside the course of employment, or otherwise discriminate against any employee on the basis of use or nonuse of tobacco products outside the course of employment, unless it is a bona fide occupational qualification that a person not use tobacco products outside the workplace. These provisions do not prohibit an employer from making distinctions in insurance coverage between employees who use or do not use tobacco products if: (1) differential rates assessed to employees reflect an actual differential to the employer; and (2) employers provide written notification to employees setting forth the differential rates imposed by the insurance carrier (Wyo. Stat. §27-9-105).

Telephone Use

10

Employers generally are free to restrict their employees' use of company telephones, even during nonworking hours. The federal and state laws that address employee telephone usage are primarily concerned with the monitoring and tape-recording of calls by employers (see Section III, Chapter 7) rather than with restricting the ability of employers to regulate employees' use of workplace telephones.

The important issue for employers, then, is not whether they lawfully can restrict telephone usage, but whether they should do so and, if so, to what extent.

Workplaces can be stressful for employees even under the best conditions. An absolute restriction on the right to use a company telephone for personal reasons, even on a limited basis or in an emergency, is likely to increase that level of stress. Employees may resent their time at work and view the company as dictatorial or uncaring. Such an atmosphere provides fertile ground for lawsuits, with some employees harboring feelings of being harassed or discriminated against, and for organizing efforts by unions.

That is not to say a policy permitting free use of the telephones is advisable. The disruption such a policy can cause is obvious. What is fairly clear, however, is that some policy is necessary. Without one, individual managers and supervisors are more likely to permit or prohibit use of the telephone on a person-by-person basis, leading to charges of favoritism or disparate treatment, which would undermine morale.

What then is a balanced policy? That, of course, may depend on the corporate environment, the particular jobs of the employees, the company's history on the issue (a sudden crackdown on telephone usage may lead to unhappiness), and other factors. The following are examples of telephone usage policies. Of course, a policy is only valuable to the extent it is enforced consistently and even-handedly.

Sample Policy

Hospital/Nursing Home
Telephone Use

Telephone lines must remain open at all times for the care of our residents and for the Hospital's business. Pay telephones are conveniently located for employees wishing to make personal calls. Such calls should be made during the employee's nonworking time except in an emergency. In addition, it is not possible to call employees to the telephone during working hours except for the transaction of Hospital business or in the case of an emergency. Please discourage your family and friends from contacting you at the Hospital except in real emergencies, in which case the call will be routed through the Human Resources Department. Failure to comply with this request may result in appropriate disciplinary action, up to and including dismissal.

Sample Policy

Professional Office
Personal Use of Office Equipment and Supplies

Proper care and use of office equipment will ensure its efficient operation.

The Company's supplies, copy equipment and postage meter are for the Company's business and should not be used for personal needs.

Personal telephone calls during business hours, both incoming and outgoing, should be confined to those that are absolutely necessary and should be kept to a minimum. Staff members are expected to pay for any personal Toll Calls. A Telephone Toll Call Record Form should be completed after each personal Toll Call and submitted to the receptionist.

Workplace Appearance

Few laws exist, at either the federal or state level, that limit an employer's ability to develop and enforce dress codes and rules governing the appearance of employees. So, what is the issue? An employer can simply adopt any policy it desires, right?

Not necessarily. Aside from employee morale implications, there can be legal issues. Consider the following hypothetical:

> The newly hired female secretary for the company president reports to work wearing beaded cornrows in her hair and sporting a nose ring. The president is surprised. At her interviews, her hair was worn down around her shoulders and there was no sign of any body piercing. He is concerned that the executive visitors to his office will have a poor impression of the company if he permits his secretary to dress in such a free-spirited manner.

Can the president require that the secretary refrain from wearing cornrows as her hairstyle? Does it matter whether the company also prohibits men from wearing that hairstyle? What if the secretary argues that her hairstyle is an expression of her ethnicity or national origin? Does it matter whether the secretary is African American or white? Can there be a religious reason why she might wear her hair that way? Does that even matter? What about the nose ring? Do the same concerns apply to prohibiting the wearing of that type of jewelry?

Suddenly, what seemed like a simple situation is more complex, calling into question a whole host of issues, mostly related to the discrimination laws.

EEOC Position

The truth is the Equal Employment Opportunity Commission (EEOC) in enforcing Title VII of the 1964 Civil Rights Act has for years disagreed with the courts on dress and grooming issues. For example, until the late 1980s, it was the commission's position that allowing female but not male employees to wear long hair, absent a business necessity, was unlawful sex discrimination that should be prosecuted.

The federal courts, however, generally disagreed, and the EEOC, while not abandoning its position, determined that, in general, it would not process charges by men involving "long-hair rules" addressed only at males. Still, the commission will treat seriously charges that an employer is discriminating against males in the enforcement of a policy, even one addressing long hair, that on its face is applicable to both sexes. Accordingly, it appears, at least as to the issue of long hair, that an employer is better off establishing a separate hair policy for men than issuing a single policy applicable to men and women but selectively enforcing it only against men.

What about the cornrows and nose ring in the above hypothetical? The EEOC generally takes the position that appearance restrictions may be unlawful if they are applied differently to similarly situated people based on their national origin, race or other protected category, or if they have an adverse impact on individuals because of their membership in a protected class. For example, in the face of a discrimination charge by the secretary, the commission would be concerned with whether any evidence showed:

- the person setting or applying the policy (*e.g.*, the restriction on cornrows) was influenced by national origin or racial considerations;

- the company permits one national origin or racial group to wear cornrows but does not permit other groups to do so, or enforces the policy more rigidly against a particular group; and

- the policy has an adverse effect on a class of individuals of the same national origin or race.

In 1981 a federal court in **Georgia** determined there was no racial discrimination when a female African-American employee was discharged after refusing to remove beads from the ends of the braids in her cornrow hairstyle. According to the court, the hairstyle was not an immutable characteristic, and it was her refusal to remove the beads, which could be noisy when clicking together, that led to her termination (*Carswell v. Peachford Hospital*, No. C80-222-A (N.D. Ga. 1981)).

Courts have found that some dress policies were really means of discriminating against women. For example, requiring a female employee to dress more femininely and wear makeup violated Title VII of the 1964 Civil Rights Act (*Hopkins v. Price Waterhouse*, 825 F.2d 458 (D.C. Cir., 1987)). Uniform requirements that applied to women, but not men who held the same jobs in a bank, were discriminatory (*Carroll v. Talman Federal Savings and Loan Assoc.*, 604 F.2d 1028 (7th Cir., 1979) *cert. denied*, 445 U.S. 929) as were those that required female lab technologists in a hospital to wear uniforms while male technologists wore white lab coats similar to those worn by doctors (*Michigan Dept. of Civil Rights v. Sparrow Hospital*, 326 N.W.2d 519 (Mich. Ct. App. 1982)).

Religious beliefs and principles also can play a role in whether a particular dress or grooming policy will be deemed unlawful. Under federal law, an employer is required to make reasonable efforts to accommodate an employee's religion-based requests regarding clothing and grooming. The failure to make an accommodation generally is justified only when the employer can show a business necessity for its refusal, or that making the accommodation would impose an undue hardship on the business.

Employers, then, should be careful to structure their dress code and grooming guidelines so that the guidelines are flexible enough to accommodate religious or ancestral practices by various ethnic or religious groups that require a certain dress either on a regular basis or, perhaps, on specially observed holidays or religious occasions.

State Laws and Cases

Although state laws and court decisions are not plentiful in the area of workplace appearance rules, there are some worth noting.

California — California enacted a "Pants Law" (Cal. Gov. Code §12947.5) that prohibits employers from requiring female workers to wear skirts or dresses, unless they are part of a uniform. In addition to the uniform exception, the statute does not prohibit an employer from requiring an employee to wear a costume while that employee is portraying a specific character or dramatic role. Employers can seek an exemption from the requirements of the law on a showing of good cause.

Kentucky — The Kentucky Supreme Court has held that it is within an employer's right to set appropriate standards of dress for its employees.

Maryland — An employer may restrict the dress of an employee as long as there is a business necessity. While the same standard applies to grooming, an additional constraint has been identified in connection with concerns of race discrimination. A grooming policy may not discriminate against African-American male employees with a certain skin condition (pseudofolliculitis barbae (PFB)) which can be cured by wearing a beard.

Michigan — In Michigan, grooming standards have been challenged under Michigan's Elliot Larson Civil Rights Act. In one case, the Michigan Court of Appeals upheld a grooming policy that required only men to cut their hair so that it did not touch their collar. The court reasoned that, because the grooming policy was not shown to be unequally burdensome or shown to be applied and enforced in an uneven manner, no discrimination was shown (*Bedker v. Domino's Pizza, Inc.*, 195 Mich. App. 725 (Mich. Ct. App. 1992)).

New Hampshire — An employer may legally require its employees to comply with reasonable grooming standards, including limitations on hair length. In one case, a federal district court upheld the termination of an employee who refused to take off his hat so that the employer could check his hair length (*McGuiness v. Federal Express*, Slip. Op. 95-CV-0124-B (D.N.H. 1997)). In another case, the New Hampshire Supreme Court upheld the termination of a security guard who claimed the employer's requirement that he cut his hair discriminated against him on the basis of his gender. Rejecting that argument, the court held the employee's loss of employment came about because of his refusal to cut his hair, not because he was a man (*Planchet v. New Hampshire Hospital*, 115 N.H. 361 (N.H. 1975)).

New York — Different grooming standards for men and women generally have been upheld when they reflect customary modes of grooming and dress, have some basis in rationality, and have only a minimal impact on employment opportunities.

Wisconsin — In Wisconsin, an employer must provide employees with notice of any grooming policy at the time of hire.

Fashioning Policy

In view of these considerations, an employer developing a dress/grooming policy should identify a legitimate business-related reason for the policy and ensure that the policy is flexible enough to accommodate religious practices and is sensitive to racial and ethnic concerns. Generally, a broad policy may be preferable to enable the company to deal with specific issues as they arise. The following sample policy is one example.

Sample Policy

Personal Appearance

Dress, grooming and personal cleanliness standards contribute to the morale of all employees and affect the business image the Company presents to the community.

During business hours, employees are expected to present a clean and neat appearance and to dress according to the requirements of their positions. Employees who appear for work inappropriately dressed will be sent home and directed to return to work in proper attire. Under such circumstances, employees will not be compensated for the time away from work.

Please consult your supervisor or department head if you have questions as to what constitutes appropriate attire.

Sent Home:
- shorty shorts
- low rider jeans, but crack
- excessive cleavage
- male/female in cargo shorts
- sandals

Nepotism and Favoritism

Instances of nepotism — favoring family members in hiring and on the job — and favoritism often can lead to hurt feelings and poor morale, fertile ground for lawsuits and union organizing efforts. For those reasons alone, policies permitting such disparate treatment generally are ill-advised. Still, despite common misconceptions, they can be lawful, particularly in the private sector, depending on the circumstances.

Nepotism

Federal law does not address nepotism and state laws that prohibit it generally are addressed to public employment. Those laws are most often concerned with preventing the appearance of impropriety that exists when one spouse is given supervisory authority over another.

Employers in the private sector, however, may be subject to state laws that prohibit discrimination on the basis of marital status. Thus, any policy permitting nepotism would need to be tailored carefully to avoid adverse effects on unmarried individuals.

A policy prohibiting nepotism, on the other hand, would have to be crafted to avoid discriminating against married women and thus violating Title VII of the 1964 Civil Rights Act. One employer had a no-spouse policy at a plant with nearly all male employees. The policy was found to discriminate against women (*EEOC v. Rath Packing Co.*, 787 F.2d 318 (8th Cir. 1986), *cert. denied*, 479 U.S. 910). Another employer avoided gender discrimination by carefully crafting a policy prohibiting spouses from working for the same supervisor so that there was flexibility as to which spouse had to transfer, and the policy was applied uniformly to all married couples (*Fitzpatrick v. Duquesne Light Co.*, 779 F.2d 42 (3d Cir. 1985)).

State Laws

The following state laws deserve mention:

Arkansas — Arkansas has several statutes prohibiting nepotism in the employment of relatives in public employment (Ark. Code Ann. §21-8-304(a); §6-11-102(c)(2) and (d)(2) and §14-47-135).

Colorado — Employers with more than 25 employees are prohibited from terminating an employee or refusing to hire an applicant because the employee or applicant is married to, or plans to marry, a current employee, except if: (1) one spouse would exercise supervisory or disciplinary authority over the other, (2) one spouse would audit or be entrusted with money received or handled by the other, or (3) one spouse has access to the employer's confidential information, including personnel and payroll records (C.R.S. §24-34-402).

Iowa — While nothing in the Iowa Civil Rights Act directly addresses nepotism, the Iowa Supreme Court has upheld, in the public employment context, a policy that prohibited the employment of spouses in the same department. According to the court, such a policy was not an unconstitutional infringement on the right to marry or the freedom of association (*Sioux City Police Officers Assn. v. City of Sioux City*, 495 N.W.2d 687 (Iowa 1993)).

Kansas — State officers and employees, other than the governor's staff, are prohibited from advocating or causing the employment or advancement of family members and from participating in any action relating to a family member's employment or discipline (K.S.A. §46-246a).

Louisiana — Strict limitations on nepotism are set in a limited number of governmental positions (La. R.S. 42:1119).

Mississippi — It is unlawful for certain public officials to hire marriage or blood relatives for public employment (M.C.A. §25-1-53). The statute does not apply to the employment of physicians, nurses or medical technicians by governing boards of charity hospitals or other public hospitals.

Montana — It is unlawful, with limited exceptions, for a member of any board, bureau or commission or employee at the head of a department of the state or any political subdivision of the state to appoint to any position of trust or emolument any person related or connected by consanguinity within the fourth degree, by infinity within the second degree (Mont. Code Ann. §2-2-302(1)). Nepotism is defined as "bestowed political patronage by reason of relationship other than merit" (Mont. Code Ann. §2-2-301).

Nebraska — With limited exceptions, no person shall be hired as an employee of certain state departments while a member of his or her family is serving as the head of that department (Neb. Rev. Stat. §81-108(3)).

Nevada — Except in certain limited circumstances, public employees and officers (including those of municipalities and school districts) are prohibited from employing members of their families (Nev. Rev. Stat. §281.210).

New Hampshire — Employment discrimination on the basis of marital status is prohibited (N.H. R.S.A. §354-a:7). The New Hampshire Commission for Human Rights has found that a school district's policy of barring spouses from employment in the same school was a violation of this statute. However, the commission allowed for the possibility that such a restrictive policy might be lawful, as a bona fide occupational qualification, when one spouse would be supervising the other.

New Jersey — Anti-nepotism policies are not per se illegal. A "no relatives" policy may be lawful, though a policy that singles out spouses for disparate treatment might violate the law against marital status discrimination (*Thompson v. Sandborn's Motor Express, Inc.*, (154 N.J. Super. 555 (App. Div. 1977)).

New York — Aside from the prohibition on marital status discrimination in the Human Rights Law (N.Y. Exec. Law §290 *et seq.*), New York generally has nothing that forbids an employer from instituting an anti-nepotism policy. Certain industries, however, may be treated differently. For example, nepotism between the director and the five highest paid officers of a savings and loan association is prohibited (N.Y. Banking §397).

Oklahoma — Oklahoma has an anti-nepotism law only with respect to persons employed by school districts (Okla. Stat. tit. 70, §5-113).

Oregon — It is unlawful for an employer to refuse to hire, or to discharge, or otherwise discriminate against an employee or prospective employee solely because another member of the individual's family works or worked for that employer. An employer is not, however, required to hire an individual, if such action would: (1) violate any federal or state law; (2) violate the employer's eligibility requirements for financial assistance; (3) place the individual in a supervisory position over a family member; or (4) cause the employer to disregard a bona fide occupational requirement (O.R.S. §659.340(2)).

Tennessee — The Uniform Nepotism Act of 1980 (T.C.A. §8-31-101) restricts the hiring of relatives in public employment.

Washington — An employer can refuse to hire the spouse of a present employee only if the employer can prove that business necessity demands the employer limit the hiring of spouses (e.g., when one spouse would have supervisory authority over the other spouse or when there is an actual or foreseeable conflict between the employer's interests and that of the spouses) (W.A.C. §162-16-150).

Wisconsin — There is an exception to the Wisconsin Fair Employment Act that allows an employer to prohibit an individual from directly supervising or being supervised by his or her spouse (Wis. Stat. §111.345).

Policy Considerations

An employer interested in promulgating an anti-nepotism policy first should identify whether there are legitimate business concerns that warrant such a policy, such as the potential for a conflict of interest. One example of such a conflict might be when the family relationship between two employees could compromise security measures designed to safeguard company assets.

An employer also should be sure to check its state's law regarding whether marital status is a protected classification. If so, the policy might be drafted to exclude any prohibition on the hiring of spouses. The following chart (see Fig. 12-1) lists those states with laws prohibiting discrimination on the basis of marital status.

Jurisdictions	Marital Status as a Protected Category	Jurisdictions	Marital Status as a Protected Category	Jurisdictions	Marital Status as a Protected Category
				Fig. 12-1 **States With Laws Prohibiting Discrimination** **on Basis of Marital Status**	
Alabama		Kentucky		North Dakota	✓
Alaska	✓	Louisiana		Ohio	✓
Arizona		Maine		Oklahoma	
Arkansas		Maryland	✓	Oregon	✓
California	✓	Massachusetts	✓	Pennsylvania	
Colorado	✓	Michigan	✓	Rhode Island	✓
Connecticut	✓	Minnesota	✓	South Carolina	
Delaware	✓	Mississippi		South Dakota	✓
District of Columbia	✓	Missouri		Tennessee	
Florida		Montana		Texas	
Georgia		Nebraska		Utah	
Hawaii		Nevada		Vermont	
Idaho		New Hampshire		Virginia	
Illinois		New Jersey		Washington	
Indiana		New Mexico		West Virginia	
Iowa		New York		Wisconsin	
Kansas		North Carolina		Wyoming	

Favoritism

There is little use denying that favoritism is rampant in most workplaces. That does not mean it is unlawful favoritism, or that, under the right circumstances, it is unjustified.

A supervisor might favor an employee with whom he or she has developed a friendship. Perhaps they golf together or enjoy the same hobbies. It would be natural for the supervisor to confide in that employee or perhaps to give the employee the more complex or interesting assignments because the supervisor knows him or her, and his or her capabilities, better than the supervisor knows other employees. Is that so bad? Perhaps not. Still, the perception of unfairness can lead to serious employee morale problems, which, in turn, generally lead to legal troubles.

Legal Risk

Suppose a male supervisor is dating a subordinate and decides to give her the best assignments and the biggest wage increases. Is that lawful?

For most, it is surprising to learn that the Equal Employment Opportunity Commission (EEOC), in enforcing Title VII of the 1964 Civil Rights Act, takes the position that such a situation is not necessarily unlawful. In the case of an "isolated paramour," the commission has said that favoritism by a supervisor to his girlfriend is not based on her gender, but on the fact that he has a relationship with her.

At least one federal appeals court has said that promotions based on an intimate relationship were not gender biased because men and women were equally affected (*De Cintio v. Westchester Cty. Med. Ctr.*, 807 F.2d 304 (2d Cir. 1986) *cert. denied*, 484 U.S. 965). On the other hand, the EEOC has emphasized, if it is clear that to get the best assignments and best increases, an employee must date the supervisor, that would most likely be unlawful sexual harassment and discrimination.

Also, if favoritism is so widespread that an atmosphere demeaning to women is created, a sexually hostile environment may exist. Thus, an employer that permits supervisor/subordinate dating and the favoritism that might result, walks a fine line between what is lawful and what is not.

The vast majority of states have no laws directly related to favoritism in employment. Of course, any favoritism that is based on a protected category such as race, gender, age, national origin, religion, disability, marital status and any other class covered by federal or state law would be clearly unlawful.

A few states have promulgated statutes that prohibit certain types of favoritism in the public sector. **Alabama** is one example, where the law provides that a public employee shall not be "appointed or promoted to or demoted or dismissed from any position in the classified service or in any way favored or discriminated against with respect to employment in the classified service because of his political or religious opinions or affiliations" (Ala. Code §36-26-38 (1975)).

Public Statements by Employees (Duty of Loyalty)

13

Despite concerns for free speech, certain states have recognized a duty of loyalty owed by an employee to his or her employer regarding statements made or actions taken that may have an adverse effect on the employer. This duty has been applied to statements made on the Internet (see Chapter 15).

Other states have laws that protect the employee from reprisal by the company for statements made by the employee in public regarding certain topics, such as religious beliefs and political associations. Some state laws are designed to protect public and/or private employees from reprisal for their political association or activity or for their testifying or otherwise providing information about the employer.

Consider the following examples:

Alabama — City, county and state employees have the right, to the same extent as other citizens of the state, to engage in political activities, including endorsing candidates and contributing to campaigns of their choosing. In addition, they have the right to espouse their public support on issues of public welfare and circulate petitions calling for or in support of referendums (Ala. Code §17-1-7). Alabama also has a statute that prohibits employer coercion, intimidation or threats of discharge to an employee for the purpose of influencing the employee's vote in any political election (Ala. Code §17-23-10).

Arkansas — Arkansas law protects a public employee's right to communicate with elected officials without the risk of employer discipline or notations in his or her personnel file (Ark. Code Ann. §21-1-503).

Colorado — Colorado recognizes a cause of action for breach of duty of loyalty. The duty commonly arises in situations when an employee begins making preparations to establish a competing business while still employed with his or her current employer. Regarding the public arena, employers may not prohibit or prevent employees from participating in the political process or running for political office (C.R.S. §8-2-108).

Florida — The Florida District Court of Appeals has recognized that, under Florida law, employees owe their employers a duty of loyalty (*Fish v. Adams,* 401 So.2d 843 (Fla. Dist. Ct. App. 1981)).

Louisiana — It is a generally recognized principle that management-level employees owe their employers a duty of loyalty and fidelity. Louisiana also prohibits employers of 20 or more employees from preventing employees from engaging or participating in politics or from becoming a candidate for public office. The law forbids employers from coercing or attempting to control or direct the political activities or affiliations of its employees (La. R.S. §23:961).

Mississippi — Employers are prohibited from interfering with the social, civil or political rights of their employees, and may be penalized $250 for every unlawful interference (M.C.A. §79-1-9).

New Jersey — An employer seeking to hold an employee liable for breach of loyalty generally must show disclosure of a trade secret or confidential information (*Boost Co. v. Faurce,* (13 N.J. Super. 63, 66 (Ch. Div. 1951)), or that the employee assisted a competitor or aided a company whose interests conflict with the employer's interests in some substantial respect (*Cameco, Inc. v. Gedicke,* 157 N.J. 504 (1999)).

New Mexico — New Mexico applies a four-part test to determine whether an employee has been unlawfully terminated for exercising his free speech rights. First, it must be determined that the employee exercised the right to speak on a matter of public concern. If so, the court will consider whether the employer's interest in the efficient performance of the employee's assigned tasks outweighs the employee's free speech interest. If it is established that the employee has a protected interest in speaking that is not outweighed by the employer's interest, the employee must prove that the protected speech was a substantial or motivating factor for the employment decision. If the employee successfully establishes that, the burden shifts to the employer to establish that the negative employment decision would have been made despite the protected speech (*Martinez v. City of Grants,* 122 N.M. 507, 514 (N.M. 1996)).

New York — In general, each employee owes his or her employer an implied duty of loyalty, good faith and obedience while employed. An employee is supposed to refrain from: (1) competing with his or her employer; (2) acting on behalf of third parties whose interests conflict with the employer; (3) using or disclosing confidential trade secrets; and (4) any other behavior that would contradict the duty of loyalty (e.g., making disloyal public statements that can hurt the employer's business). The duty of loyalty generally ends when the employment ends, absent an agreement to the contrary.

Tennessee — It is unlawful for an employer to coerce an employee to vote for any measure, party or person or to threaten to discharge the employee if he or she fails to vote in the manner sought by the employer (T.C.A. §2-19-134).

Notwithstanding any state laws that establish a duty of loyalty on behalf of an employee or that would permit an employer to take action against an employee for a breach of this duty, the National Labor Relations Act (see Chapter 14) protects employees when they act in concert for their "mutual aid or protection," whether or not they are represented by a labor union. Accordingly, statements made in public by employees about their terms and conditions of employment, even if disparaging to an employer, may nonetheless be protected.

SECTION V:
The Electronic Workplace

It is possible that the computer and the Internet have had the most profound impact on the workplace since the introduction of electricity. With computer technology progressing by leaps and bounds, businesses are continuing to take advantage of the benefits associated with increased productivity and faster communications. Although e-mail and the Internet both offer a rapid and effective way to communicate business information, they also can present serious challenges to any employer. New demands on time that increased accessibility creates, brings new opportunities for intrusions on people's private lives. New opportunities for mobility invite the intrusion of work into venues never before imagined as "workplaces."

E-mail and Internet access is now ubiquitous in the contemporary workplace. A computer is as common a feature of the office as the phone. But the opportunities to access cyberspace inevitably raise questions as to what all these workers are doing with these computer systems, as well as what employers can do to control their employees' computer-based activities.

Chapter 14 examines the major privacy issues and possible solutions for fashioning a workplace computer use and monitoring policy. We have moved beyond the days of prohibiting personal use of the computer and hope now to control it. Chapter 15 addresses blogging and instant messaging by employees, including cybersmearing. Indeed, the advent of blogs, cell phone cameras and other means of publishing private thoughts and moments have created new areas of workplace concern. Just when, for example, do comments on private blogs or questionable activities shown on all–too-public sites become a basis for an employer to take adverse action against a worker? This chapter also provides some tips for creating an electronic communication policy. Chapter 16 provides sample computer and electronic communications systems policies to help you regulate and keep control of this exploding world of electronic information.

Computer Monitoring

14

Consider the following hypothetical:

> A company prides itself on remaining current with the latest developments
> in technology. Every employee is provided with a desktop computer out-
> fitted with up-to-date communications and word processing software. The
> computer usage policy allows employees to use their computers for personal
> reasons, provided such use does not disrupt the workplace or their ability to per-
> form their jobs. Many employees, with the company's knowledge and acquiescence,
> have placed private passwords on personal files, thereby restricting access to those files.
> One employee is under investigation for possible wrongdoing. The human resources
> director conducting the investigation has been made aware that possible incriminating
> evidence might be found in the employee's password-protected computer files.

Can the company search those files? Does the nature of the wrongdoing for which the
employee is under investigation matter? Is there a more compelling case for the search if
the employee has been accused of plotting violence against a manager or supervisor? Does
the employee in that case have any less of a privacy right? Or is it simply an issue of the
property rights of who owns the computer? Does it matter whether the employee created
a particular personal file while on company time? Should it?

Employee Privacy or Employer Property?

These are not idle questions. Employers are facing them daily and will be even more frequently in the months and years to come. And yet, there is wide disagreement of opinion
on whose interests should prevail.

Technology has advanced to the level where users often believe they are operating in complete privacy and anonymity. Messages can be sent to other computers miles away without
revealing the source. People can log on to chat rooms using only aliases and without ever
revealing their true identities. Files of any nature can be downloaded and stored in files
that are protected by passwords, presumably safe from the prying eyes of others. In other
words, though the converse may be true both legally and technologically, employees often
consider their computer use private.

On the other hand, employers still have a property interest in the computer systems they maintain. A computer system is intended to be a valuable business asset, not an entertainment venue for employees. The efficiency of rather expensive systems can be hindered as employees use them to shop, play games and carry on non-business-related conversations. Further, illicit activity on workplace computer systems can catch employers unaware and subject them to unforeseen liability. The question is which interest wins: the employee's privacy interest or the employer's property interest?

Federal Court Cases

The federal appeals courts have not as yet agreed on a definitive test for when an employee's right to privacy makes the search of his or her computer files unreasonable when government action is involved. Government action occurs when the employee works for a governmental entity or when it is a law enforcement agency that searches the employee's computer. The Fourth Amendment to the Constitution protects individuals from unreasonable searches and seizures by their government. For the amendment's protections to apply, the individual must have a legitimate expectation of privacy in the place searched or item seized. That is, the person must have a subjective expectation of privacy that society would regard as objectively reasonable.

Most courts that have ruled on the issue of computer privacy agree that computer users have a subjective expectation of privacy in their computer files. Whether that expectation is objectively reasonable often depends on the employer's publicized policies. For example, in *United States v. Angevine* (281 F.3d 1130 (10th Cir. 2002)), the warrantless search of a public employee's workplace computer did not violate the Fourth Amendment because the employer had a widely advertised computer policy that kept employees from having a reasonable expectation of privacy in their office computers. The company even had a logon banner that informed employees that e-mails contained no right of privacy or confidentiality.

The 10th Circuit ruled more recently that a city employee who brought his personal computer to the office to use during business hours did not have a reasonable expectation of privacy in his computer files, making a warrantless search permissible. Pointing out that details are key in these situations, the court based its decision on the fact that the employee shared his office space, hooked his computer up to the city's network for the purpose of sharing files, and did not protect his files with personal passwords or take any other steps to prevent third-party use of his PC (*Barrows v. City of Glencoe*, (10th Cir. 2007)).

In *United States v. Zeigler* (456 F.3d 1138 (9th Cir. 2006)) the court held that the employer had a right to consent to an FBI search of the employee's office computer because "the computer is the type of workplace property that remains within the control of the employer 'even if the employee has placed personal items on it,'" (quoting *O'Connor v. Ortega*, 480 U.S. 709 at 716 (1987)). Moreover, the employer told employees about its computer monitoring through training and its personnel manual, and told employees that the computers were company-owned and not to be used for personal activities.

On the other hand, the U.S. Court of Appeals for the Armed Forces held that a U.S. Marine had an objectively reasonable expectation of privacy in e-mail messages transmitted over a government computer network. The service member in *United States v. Long* (C.A.A.F., No. 05-5002, 9/27/06) had protected her e-mail account with a private password and the system administrator stated that she and other service members had a privacy interest in their accounts. Although there was a logon warning, it stated only that the computer files were subject to monitoring, not searching for law enforcement purposes.

State Cases

The law is still developing. Those state courts that have considered the monitoring issue generally have recognized the need to balance the two interests. They have focused primarily on whether an employee has a reasonable expectation of privacy in his or her computer activity and, if so, whether that interest outweighs the employer's property interest.

Thus far, courts have tended to side with employers. In a **Texas** case (*McLaren v. Microsoft Corp.*, 1999 WL 339015 (Tex. Ct. App. 1999)) with facts similar to those outlined in the hypothetical above, a Microsoft employee was suspended while under investigation for sexual harassment and "inventory questions." The employee notified Microsoft that several e-mails found in his own password-protected files could vindicate him, but instead of allowing him to retrieve the e-mails, Microsoft decrypted the employee's password and read his personal files. When the employee was terminated, he brought suit against Microsoft for invasion of privacy.

As a foundation for his suit, the employee relied on a previous Texas case (*K-Mart Corp. Store No. 7441 v. Trotti*, (677 S.W.2d 632 (Tex. App. 1985)), in which the court held that employees have a reasonable expectation of privacy over the contents of employee lockers that are secured with personal padlocks. The McLaren court disagreed with the employee. In its view, the computer workstation through which the employee stored files and sent e-mails was provided by Microsoft so that he could perform the functions of his job, not to store personal items. Therefore, the e-mail messages contained on the computer workstation were not the employee's personal property, but part of the office environment. Even if the employee could establish a reasonable expectation of privacy, the court added, his expectation would not outweigh Microsoft's interest in preventing inappropriate comments and illegal activity over its own computer/e-mail system.

A federal court in **Pennsylvania** went even further (*Smyth v. Pillsbury Company Co.*, (914 F. Supp. 97 (E.D. Pa. 1996)). It determined an employee never can have a reasonable expectation that electronic transmissions are confidential, even when the employer provides assurances that they are. The employee had received e-mails from a supervisor on his home computer. Acting on assurances from his employer that all e-mail was confidential and could not be intercepted and used as a ground for termination, the employee responded by threatening to "kill the backstabbing bastards" in sales management.

The e-mail messages were in fact intercepted and the employee was discharged, at which time he brought suit against his former employer for unlawful discharge in violation of public policy. In dismissing the action, the court noted that once an employee communicates a comment over an e-mail system used by an entire company, he loses any claim of reasonable expectation of privacy, despite any assurances that may be made by the company. Further, as in McLaren, the court stated that even if there were a reasonable expectation of privacy, it did not outweigh the company's interest in preventing inappropriate and unprofessional comments from being transmitted over a company e-mail system.

Not all courts are so sure. In **Massachusetts**, an employee was terminated for excessive and inappropriate use of a company's e-mail system. At least some of the messages criticized a supervisor and implied that he was having an extramarital affair. The company had no policy against using the e-mail system for personal messages, although there was a policy against excessive chatting, and employees were never notified that their e-mail could be monitored by supervisors.

The Superior Court of Massachusetts determined there were genuine issues of material fact warranting a trial on the issue of whether the former employee had a reasonable expectation of privacy in her e-mail messages, particularly because of the failure of the company to notify its employees about the potential for monitoring (*Restuccia v. Burk Tech. Inc.*, 1996 WL 1329386 (Mass. Super. Ct. 1996)).

Reasons for Monitoring

There are significant reasons why an employer would, and perhaps should, want the right to monitor employee computer use.

According to a survey conducted in early 1998 (Technology and Ethics in the Workplace by the American Society of Chartered Life Underwriters & Chartered Financial Consultants and Ethics Officers Association), 45 percent of 726 employees surveyed reported they had engaged in unethical actions related to new technologies such as e-mail, voice-mail and pagers, while 27 percent admitted they had committed a "highly unethical or illegal act." Those are frightening statistics considering that, with a quick point-and-click, trade secrets and other sensitive information can be sent directly to a competitor or posted on a Web site for all to see.

The risk of information theft and disclosure aside, uncontrolled employee e-mail and Internet usage can provide distractions that result in a costly decrease in productivity. It is common for computer games and even some Web sites to have "boss keys," enabling the errant game player or Web-surfer to quickly cover his or her activity with an official-looking spreadsheet should he or she be interrupted by a co-worker or supervisor.

What is more, employees, it seems, tend to be less careful in their choice of words and what they say when using e-mail than when speaking. Perhaps it is the fact that there is no "looking someone in the eye" when composing an e-mail message. But, by the same token, there is less control over who sees the message. Private jokes that, if said in person or by telephone, might never have seen the light of day, can fall into the hands of someone who becomes offended, or feels harassed or the victim of a hostile work environment.

It is not surprising, then, that employers are resorting to monitoring their employees' computer usage. A 1999 survey conducted by the American Management Association found that 27 percent of major U.S. firms regularly check their employees' e-mail. This represents a 12 percent increase from 1997. In all, the survey concluded, approximately 67 percent of companies conduct some form of electronic monitoring.

More than that, employers are acting on their findings. In 1999, the *New York Times* fired 22 people at a pension office in **Virginia** for distributing potentially offensive e-mails, some of which included sexual jokes and pornographic images. A month earlier, Xerox Corporation fired 40 workers for spending up to eight hours a day surfing pornographic and shopping sites on the Web. Such recent actions have raised significant legal issues, particularly with respect to employee privacy, and indications are that employees are becoming increasingly protective of their computer privacy. A *USA Today* article reported that in increasing numbers, workers believe it is more unethical for companies to monitor their e-mail than to surveil them with video cameras (*USA Today*, p. 1B (March 27, 2000)).

Electronic Harassment and Discrimination

One threshold problem with e-mail and Internet technology that increases the risk of employer liability is that while both mediums are easy to use and master, relatively few employees have a clear idea about how the technology actually works. The common perception is that e-mail is both informal and private, even when it is sent and received through company property. Emboldened by a false sense of anonymity, employees are more likely to transmit inappropriate verbal and visual messages through e-mail and Internet systems than they would through other forms of communication (*Anne L. Lehman, Comment, E-mail in the Workplace: Question of Privacy, Property or Principle?* 5 Commonlaw Conspectus 99, 109 (1997)).

Likewise, employees — and some unfortunate employers — often believe that when the delete key is pressed, all traces of inappropriate material are erased permanently. In actuality, electronic data of any kind often can be stored and retrieved even after an employee deletes it.

In view of the casual tone most people use when utilizing computer technology, employees may inappropriately send e-mails that, intentionally or unintentionally, offend other employees with respect to race, gender, national origin or religion without ever considering that the message will be viewed by anyone other than the designated recipient. However, these messages can be quickly and easily transmitted throughout a company's e-mail system, quite often by mistake. Also, with multiple employees having access to the same files and computer terminals, there always remains the likelihood that someone's Web surfing or chat room conversations, inappropriate or otherwise, will be stumbled on by someone else.

Indeed, the lawsuits spawned by employee use of e-mail and the Internet have given rise to a whole new language in the litigation arena. "E-harassment" was the term one court used in referring to the claimed sexual harassment of an employee by a supervisor who sent the employee graphic e-mails remarking on her physical characteristics and professing his sexual desire for her (*Rudas v. Nationwide Mutual Ins. Co.*, 1997 WL 11302 (E.D. Pa. 1997)). Another court suggested that spamming — sending a large number of annoying but not improper e-mail messages to someone — when engaged in by a supervisor could be evidence of an unlawful hostile work environment (*Griswold v. Fresenius USA, Inc.*, 978 F. Supp. 718 (N.D. Ohio 1997)).

ESI Preservation Rules

Because e-mail messages are often printed or electronically stored, proving e-harassment may be easier for plaintiffs than proving other types of harassment or discrimination. Even deleted e-mail can haunt a company involved in litigation because, despite the belief of many employers, deleted e-mail is not immediately erased and may be retrieved later.

Plaintiffs' lawyers have quickly learned to seek out this type of evidence and are armed with the technological tools to determine the retrievability of deleted e-mails or logs of Internet activity (Joseph P. Zammit and Lynnett A. Herscha, *Litigation Issues in a Cyber World*, 707 Prac. Law Inst. 107 (1998)). Amendments to the Federal Rules of Civil Procedure that took effect Dec. 1, 2006, require parties who know or have reason to believe that litigation will commence must preserve all information, including electronically stored information, or ESI, of possible relevance to that litigation. Rule 34(a)(2) explicitly recognizes a requesting party's right, under limited circumstances, to search the responding party's computer.

Even before the rules change, some employers were sanctioned for destroying or failing to preserve ESI files. In *Zubulake v. USS Warburg LLC* (220 F.R.D. 212 (S.D.N.Y. 2003)), for example, the court ruled that the employer had a duty to preserve computer files from the moment an employee threatened to sue for discrimination under Title VII of the 1964 Civil Rights Act, and imposed severe sanctions for its failure to do so.

Employers should want ESI to be routinely preserved not only to be able to produce them in case of a lawsuit by an employee, but to protect their intellectual property or enforce rights against departing employees. Data in a departing employee's files may be important to future business operations to provide other employees with necessary information, or ESI may be needed to bolster the employers own suit against a departing employee it suspects of violating a non-disclosure or non-compete contract.

Union Solicitation and Other Protected Concerted Activity

Just as e-mail can rapidly disseminate business information, it also can be an efficient vehicle for employees and labor unions to use in transmitting employee communications such as organizing campaign literature and grievances over terms and conditions of employment that are protected by federal law.

Consider the following hypothetical:

> The company's chief operating officer writes to all employees via their company e-mail to explain a proposed change in the vacation policy. One employee vehemently opposes the change and replies, sarcastically and bitterly, sending copies of his reply through the e-mail system to his fellow employees.

Can the company discipline or terminate the employee for using the company e-mail to vent his anger at the company or the chief operating officer? Or for his discourteous tone? Does it make a difference if there is no labor union representing the employees?

Under the federal National Labor Relations Act (NLRA), employees, union or non-union, have a right to engage in "protected concerted activity," that is, concerted activity for the "purpose of mutual aid or protection" (NLRA §7). In the situation posed above, the National Labor Relations Board — the government agency charged with enforcing the NLRA — decided the employer did not have the right to terminate the employee, even when there was no union representing the employees (*Timekeeping Systems, Inc.*, 323 N.L.R.B. 244 (1997)). According to the labor board, the employee's "effort to incite the other employees to help him preserve a vacation policy which he believed best served his interests, and perhaps the interests of other employees, unquestionably qualified his communication as being in pursuit of 'mutual aid or protection.'"

What does this mean? Do disgruntled employees have a license to rail against the company through the e-mail system, even if their remarks are offensive? And what about statements made about the company in an Internet chat room, accessible by hundreds, perhaps thousands, of individuals?

While the right of employees to engage in protected concerted activity is a broad one, protecting a wide variety of communications concerning wages, benefits and other terms and conditions of employment — particularly when inciting group action is the purpose of the communication — not all statements made by employees are shielded from management's control. If the communications are violent or "truly insubordinate or disruptive of the work process," for example, they lose their otherwise protected status and allow for the possibility of discipline or, in appropriate cases, discharge (*Timekeeping Systems, Inc.*, 323 N.L.R.B. 244 (1997)). Further, employees do not have the right to divulge company secrets and internal memoranda through e-mail or publication on the Internet (*Pratt & Whitney*, 1999 WL 381115 (N.L.R.B. Gen. Counsel Memorandum Feb. 10, 1999) (Kearney)).

On the other hand, the Labor Board has given great leeway to employees in applying the standard, refusing to remove protection for employee letters describing management as "a-holes" (*Postal Service*, 241 N.L.R.B. 389 (1979)) or "hypocritical," "despotic" and "tyrannical" (*Harris Corp.*, 269 N.L.R.B. 733 (1984)). Even a statement by one employee to others that the chief executive officer was a "cheap son of a bitch" was deemed protected concerted activity (*Groves Truck & Trailer*, 281 N.L.R.B. 1194 (1986)). Accordingly, employers contemplating action against employees who use the company e-mail or Internet chat rooms to criticize the company, supervisors or fellow employees must consider whether the employees' actions are protected by law.

Courts, too, have supported the right of employees to use employer e-mail systems to discuss union matters, particularly when the employer did not prevent other non-business uses of the system (see *Media General Operations, Inc. d/b/a Richmond Times-Dispatch v. NLRB*, Nos. 06-1023, 06-1061 and 06-1213, unpublished (4th Cir., March 15, 2007)).

'Personal' PCs

Whether employers can reach into their employees' and others' hard drives is not completely clear as yet, but at least one federal court in **Minnesota** allowed an employer to do just that. According to a page one article in the May 26, 2000, edition of the *Wall Street Journal* ("Data Raid: In Airline's Suit, PC Becomes Legal Pawn, Raising Privacy Issues"), the court approved a search by Northwest Airlines of the computers of certain employee union activists the airline had suspected of using e-mails to spearhead a sick-out by flight attendants.

The airline employed a team of specialists to pull from the activists' hard drives deleted files, portions of Web searches and other data and communications. The volume of material that could be retrieved apparently surprised even the airline, which remarked to one judge that printouts of the documents would produce a pile of paper five times as tall as the 555-foot Washington Monument. The activists, who complained they were forced to turn over irrelevant personal documents, accused the airline of violating their privacy.

The issues raised are serious ones. They could impact what employees, particularly outspoken ones, keep on their computers, and what labor unions might do to guard against the risk that invasive searches could uncover sensitive union information. Will these issues prompt the states or the federal government to become more active in creating legislation designed to deal with these and other privacy issues? The answer almost certainly is "Yes." As far as computers go, most agree the industry is still in its infancy.

One thing is certain even today. In creating any limitations on the ability of employees to use company e-mail, an employer must be careful not to give rise to claims of unlawful discrimination, particularly in light of attempts to use an employer's own e-mail system as a tool for union organization.

Limiting 'Union Talk'

The rules governing when and to what extent an employer can limit "union talk" among its employees are well settled. They depend primarily on whether employees are soliciting other employees verbally, so-called "solicitation," or through the distribution of literature. Employers are given greater leeway in controlling distribution because literature quite simply can cause a litter problem and because its permanent nature, allowing employees to read it at their convenience, eliminates the need for employees to be able to distribute it in real time throughout a company.

The rules are as follows:

1. Solicitation generally can be prohibited during work time, but unless a broader restriction is necessary to maintain production or discipline (a difficult standard to meet), it cannot be prohibited on nonworking time, even in work areas. Thus, a policy that bans employee solicitations during break times is presumptively invalid.

2. Distribution, on the other hand, can be prohibited during work time and in work areas.

3. Whether the prohibition is addressed to solicitation or distribution, even a valid rule will be deemed unlawful if applied in a discriminatory manner. If, for example, an employer's "no distribution" policy prohibits the distribution of non-business-related literature during work time, but employees in fact are permitted to distribute bulletins soliciting money for bake sales or political campaigns or other reasons, any attempt to ban union organizing materials likely would be considered discriminatory and unlawful.

What Is E-mail?

The introduction of e-mail to the workplace has raised some significant issues. Is e-mail more similar to verbal conversation, so that e-mail solicitations will enjoy the same, broader protections as solicitation generally? Or is it akin to documentation, so that the employer has greater freedom to impose a ban?

In *E.I. du Pont & Co.* (311 N.L.R.B. 898, 919-20 (1993)), one of the first decisions of significance by the Labor Board on the issue of e-mail solicitations, the board did not need to resolve this issue because the employer applied its no-distribution policy in a discriminatory manner. While it prohibited employees' use of the company's e-mail system to distribute union literature, it allowed use of the system by employees to distribute material on a wide variety of other personal matters.

Still, the case raised concerns. Most employers feel that a total ban on employee use of the company computer system for all but business-related communications is unrealistic and draconian. Does that mean that, as a practical matter, a company can never really hope to ban union solicitations from its e-mail system? Maybe ... or maybe not. The law is far from settled.

More recent pronouncements from the Labor Board's Office of the General Counsel, while not having the force of law of Labor Board decisions, seem to indicate the general counsel's view that, under some circumstances, even a very restrictive policy on e-mail usage might not be sufficient to prevent use of the system for union organizing.

In a 1998 memorandum, *Pratt & Whitney* (1998 WL 1112978 (N.L.R.B.G.C. Feb. 23, 1998)), the general counsel explained that some employee e-mail is akin to verbal solicitation while other e-mail may seem more like literature. He noted:

> [I]t has been widely recognized that at least some e-mail messages are not merely analogues of printed messages; rather, they have been characterized as "a substitute for telephonic and printed communications, as well as a substitute for direct oral communications" [In Re: Amendments to Rule of Judicial Administration, 651 So.2d 1185 (Fla. Sup. Ct. 1995)]. There has even been Congressional recognition that e-mail "is interactive in nature and can involve virtually instantaneous 'conversations' more like a telephone call than mail" [H.R. Rep. No. 647, 99th Cong., 2d Sess. at 22, discussing the Electronic Communications Privacy Act of 1986].

Other e-mail, he explained,

> may seem more like the printed documents classified as distribution. While e-mail does not cause the physical litter problems that written literature can create, it can take up cyberspace and thus has the potential to affect the performance of an employer's computer network. Moreover, even if the message is composed and sent on the sender's nonworking time, it may well appear during the recipient's working time, thereby possibly causing disruption and affecting production.

The employer's policy at issue in the case was a broad ban on all non-business use of e-mail by employees. The employees, moreover, used the computer system to such a degree in their work that the system really became their work area. Because some of the banned e-mail could be of the type deemed solicitations, such a broad ban, the general counsel concluded, would have the effect of prohibiting solicitation on nonworking time and in work areas and is thus unlawful as overbroad. The general counsel made clear, however, that his opinion did not mean all e-mail messages must be treated as solicitation.

Open Issues

The general counsel listed the issues not addressed in Pratt & Whitney that are likely to arise in future cases: employee use of company electronic bulletin board systems; non-employee (*e.g.*, union) access to e-mail addresses maintained by the company; and "reasonable rules limiting e-mail to narrowly address particular problems, such as rules that only prohibit 'mass' distribution of non-business e-mail messages, which require that any non-business e-mail message include 'non-business' in the title of the message, or which require any non-business e-mail message to be sent by lowest priority or otherwise treated so as to limit its interference with business-related e-mail."

In a later memorandum, *IRIS-USA* (No. 32-CA-17763, 2000 WL 257107 (N.L.R.G.C. Feb. 2, 2000)), the general counsel approved, as lawful, the following employer policy:

> Employees are expected to use the voice mail, electronic mail and computer systems for company business only and not for personal purposes. Personal purposes include, but are not limited to, soliciting or proselytizing for commercial ventures, religious or political causes, outside organizations or other non-job-related solicitations.

He distinguished *Pratt & Whitney* by noting that in that case, unlike the one before him, the employees had performed a significant amount of their work on the computer network so that the network truly had constituted the employees' "work area." The bargaining unit employees in *IRIS-USA*, however, generally were production workers with essentially no access to electronic mail or computers as part of their regular work. A "computer work area" did not exist for them.

Confused? Do not be too upset. There undoubtedly will be more and more developments, including further clarification of the labor board's position and court decisions weighing in on what the law is and should be, in the months and years to come. For now, the debate rages on.

Defamation and Copyright Infringement

With loose talk, an earmark of e-mail generally, comes the increased potential for defamation and another reason for employers to consider implementing e-mail and Internet use policies.

While the proof required to state a claim of defamation (libel or slander) may vary by state, a plaintiff generally must show that a false, defamatory statement caused him or her injury and was communicated (or "published") to a third party (see Chapter 5). Significantly, an employer can be held liable for defamatory statements made by an employee within the scope of his or her employment.

The very nature of company e-mail systems is conducive to defamation claims for reasons discussed earlier. Employees tend to be careless in what they say in e-mail messages, considering it more like casual conversation than documentation. E-mail messages can be effortlessly distributed to third parties either inadvertently by hitting the wrong reply button or intentionally by forwarding the message at the click of a mouse to any number of recipients. E-mails frequently are stored by the writer and/or recipient, so that one employee's defamation of another — including the exact language of the defamatory statement and the fact that it was communicated to a third party — may be perfectly preserved for use as evidence in a later litigation.

Trade Secrets and Confidential Information

The risks posed to employers by employee use of company e-mail and the Internet are perhaps no better illustrated than in the case of trade secrets and other confidential and proprietary information. Employers face exposure on two fronts, as creators of information they need to protect and as recipients of information that may have been pirated by their own employees or new hires.

From the creation side of the equation, it is clear that company documents, marketing strategies, price lists, customer lists and a panoply of other types of sensitive business information can easily be downloaded to the Internet or transmitted via e-mail by a disgruntled employee. Unfortunately, once the information has made its way into cyberspace, it is not only technologically impossible to get it back, but courts are reluctant to interfere.

Take, for instance, the case of Ford Motor Company. The company became aware that some of its internal documents were being quoted on a Web site maintained by an individual who had never been an employee of Ford. When Ford threatened legal action, the Web site owner posted another 40 of Ford's confidential documents on the site. Ford was able to obtain a temporary restraining order against the individual, but less than two weeks later, a federal judge refused to issue a preliminary injunction based on First Amendment grounds (*Ford Motor Co. v. Robert Lane d/b/a Warner Publications*, 67 F. Supp. 2d 745 (E.D. Mich. 1999)).

An employer also may be held vicariously liable for an employee's infringement, particularly when it can be shown that the company enjoyed an obvious and direct benefit from the employee's use of protected information. (See Barbara Kolsun, *Drafting, Negotiating and Enforcing Trademark, Copyright and Software Licensing Agreements*, 517 Prac. Law Inst. 533 (1998).) Thus, employers need to be concerned about employees who suddenly come up with that "new" idea or "unique" concept, especially when those employees recently were employed by competitors.

Reducing Liability Risk

Though no plan of action is foolproof, there are steps an employer can take to reduce the risk of liability. Consider the following:

- Developing written nondisclosure and confidentiality agreements that must be signed as a condition of employment. These agreements must be carefully tailored so as to avoid being overbroad. The courts still struggle with developing technologies and, absent clear direction from legislators, are hesitant to enforce broad restrictions on individuals' freedom of expression. In addition, the dividing line is not always clear between what is confidential and the property of an employer, and what an employee knows by virtue of his or her skill.

- Requiring applicants to sign representations, on the application form or elsewhere, that they are not parties to any non-compete or confidentiality agreements and that they will not use information or materials that are protected by law as the property of others.

- Requiring employees to agree to indemnify the company for any liability resulting from their infringement of any copyright or other protections.

Legal Restrictions on Employer's Ability To Monitor

Given the many sources of potential liability if employee computer activity is not adequately monitored, it seems clear some safeguards are necessary and prudent. This does not mean an employer should immediately begin routinely reading e-mail messages. There are several federal and state restrictions that mandate the development of a written policy before a business can institute any form of monitoring program.

Federal Law

In response to the development of communications and computer technology, Congress passed the Electronic Communications Privacy Act of 1986 (ECPA), amending the federal Omnibus Crime Control and Safe Streets Act that is most often applied in regulating the interception of telephone calls and other "sounds" by employers (see Chapter 6 for a fuller discussion of that act, sometimes called the federal Wiretapping Act). The ECPA prohibits both the intentional unauthorized access of stored e-mail communications, as well as the interception of communications. Without formulating appropriate monitoring policies, employers can incur criminal and civil liability under the act.

The ECPA has two main sections: Title I, which addresses the interception of data being transmitted, and Title II, which addresses accessing stored data. (See 18 U.S.C. §2510-§2522 (intercepting data) and 18 U.S.C. §2701-§2711 (stored data).) Violations of Title I carry criminal fines and the possibility of up to five years in prison. Title I also allows for private civil actions and the recovery of actual damages, attorney's fees and costs, and punitive damages. In lieu of actual damages, a private plaintiff may recover statutory damages of the greater of $100 a day for each day of the violation or $10,000.

Title II carries criminal penalties of up to two years in prison or fines of up to $250,000. Title II also allows for civil actions with the availability of attorney's fees and costs and actual damages, as well as any profits made from the stored information. Though a plaintiff has the ability to receive any amount of actual damages proven, the minimum award under Title II is $1,000 and a plaintiff cannot receive punitive damages.

Due to the penalty differences, including the ability to receive punitive damages under Title I, the distinction between whether an employer intercepted an e-mail message or merely accessed stored e-mail can be critical when assessing liability. In the case of *Steve Jackson Games, Inc. v. United States Secret Service* (36 F.3d 457 (5th Cir. 1994)), the court ruled that e-mail that was delivered but not yet read was actually stored data and, therefore, fell under Title II rather than Title I.

Three exceptions exist to the ECPA's restrictions on improper interception and access. An employer can intercept e-mail if:

- an employee consents;
- the employer is a provider of the e-mail service; or
- the employer intercepts the e-mail during its routine business on a component of the system.

If an employer maintains its own computer communications system it may qualify as a provider (*Bohack v. City of Reno*, 932 F. Supp. 1232 (D. Nev. 1996)). However, an employer that merely contracts with a commercial service such as Prodigy or America Online to provide e-mail to its employees probably will not be considered a provider of electronic communication. A provider is allowed "to intercept, disclose, or use that communication in the normal course of his employment." Under Title II, a provider also is allowed to access stored communication, although the provider cannot divulge the information to outside sources.

Consent of the employee is necessary to intercept or access an employee's e-mail if the employer is not a provider. Consent also is required before an employer-provider can divulge the contents of e-mails to others. Of the three exceptions, express consent in which the employer informs employees of its intention to intercept or access e-mail or Internet communications may be the best way to avoid litigation involving e-mail and Internet privacy matters.

State Laws

For the most part, states have yet to react to developing technology in the same manner as the federal government. On the whole, most states have wiretapping statutes patterned after the older federal Wiretapping Act, which, prior to the passage of the ECPA, primarily addressed the aural acquisition of wire and oral communications. Applying standards developed for telephone and outmoded wire communications to continually advancing technology will not be an easy task as state governments, employers, employees and civil rights groups continue to battle over the tension between employer property and employee privacy that is endemic to the area of computer monitoring.

For example, the **California** legislature passed a bill that would have required employers to prepare and distribute copies of electronic monitoring policies to all employees by March 1, 2000. Those employers that failed to distribute copies would have been precluded from monitoring employee computer use. The bill had support from such groups as the American Civil Liberties Union and the Privacy Rights Clearinghouse. It was opposed by the California Employment Law Council. When the bill was presented to Gov. Gray Davis for his signature, it was vetoed.

Still, a handful of states have begun to modify their monitoring statutes to encompass other forms of electronic communication, including e-mail and Internet use. In **Georgia**, for example, the Computer Systems Protection Act declares that "any person who uses a computer or a computer network with the intention of examining any employment, medical, salary, credit or any other financial or personal data relating to any other person with knowledge that such examination is without authority shall be guilty of the crime of computer invasion of privacy" (Ga. Code Ann. §16-9-93).

Florida appears to have one of the strictest policies regarding electronic monitoring. Under the Florida Security of Communications Act, it is unlawful to intercept or disclose the contents of any electronic communication without obtaining the consent of both the sender and the recipient (Fla. Stat. §934.01 *et seq.*).

Unlike the Florida law, most state statutes permit interception with the consent of the employee alone. Other states grant employers the ability to intercept employee communications simply because the communication was transmitted through the use of company property. For example, the **Nebraska** Telecommunications and Technology Act allows an employer to intercept, disclose and use communications made on its premises in the normal course of its business, while engaged in any activity that is necessarily incident to the rendition of its service (Neb. Rev. Stat. §86-702(2)(a)).

Monitoring statutes

The following states currently have legislation addressing e-mail and other computer monitoring by employers:

- **Colorado** — An employer is prohibited from intercepting telephone or other electronic communications without the consent of either the sender or receiver (C.R.S. §18-9-303). However, an employer may use monitoring devices on its own premises for security or business purposes provided that the employer gives reasonable notice to the public of their use.

- **Connecticut** — An employer must give prior written notice of electronic monitoring to all employees who may be affected, informing them of the types of monitoring that may occur (Conn. Gen. Stat. §31-48d). Electronic monitoring refers to the collection of information by any means other than direct observation. Each employer also must post, in a conspicuous place, a notice concerning the types of electronic monitoring that the employer may use. Such a posting constitutes prior written notice. Employers may monitor employee computer use without notice if they have reasonable grounds to believe that employees are engaged in conduct that is (a) illegal; (b) violating the legal rights of the employer or the employer's employees; or (c) creating a hostile workplace environment, and the monitoring will provide evidence of the misconduct.

- **Florida** — Under Florida's Security of Communications Act, it is likely that an employer cannot monitor employee computer use without first getting the consent of the employee (Fla. Rev. Stat. §934.01). Under the act, a person is prohibited from intercepting or disclosing the contents of any private wire, oral or electronic communications without the consent of both parties to the communication.

- **Georgia** — Under the Computer Systems Protection Act, employers are prohibited from using a computer or computer network with the intention of examining employment, medical, salary, credit or any other financial or personal data without prior authority from the subject (Ga. Code Ann. §16-9-93(c)).

- **Nebraska** — Nebraska's Telecommunications and Technology Act prohibits the interception, disclosure and use of wire, electronic and oral communications and is broad enough to encompass computer, e-mail and Internet use. However, the act allows an employer to intercept, disclose and use such communications made on its premises, and random monitoring for performance control is lawful when reasonable notice is provided to employees (Neb. Rev. Stat. §86-702(2)(a)).

- **Ohio** — The Ohio Wiretapping Act (Ohio Rev. Code §2933.51 et seq.) generally tracks the provisions of the federal Wiretapping Act outlined in Chapter 6, and is applicable to the monitoring of an employee's computer use.

- **Wisconsin** — The interception or monitoring of electronic communication generally is prohibited without a party's initial consent (Wis. Stat. §968.31). As such, an employer in this state should obtain employee consent before monitoring.

- **Wyoming** — Similar to other state monitoring statutes, the interception of an electronic communication is permitted if a party to the communication has given his or her prior consent to the interception (Wyo. Stat. §7-3-602(b)).

Invasion of Privacy

The most likely claim that will be faced by employers as the law and technology continue to develop is that of invasion of privacy. In some states, such as **South Carolina** and **Wisconsin**, a private right of action for invasion of privacy is guaranteed by the state constitution or in laws promulgated by the state legislature (S.C. Const. art. I, §10; Wis. Stat. §895.50). In others, it may simply be recognized by the courts for public policy reasons.

The action of invasion of privacy is discussed in more detail in Chapter 5, but generally speaking, to prevail on such a claim, an employee often must show that he or she had a reasonable expectation of seclusion or privacy. Thus far, as stated above, courts have tended to find that employees' expectations of privacy in e-mail communications sent over an employer's internal system, if they exist at all, do not outweigh the employer's compelling interest in controlling what is placed on and sent through its property.

In *United States v. Simons* (206 F.3d 392 (4th Cir. 2000)), a federal employee was arrested for the transmittal and downloading of child pornography. The agency for which the employee worked maintained a policy that stated employees were to use the Internet for official government purposes only. Accessing unlawful material was specifically prohibited, and the agency announced it would conduct electronic audits to ensure compliance with the policy. A network administrator, conducting a routine check of the computer system's firewall, noticed an unusually large number of Internet "hits" coming from one computer contained the keyword "sex." Agency managers ordered the administrator to conduct a remote search of the employee's computer files, at which time the unlawful child pornography was found.

The court found that no warrant for the remote search was necessary as the employee never had a reasonable expectation of privacy with regard to those computer files, principally because the employee had notice of the employer's policy of conducting random electronic audits.

Internal e-mail systems often provide the system administrator with access to all e-mail communications and employees generally will be found by the courts, even absent express notice from the company, to have had knowledge that e-mail communications were subject to monitoring. Of course, any steps that can be taken to diminish employees' expectations of privacy can only help. The importance of an e-mail and Internet usage policy and employee agreement that clearly permit employer access, review and disclosure of messages cannot be ignored.

Blogging and Instant Messaging

15

Communication goes far beyond the telephone in today's workplace. Blogging, text and instant messaging are all very common, especially among younger workers. For the uninitiated, the word "blog" is short for "Web log." It is essentially an interactive diary in which anyone with access to the Internet can post his or her thoughts, criticisms and other information. Unless the blog is password-protected, anyone else on the Internet can read what is posted.

Blogs can contain anything the writer, who may or may not be identified, decides to include in the series of entries. Links to Web sites are common, especially to news or entertainment stories and other blogs. Many blogs permit readers to comment on the postings, which creates an online dialogue. Blogs are searchable, interactive public message boards that can be read by millions of people.

Technorati, a Web site that tracks blogs, reported that in 2006, the blogoshere was doubling in size every six months. On average, a new blog was created every second of every day! Blogging is a powerful tool that provides quick and easy access to the vast audience of Internet users worldwide and employers are beginning to see its usefulness and its danger.

Some employers incorporate a review of personal blogs or other Internet postings made by job applicants as part of routine pre-hire background checks. Some companies maintain their own blogs as a means of communicating with customers, employees and the public. There are blogs authored by high-level company executives and company-sponsored blogs by employees. The latter category includes blogs by reporters and columnists for news media organizations that appear on the company's Web site.

Cybersmearing

The downside of blogging for employers involves "cybersmearing" — using personal blogs to complain about companies and post negative or damaging information or even reveal company secrets. Anonymous employee bloggers criticize supervisors and managers, say negative things about competitors, disclose proprietary information and tarnish employer goodwill by disparaging company products or services.

While employers can sue anonymous online posters for defamation or disclosure of confidential information, doing so can backfire by encouraging even more online postings and attacks. Internet service providers usually are not liable for defamation because they are considered the distributor, not the publisher of the information. Obtaining the identity of the poster is a major hurdle.

Blogs can do damage in other ways as well. Because the postings are a form of publication, they can defame individuals with false statements that subject them to hatred, contempt or ridicule, or tend to diminish the esteem, respect, goodwill or confidence in which the person is held by others. Blogs can be a form of harassment, especially in the workplace. They can invade an individual's privacy, violate copyright and trademark laws, and jeopardize private securities offerings or violate securities laws.

Discipline for Blogging

The First Amendment's prohibition against governmental restriction of free speech does not prevent private employers from taking disciplinary action against employees based on the content of their blogs. Delta Airlines, Google, Wells Fargo and Harvard and Boston Universities have fired employees for negative blog postings. There is even a term for such terminations — dooced. It is derived from the case of a Los Angeles software company employee who was fired for making critical comments about her employer on her blog, "dooce.com."

There are some limits employers need to be aware of, however. The National Labor Relations Act protects employees' right to engage in "concerted activity for the purpose of ... mutual aid and protection," and it applies to nonunion as well as unionized employees. Blog discussions of wages, benefits or the like that affect a group of workers arguably are protected concerted activity for which employers cannot impose discipline (see the section on union activity in Chapter 14).

Bloggers also may be protected by whistleblower laws if their postings are critical of company practices that violate laws or regulations.

Some states, including **California**, **Colorado**, **Connecticut** and **New York** protect employees from adverse actions by their employers for lawful off-duty activities, which blogging done on personal time arguably is. Blogging also may be protected political activity.

California also permits "strategic lawsuits against public participation," or SLAPP suits. These suits, available in about 20 states, permit individuals to sue anyone who attempts to deter or punish them for exercising their political or legal rights. In the case of a blog, the suit would be for the attempt to quell speech.

Employers should decide whether they want to have a policy focused just on blogging, or to incorporate references to blogging in existing policies that deal with e-mail and other electronic communications (see Chapter 16 for sample computer and electronic communications policies). Policies on issues such as confidentiality and trade secret protection, securities law compliance, harassment and discrimination should be examined to see if they are sufficiently broad to cover blogging.

Instant Messaging

Instant messaging, or IM, is an innovation used both for personal and work-related communication. IM usually involves short messages exchanged between users in real time, just like a face-to-face conversation. IM can include voice an audio conversations as well as the transfer of files. Messages can be conveyed via computers, cell phones and PDA devices such as BlackBerries and Palm Treos.

IM is even more widely used than blogging. Moreover, it is widespread in the workplace, with some companies issuing devices to their employees so they can be reached anywhere, any time.

IM has the same legal issues for employers as e-mail and blogging — potential harassment, defamation, invasion of privacy, disclosure of proprietary information and the like. As with e-mail, IM can carry computer viruses and worms and is subject to spamming. IM also can severely impact employee production in the same way regular Internet use can.

Employer-owned IM equipment has the same employee privacy/employer property issues as computers (see Chapter 14). Employers must decide how, if at all, they want to limit the use of IM on company computers, networks, cell phones and PDAs. If IM is used in the workplace, employers should require employees to use company software that has appropriate security, encryption and logging/archiving features.

As with blogging policies, IM policies can be included in existing policies on e-mail and other electronic communication, or employers can have a separate IM policy.

Tips for Creating Electronic Communication Policies

1. Do an audit of all aspects of electronic communication in the workplace.

2. Create, implement and distribute written policies to manage electronic communication. Policies should include provisions on permissible uses, a clear statement that personal blogs, e-mails and IMs are not private and that the employer may review those communications and all other aspects of an employee's computer use in the workplace at any time.

3. Train employees about company policies.

4. Use software designed to secure electronic communication systems.

5. Develop a procedure to monitor Internet, e-mail and IM use.

6. Control inappropriate incoming and outgoing communications.

7. Develop a policy to save information when required and to purge other information on a regular basis.

Sample Computer and Electronic Communications Systems Policies

16

The liabilities employers face if they choose not to establish some form of e-mail and Internet usage monitoring can be significant. However, legal liability is not the only consideration.

Before formulating any sort of monitoring plan, it is advisable to consider the implications a plan may have on employee morale and productivity. A draconian, "business-use only" type of policy might provide the greatest protection from liability if lawful under the circumstances, but is it realistic or even desirable? For most businesses, a middle-ground approach, limiting usage to business-related purposes as much as possible but recognizing employees' need and desire for some personal e-mail use, at least during break and lunch times, will make the most sense.

Need for Written Policy

Any monitoring policy should be reduced to writing. Providing written notification to employees that their e-mails or Internet access may be monitored helps to diminish any claim an employee may later make of an expectation of privacy. Moreover, requiring employees to execute agreements acknowledging their awareness of the monitoring generally will satisfy the consent requirement typically found in federal and state statutes.

In addition to a written policy, employers may want to consider other means to alert employees that their e-mail messages and use of the Internet through the company's computers is not private and confidential. For example, most of today's e-mail programs can be modified to flash a notice to employees, whenever a program is opened or used, that their e-mail is subject to being monitored.

Contents of Policy

Any written policy should explain the purpose for the policy and the importance of adherence to it. Employees must be told e-mail and Internet access may be monitored. The general restrictions on usage — whether an employee can use the e-mail systems for any purpose, business purposes only or mostly for business purposes — should be made clear. Even those policies that allow some sort of personal use need to emphasize that transmissions are not private and as such, employees should be mindful to avoid the use of statements or material that may be offensive to other employees. Further, employers should be careful to mandate that all e-mail correspondence must otherwise comply with the company's discrimination and harassment policies.

The following are several sample policies that vary in scope and approach. Of course, they are only samples and should be tailored in accordance with advice of legal counsel to the laws of the jurisdiction(s) in which the employer does business. E-mail and the Internet both have the potential to be tremendous assets. However, careful planning and policy drafting are essential to ensure these assets do not turn into liabilities.

Sample Use Policies

Policy 1 — Broad Computer and Electronic Communications Systems Policy

This policy applies to all electronic communications systems owned, licensed or operated by the Company, including e-mail, connections to the Internet and similar networks. This policy applies to all employees.

General Use of Systems

The Company's computer network is equipped with e-mail capability and employees are urged to use e-mail to communicate with others when it is appropriate to do so. Use of e-mail messages is not, however, intended to be a substitute for communication through speaking with another employee, client, or party or sending a written memorandum when such communication is needed to properly service clients or carry out the Company's business. Each person should access his or her e-mail several times per day to ensure prompt receipt of any messages.

Electronic communications are considered part of the Company's business records and may be subject to disclosure to third parties for use in litigation. It is important to compose messages in the same professional manner in which any other written communication or memorandum would be composed. Sarcasm and derogatory language must be avoided.

Prohibited Use of Systems

The Company's electronic communications systems are for the purpose of conducting the Company's business. Personal or other non-business use is prohibited during working time. In addition, any use of the Company's electronic communications systems connected with the sale of any goods or services for profit is strictly prohibited at any time. Nonemployees are strictly prohibited from utilizing the Company's electronic communications systems at any time.

Electronic communications systems must not be used in a manner that is contrary to the Company's policies and procedures, as expressed in this handbook or elsewhere. Thus, employees are prohibited from engaging in the inappropriate use of the e-mail systems and are prohibited from transmitting any material that could be construed as illegal harassment in violation of the Company's Equal Employment Opportunity Policy and/or Harassment Policy. Any offensive or otherwise inappropriate material received by an employee must be immediately reported to a supervisor and should not be transmitted further through the system.

Employees may not use the Internet to gain access to Internet sites that contain content that may be perceived as discriminatory, harassing or offensive to others. Use of the Company's access to the Internet for purposes of gaining access to sites containing pornography or other material embarrassing to the Company is strictly prohibited.

Employees shall refrain from transmitting or accessing the personal information of others, false or otherwise. This includes medical records, salary information, disciplinary action or any other material that a reasonable person would deem confidential.

Employees may not download any program onto the Company's computer equipment or diskettes without prior approval from the appropriate personnel.

No Right of Privacy

All employees should be aware that, because the electronic communications systems are designed for business use to serve the Company's clients or customers and conduct other Company business, the Company may from time to time access and review e-mail messages. In addition, because of the nature of the computer system's technology, the e-mail system stores e-mail messages sent and all messages likewise are maintained on tape backup. For this reason, e-mail messages cannot be considered private by the employee.

Employees using any Company electronic communication systems for personal purposes do so at their own risk and expressly consent to Company monitoring, recording, transcribing, copying or storing of communications in a separate location.

Security

In using all electronic communications systems, employees are required to protect the integrity of confidential, sensitive and privileged information. Employees utilizing the Company's electronic communications systems to send materials or messages outside of the Company must exercise great care to protect sensitive, privileged or confidential information from being intercepted. Information sent through the Internet can be monitored by external systems. If necessary, sensitive, confidential or privileged information can be transmitted through the Internet only when the sender and recipient can use encryption.

Acknowledgment:

Through his or her signature below, the employee acknowledges that he or she fully understands the policies set forth above and, as a condition of access, hereby consents to the monitoring of e-mail and electronic transmissions sent through the Company's computer system.

_____

Employee's Signature   Date

Policy 2 — E-Mail, Voice Mail and Internet Usage

Electronic and voice mail communications are the property of the Company and should be used for business purposes only. They are not to be used for personal communications (e.g., political messages, charitable announcements or solicitations, for sale ads, recipe exchange, or personal or vulgar remarks/criticisms relating to the Company or its employees). The misuse of Company time, equipment, facilities or telephones for personal purposes, including personal gain, is a violation of Company policy and may result in disciplinary action.

Electronic mail, voice mail and Internet communications are subject to the same confidentiality and ethical conduct rules that apply to any other form of Company communication. All Company communications, including electronic mail, facsimiles, voice mail and Internet communications, shall be made with due regard to the interests of the Company, its employees and customers.

Expressly prohibited are false and/or malicious communications, and communications of a sexually or racially offensive nature. In that regard, the Company's policies against harassment, including sexual harassment, apply to electronic communications as well as any other form of communication.

E-mail should not be considered a private method of communication and messages may be monitored without prior notice, to prevent personal use of these systems as well as to monitor the quality of our services. Therefore, employees should not have an expectation of privacy with regard to e-mail messages or computer files that they use at work and should refrain from using the e-mail system or computer files for any messages that they consider private or confidential.

Employees having questions concerning the application of the foregoing principles should speak with their supervisor or any officer of the Company.

Policy 3 — Computer Use

Computer equipment and computer software provided by the Company is for business use only. Use of the computer equipment or computer software for personal reasons is prohibited unless such use is approved by a supervisor.

The Company has the capability to access, review, copy or delete information prepared on, stored on, or in any other manner or status maintained on computer equipment, computer software or computer discs, notwithstanding the use of passwords, "fire walls" or other measures intended to protect the security or confidentiality of the information. The Company reserves the right to access, review, copy or delete all such information, including such information to any third party (inside or outside the Company) it deems appropriate.

Accordingly, an employee cannot have an expectation of privacy in any such information. Deleting information from computer equipment, computer software or computer discs does not guarantee that it has been erased or is not capable of being accessed.

Should an employee make approved use of the Company's computer equipment, computer software or computer discs to prepare, store or otherwise maintain personal information, such information will be treated no differently from other information. That is, the Company reserves the right to access, review, copy, delete or disclose it for any purpose.

Also, the copying of computer software of the Company, or the installation of computer software on the computer equipment of the Company, may violate copyright laws, otherwise be illegal, or result in the introduction of computer viruses or other defects in the computer systems of the Company. Accordingly, employees are absolutely prohibited from copying software of the Company for any reason, or installing personal software of any kind in a computer of the Company, without the prior written approval of the President of the Company, or his or her designee.

Computer software purchased by the Company is purchased for specific uses and machines. Unauthorized copying of computer software for installation on other machines of the Company also is expressly prohibited. Before any software is installed into a computer of the Company, or any computer disc that has not been in the exclusive use, custody and control of the Company is placed in a computer of the Company, appropriate measures must be taken to ensure that said computer software or disc does not contain a "computer virus" or other defect.

If you have any questions or concerns regarding the Company's computers and computer software, or this policy, please contact either your supervisor or the Company system administrator.

Policy 4 — E-Mail Use

The Company maintains an e-mail system that is intended solely for the conduct of Company business. The Company treats all messages (or records of such messages) prepared, transmitted, received or stored in the Company e-mail system as business messages of the Company.

The Company has the capability to access, review, copy or delete messages (or records of such messages) prepared, transmitted, received or stored on these communications systems. It reserves the right to access, review, copy or delete all such messages (or records of such messages), including messages of a personal nature, for any purpose and to disclose them to any third party (inside or outside the Company) it deems appropriate, without notification to or permission from the employee who prepared, transmitted, received or stored the messages (or records of such messages).

Accordingly, employees have no right or expectation of privacy in any electronic communication and deleting a message (or record of such message) from an electronic communication system does not guarantee that it has been erased from the system.

As a condition of continued employment, all employees consent to the access, review, copying, deletion or disclosure of electronic communication messages (or records of such messages).

The use of the Company's e-mail systems for personal matters is strictly discouraged. No e-mail communication, personal or otherwise, should include the following:

A. Offensive communications, such as those involving defamatory, obscene, racial or sexual messages, or messages that disclose personal information about other individuals without authorization; and

B. Any references to outside business ventures, political campaigns or similar non-business-related activity.

Should employees make incidental use of the Company e-mail system to prepare, transmit, receive or store personal messages, such messages (or records of such messages) will be treated no differently from other messages. That is, the Company reserves the right to access, review, copy, delete or disclose them for any purpose.

In addition, Company records are subject to disclosure to law enforcement and other governmental agencies, as well as third parties, through subpoena or other process. Moreover, any electronic communication is subject to being intercepted by third parties.

Consequently, employees always should ensure that the business information contained in electronic messages is accurate, appropriate and lawful. When the certainty of confidentiality is important, other means of communication should be used.

Any violation of this policy, or any abuse of the Company's communications systems will result in disciplinary action, up to and including discharge.

Policy 5 — E-Mail Systems

Policy

E-mail is provided by the Company to assist employees as they conduct daily Company business. The e-mail system, its contents and passwords are the property of the Company. This policy outlines the following:

A. appropriate and inappropriate use of e-mail;

B. management's rights and responsibilities; and

C. employee responsibilities.

Procedure

1. E-mail may be used for Company business only. Appropriate use of e-mail includes sending:

   A. work-related correspondence;

   B. approved Company announcements; and

   C. meeting schedules and announcements.

2. Inappropriate use of the e-mail system includes sending:

   A. messages that contain trade secrets or other confidential information;

   B. personnel information (e.g., discussions of performance reviews, disciplinary actions, Employee Relations inquiries, etc.);

   C. Company financial records;

D. copyrighted software or copyrighted documents as e-mail attachments;

E. any form of solicitation for commercial ventures, religious or political causes or non-business-related messages;

F. e-mail that contains ethnic slurs, racial epithets, or anything that may be construed as harassment or disparagement of others based on their race, national origin, gender, sexual orientation, age, disability, or religious or political beliefs;

G. sexually explicit images, messages or cartoons; and

H. messages that are disruptive, excessive, offensive to others or harmful to morale.

Management's Rights and Responsibilities

1. E-mail is not private and messages are considered Company records. E-mail, under the appropriate circumstances, may be accessed and read by designated Company employees or outside individuals for business purposes. The Company reserves the right to enter an employee's e-mail files whenever there is a business need to do so, including the following:

    A. when the Company has a business need to access the employee's mailbox or computer because the employee is absent and the supervisor has reason to believe needed information is located in the employee's e-mail;

    B. when the Company receives a legal request from law enforcement officials to disclose e-mail messages or in ongoing legal proceedings;

    C. when the Company has reason to believe that the employee is using e-mail in violation of Company policy; or

    D. during periodic audits of the e-mail system.

2. Managers are responsible for communicating, monitoring, and enforcing this policy.

Employee Responsibilities

1. Employees are required to use the e-mail system in a responsible and productive manner. Employees will be held accountable for the content of all text, audio or visual images that they place, or transmit, via the Company's e-mail system.

2. Employees should immediately delete inappropriate e-mail or attachments that are sent to them. Such messages should not be printed or forwarded. In addition, employees receiving inappropriate e-mail or attachments shall notify their immediate supervisor.

3. Misuse of the e-mail system is a serious offense that may expose the Company and employee to criminal and/or civil liability. Violations of this policy will result in disciplinary action up to and including termination.

Policy 6 — Sample Release

I, _____, having read the above policy, understand that the Company's computer systems, including e-mail and Internet access, is provided for business use only, and is not to be used for personal reasons. I understand that all files are deemed to be Company property and that the Company can, and on occasion will, exercise the right to review, transmit, intercept and generally access any and all files, including e-mails that are found on the Company's system. I understand that this access can take place at any time and without further notice.

By my signature, I acknowledge that I have read the Company policy regarding computer use. I further acknowledge that I have been given notice that computer files and personal e-mails may be accessed at any time by the appropriate Company representative. I hereby release and hold harmless the Company and its employees and agents from any liability whatsoever arising from a request for access and any decisions made concerning my continued employment based on the results of such access. I also understand that in certain circumstances law enforcement officials may be notified.

_____

Employee's Signature   Date

SECTION VI:
Disclosure of Workplace Records

This section examines how employers should manage the collection and disclosure of workplace records, such as personnel files and medical information. In our emerging world of electronic record-keeping and its apparently constant companion, hacking into computers, knowing what records you must keep and for how long has become a critical employer function.

Chapter 17 explores the various statutory and regulatory issues employers should understand in their management of employee personnel files: What must be retained as a matter of law? Is there an accepted definition among employers as to what ought to be included in personnel files? What should employers include and exclude in files such as medical records, immigration documents and privileged information? What recordkeeping requirements should employers follow? How should employers fulfill requests for employee personal information by government agencies, attorneys and others? What right does an employee have to access his or her personnel file? A Record Retention Chart is included to assist you in these important tasks.

Maintaining employee medical records is a matter of law and can be a potential minefield of liability. Chapter 18 shows employers how this liability can be limited, including a review of the often complicated rules under HIPAA. For example: How should employee medical records be kept? Which employee health documents are actually considered "medical records" and which are subject to restrictions from disclosure? These are all discussed in clear and concise language.

Personnel Files

17

Few workplace issues seem more clear-cut to employees — and even to many employers — than the right of employees to see what has been placed in their personnel files. The information will be used to make decisions regarding their employment and may contain clues to some of the most intimate details about them, such as their race, age, emergency contacts, the health plan used by them and their families, their addresses, the names of their children, their Social Security numbers, and accusations made against them by fellow employees, customers and others, founded and unfounded.

Despite the sensitive and confidential nature of the information contained in it, the file may wind up being turned over to some government agency during an audit, or to a union pursuant to its processing of grievances or to an attorney representing some other employee in a lawsuit against the company.

In short, the argument goes, the information contained in personnel files relates to employees and they have every right to ensure that what is being kept by the employer is accurate and fair. Don't they?

Not necessarily.

What must be shown to employees generally depends on the jurisdiction in which the employer does business and that governs the employment relationship. Very often, as has been seen with so many of the privacy issues affecting the workplace, the employer's obligations with regard to the personnel file depend on whether the state or locality recognizes a general or common law privacy right for employees emanating from the state constitution or public policy, or a statutory or regulatory right (see Chapter 5 for a discussion on common law rights to privacy).

Still, even in those jurisdictions where employers have greater legal entitlements to refuse disclosure of workplace records to employees and others, there may be overriding business considerations that warrant disclosure, or disclosure may occur inadvertently.

Of course, the disclosure of workplace records, whether intentional or inadvertent, is not always free from risk and an employer must be certain to implement policies that will minimize potential liability. Depending on the circumstances, employers may expose themselves to claims of defamation, invasion of privacy, interference with contractual relations, wrongful referral or negligent or intentional discrimination. Laws such as the Americans With Disabilities Act (ADA), the Family Medical and Leave Act (FMLA) and the Health Insurance Portability and Accountability Act (HIPAA) include their own sets of record management requirements.

The presence of a union may add a further wrinkle in view of the competing obligations of employers to both recognize employee privacy concerns and to hand over to the union information relevant and pertinent to the union's role as the employees' bargaining representative. Finally, with advances in technology that have made employee records more transferable than ever, the risk of improper, or at least unmonitored, disclosure and identity theft is very real.

Defining 'Personnel File'

Perhaps the single most sought after item by government agencies investigating workplace claims and by disgruntled employees' lawyers is the personnel file. Yet, there is no universally accepted definition among employers as to what ought to be included in this file.

Some employers even question whether it is wise to have a personnel file. In many jurisdictions there is no legal requirement to have such a file, but if a company does have one, the law generally requires the employer to maintain it and a whole host of rules may govern how to do that.

Nonetheless, there are significant benefits to keeping personnel files. They can be an effective tool for organizing and maintaining employment-related records that must be kept as required by state and federal law. For example, the Fair Labor Standards Act (FLSA) and the FMLA each require that employers keep records on employee identity, occupation, wages, hours of work, and other terms and conditions of employment. Moreover, if done correctly, the preservation of employee performance and disciplinary records in up-to-date, properly maintained files can make the difference in being able to prove that an employment action was legitimate and not a pretext for unlawful discrimination.

Other employers take the position that it is best to keep very little in the file — perhaps the employment application, evidence of wage increases, some payroll information and little else. The rationale is that if there is little in the file, there is little that must be produced when the file is requested or subpoenaed.

Of course, those who have been through a government investigation or who have had to respond to subpoenas by opposing lawyers know that the recipients of thin personnel files generally will respond with a supplemental, much broader request such as for "all documents related to the complainant's employment with the company." Moreover, a skimpy personnel file may lead the recipient to believe that the company has something to hide, thus provoking a more thorough investigation (see Fig. 17-1 for information on unofficial files that may be lurking in managers' desk drawers).

Fig. 17-1
Unofficial Personnel Files

It is not unusual to find that supervisors maintain supplementary information files and/or diaries on employees under their supervision. Often, the human resources department is unaware either of their existence or their content. Such records, however, complicate both the investigation and the decisionmaking process. The investigator, decisionmaker and any person(s) reviewing the personnel decision internally must be familiar with these additional records to understand the issues fully, conduct a proper investigation and make an informed decision.

Accordingly, employers should take steps to ensure that all records on an employee are kept centrally, with the full knowledge of the human resources department or any other department or individual responsible for employee relations at the company.

What To Include and Exclude

Though there are documents that should, or must, be excluded from the personnel file, these files generally should contain all documents related to the employee's employment with the company, including, for example:

- job applications and resumes;
- documentation of benefits;
- compensation data;
- employee authorizations (e.g., for deductions from wages);
- performance evaluations;
- workplace investigation notes and incident reports;
- records regarding promotions or demotions;
- transfer records;
- attendance and leave records; and
- discipline and termination records.

As stated, there are certain documents that should not, or by law cannot, be kept in the personnel file.

Medical records

The ADA, FMLA and HIPAA require that information and documentation resulting from medical examinations or inquiries be treated as confidential medical records and maintained on separate forms and in separate files. Indeed, the Equal Employment Opportunity Commission has suggested employers keep such information in a separate, locked cabinet. Under the ADA, employers are required to limit access to this information to supervisors and managers (as to necessary restrictions on work duties and potential accommodations that can be made for employees), first aid and safety personnel (as to information concerning emergency treatment) and government officials investigating compliance with laws. (For more information on medical records, especially with regard to HIPAA and state laws, see Chapter 18.)

Why the need for such restrictions? First, individuals are highly sensitive about information relating to their medical conditions. Such information is private and should remain confidential to the extent possible. Moreover, the government does not want workplace decisionmakers such as managers and supervisors to base their decisions — regarding performance reviews, wage increases, discipline and discharge — on the protected characteristics of employees such as whether an employee has a disabling medical condition.

These restrictions often benefit the employer for this very reason. When faced with a claim that the company took an action against an employee because of his or her disability, rather than based purely on poor performance, the company is far more likely to succeed if it can show it had no knowledge of the alleged disabling condition. While such a showing can be difficult even under the best set of facts, it is much more problematic when the employee's personnel file — to which the manager had access — contains documentation evidencing the employee's disability.

Immigration documents (I-9)

For similar reasons, employers would be well advised to keep records regarding an employee's national origin and immigration status such as the I-9 Form apart from personnel files to avoid making, and creating the appearance of making, discriminatory employment decisions. In fact, maintaining a separate file cabinet for I-9 forms should assist employers in responding to an audit by the Immigration and Naturalization Service. Few employers relish having to search through personnel files to retrieve intermingled I-9 forms or permitting INS officials leave to search through those files themselves.

OSHA records

Information relating to workplace injuries might also be kept separate, for many of the same reasons.

Privileged information

Too many employers keep documentation of their discussions with attorneys in the personnel file. Normally, these documents can be protected from disclosure, even in the face of a subpoena, as attorney-client privileged information. However, their disclosure to low-level supervisors or employees, even if inadvertent, may destroy the privilege and remove this protection.

Permitted exclusions under state law

Certain state laws expressly allow the exclusion of specified documents from the personnel file.

In **Delaware**, for example, the following documents may be excluded: documents relating to criminal investigations; letters of reference; documents used in preparation for criminal or civil proceedings; medical records; materials used by the employer to plan its future operations; and documents available pursuant to the federal Fair Credit Reporting Act.

Illinois, while permitting the inspection of personnel files by employees under certain circumstances, has enumerated those documents that need not be included for inspection by the employee: letters of reference; portions of testing documents (other than the cumulative score); materials related to staff planning and overall business development;

personal information about another employee; records relevant to any pending claim between the company and the employee; and investigatory or security records maintained by the company to investigate criminal conduct or other activity of the employee that could reasonably be expected to harm the employer's property, operation or business.

Michigan law contains similar exclusions as well as materials related to staff planning with respect to more than one employee such as salary increases, bonus plans and job assignments and information of a personal nature that would constitute a clearly unwarranted invasion of privacy.

In **Minnesota**, non-personnel records, which employees have no right to review, include written references, information from criminal or civil law investigations, education records maintained by an institution, test results (other than test scores), personal information regarding another individual, information regarding business plans and medical reports and records.

Recordkeeping Requirements

In addition to regulating which records must be kept and where, federal and state laws in some instances mandate the length of time these records must be maintained. The table, Fig. 17-2, is a summary of federal recordkeeping requirements for certain employment records.

Fig. 17-2 Federal Requirements for Employee Records		
Type of Record	**Retention Period**	**Statute or Regulation**
Payroll records; collective bargaining agreements; individual contracts; and certificates	3 years	FLSA 29 C.F.R. §516.5
Earnings records, wage rate tables, work schedules, timesheets, and records of additions to or deductions from wages paid	2 years	FLSA 29 C.F.R. §516.6
Dates of leave taken, hours of leave (if less than full day), copies of employee notice of leave, documents describing employee benefits, and records of disputes over FMLA benefits	3 years	FMLA 29 C.F.R. §825.500
Requests for accommodation	1 year*	ADA 29 C.F.R. §1602.14
General records (including summary of occupational injuries and illnesses)	5 years	**OSH Act 29 C.F.R. §1904.2
Exposure to hazardous waste materials records and medical examinations records required by law	30 years	OSH Act 29 C.F.R. §1910.1020
*One year from the date of making the record or date of personnel action, whichever occurs later. **OSH Act is the Occupational Safety and Health Act.		

As a practical matter, employers should treat the time frames set forth in the laws as minimum retention periods. The most important consideration for the company should be how long it must keep the records to be able to make out a defense should it be sued for a workplace wrong. For example, suppose a New York company fired an employee for misconduct and five years later was sued by that employee for an alleged failure to pay for overtime hours worked.

Had the company destroyed its earnings records after only two years, consistent with the FLSA's regulations, it would have no documentation to demonstrate it had indeed paid the employee for overtime. In **New York**, it so happens, a claim for unpaid wages, including unpaid overtime, may be brought for six years following the alleged violation of law. New York employers, then, would be well advised to retain wage records for at least six years after an employee's termination.

Employee Requests for Access

The right of an employee, or even a former employee, to have access to his or her personnel file generally is a matter of state law. As illustrated by Fig. 17-3, 17 states have statutes that grant such access to employees in the private sector; some of those statutes also address former employees and permit access by public employees. Approximately 13 states have laws that restrict the right to inspect personnel files to public employees.

Bear in mind that laws addressing access rights typically provide detailed information as to the types of records that may be accessed, the time and place for any inspection, the right to make copies, the right of employees to object to certain contents and to demand their own written explanation or rebuttal be kept in the file, and remedies for an employer's failure to comply. In addition, certain states have "open records" laws that provide for public disclosure of certain items in government employee files provided such disclosure would not constitute an unwarranted invasion of privacy.

Employers with employees in more than one state should consider adopting a separate plan for each state or, if creating a uniform plan, ensuring the plan complies with all applicable state laws.

In those states that do not have laws specifically addressing access rights, the employer generally will be bound by its own policy and practice. In **New York**, for example, where there is no statutory right of employees to view their personnel files, an employer's practice of permitting employee inspections will be enforced against the employer should it deny access in a given circumstance.

That is not to say an employer is bound to permit inspections forever once it has set a policy or practice permitting them. However, any change in such a policy must be done carefully, preferably in writing, with due regard for the morale problems that might result.

Fig. 17-3
State Personnel File Access Statutes

Alabama	Public (school board employees may access records)	**Montana**	None
Alaska	Private and Public	**Nebraska**	Public
Arizona	Public	**Nevada**	Private and Public
Arkansas	Public	**New Hampshire**	Private and Public
California	Private and Public	**New Jersey**	None
Colorado	None	**New Mexico**	None
Connecticut	Private	**New York**	None
Delaware	Private and Public	**North Carolina**	Public
District of Columbia	Public	**North Dakota**	Public
Florida	None	**Ohio**	None
Georgia	None	**Oklahoma**	Public
Hawaii	None	**Oregon**	Private
Idaho	None	**Pennsylvania**	Private and Public
Illinois	Private and Public	**Rhode Island**	Private and Public
Indiana	Public	**South Carolina**	None
Iowa	Private and Public	**South Dakota**	Public
Kansas	None	**Tennessee**	Public
Kentucky	Public	**Texas**	None
Louisiana	None	**Utah**	Public
Maine	Private and Public	**Vermont**	Public
Maryland	None	**Virginia**	None
Massachusetts	Private and Public	**Washington**	Private
Michigan	Private and Public	**West Virginia**	None
Minnesota	Private	**Wisconsin**	Private
Mississippi	None	**Wyoming**	None
Missouri	None		

State Law Examples

California — Employers are required to permit employees to inspect their personnel files "at reasonable times, and at reasonable intervals" (Cal. Lab. Code §1198.5). The employer is required to maintain a copy of the file at the worksite where the employee reports or otherwise make the file available at that site within a reasonable time after the employee requests to see it. Employees or applicants, on request, are entitled to a copy of any document they have signed that relates to their "obtaining or holding of employment" (Cal. Lab. Code §432).

Connecticut — Employee records are protected from disclosure to individuals other than the employees themselves by Connecticut law. After receiving a written request from an employee, the employer must allow the employee access to his or her file, but may require that the inspection be performed on site (Conn. Gen. Stat. §31-128).

Maine — Under Maine law (26 M.R.S.A. §631), an employee and a former employee have the right to review their personnel files at the company's offices. The employer must allow the employee or former employee to copy the file at the employee's or former employee's expense.

Minnesota — Current employees of covered employers have the right to review their personnel files every six months and former employees have the right to review their files within one year of separation (Minn. Stat. §181.960 *et seq.*). On request, the employer must make the records available within seven days during the employer's normal hours of operation at or near the employee's work location and in the presence of a management representative.

Rhode Island — An employer must permit an employee to inspect his or her personnel file at a location chosen by the employer within seven days of the employee's request. The company can refuse to allow the employee to copy or remove any documents. The company, moreover, need permit such an inspection only up to three times in one year (R.I. Gen. Laws §28-6.4-1).

Wisconsin — An employer must grant an employee at least two requests each year (unless a collective bargaining agreement specifies otherwise) to inspect his or her personnel file. If the employee disagrees with information contained in a record in the file and the company does not consent to a modification or removal of the record, the employee must be allowed to submit a statement for attachment to the disputed portion of the record. That attachment, moreover, must be included any time the record is released to a third party (Wis. Stat. §103.13).

Disclosure to Former Employees

In a number of states — including **Alaska, Connecticut, Illinois, Massachusetts, Michigan, Minnesota, Nevada, Oregon, Washington** and **Wisconsin** — former employees have the right to review their personnel files within a specified period of time following separation of employment. In **Delaware** and **Pennsylvania**, employees who are laid off but have reemployment rights and employees on leaves of absence also are entitled to access their personnel files. As the criteria for access may vary from state to state, employers should consult their applicable state law before making disclosure decisions.

Protecting Against Identity Theft

Identity theft involves the fraudulent use of another person's identifying information — name, address, Social Security number, birth date, mother's maiden name and the like — to establish credit, incur debt or take over financial accounts. Individuals whose identities are stolen can spend years and thousands of dollars clearing their names. In the meantime, they can be refused loans, lose job opportunities and even be arrested for crimes they did not commit.

In today's work environment, with direct deposit arrangements and pension and Social Security accounts, which often includes birthdates and maiden names, employers have all the personal information in their employee records a criminal needs to completely steal an identity. Protecting that information and maintaining its privacy should be of prime importance. Security should be included in every facet of the human resources process, from recruiting to terminating employees.

The first step in a plan to prevent the breach of private employee information is to do an analysis of how the information is collected, stored, accessed, shared and managed. Practical measures that can be taken to protect the information include:

- limiting what is collected:

- limiting the time data is retained;

- limiting access to the information;

- training employees about the importance of data protection; and

- using controls such as password protection and encryption, especially when data is stored on transportable devices such as laptop computers.

In addition, employers are advised to take proactive steps to assure themselves and their employees that sensitive personal data is secure. For example, a prudent employer should periodically assess the risk of a breach and the magnitude of harm that could result from the unauthorized use of personal information. Periodic tests and evaluations of the effectiveness of the information security policies that have been put in place should be conducted. Finally, an employer should have a process for assisting employees in the event there is a breach of security and a means for evaluating and documenting remedial action addressing any deficiencies.

Only information that is absolutely necessary should be collected from employees. Moreover, information that is needed for payroll purposes may not be needed for performance evaluation files. Compensation and benefits databases can be kept separate from other employee records with even higher levels of security.

Employers often keep information on employees long after the need for it has passed. Personal data should be kept for as short a period as possible and the files should be routinely purged of dated information. Having information in segregated files will assist in this effort. For example, there is a need to keep certain pension-related information for years, but that information should no longer be part of other elements of a human resources information system. And access should be on a strictly need-to-know basis, as with medical and health data under HIPAA and the ADA. The fewer people with access, the fewer chances there are for a breach to occur.

Sensitive personal data in electronic form is best kept on company-controlled servers rather than on individual computer memories, especially those on portable devices. In that way, access can be limited and the information will not be lost if a device is lost. If information needs to be available on portable devices such as a laptop computer, the risk of data being accessed by unauthorized individuals is lessened if encryption is used.

Security Breach Notification

If a data breach does occur, the employer should notify its affected employees as soon as possible. Some states, **California** being one, require businesses to notify consumers about security breaches that could directly affect them (Cal. Civ. Code §1798.81.5). At last count, 34 states had laws requiring some form of notification when personal information is compromised. Many more have introduced notification bills. Affected employees should be treated in the same way. Prompt notification will also permit affected individuals to take steps, such as "freezing" credit, when permitted by state law. Currently, 25 states permit a "consumer" (which would include an employee) who has been victimized by ID theft to freeze credit cards.

States that have adopted notification requirements when personal data is compromised include: **Arizona, Arkansas, California, Colorado, Connecticut, Delaware, Florida, Georgia** data brokers only), **Hawaii, Idaho, Illinois, Indiana** (state agencies only), **Kansas, Louisiana, Maine, Minnesota** (does not apply to financial institutions or HIPAA entities), **Montana, Nebraska, Nevada, New Hampshire, New Jersey, New York, North Carolina, North Dakota, Ohio, Oklahoma** (state agencies only), **Pennsylvania, Rhode Island** (does not include HIPAA entities), **Tennessee, Texas, Utah, Vermont, Washington** and **Wisconsin**.

Most are similar to **California's** law. They cover computerized data (a few states include breaches of personal information contained in paper records as well as electronic ones) that contains individual names combined with Social Security numbers, driver's license or state identification card numbers, or account, credit card or debit card numbers together with required security codes or passwords when either the name or one of the data elements is not encrypted.

Most states have an exception for information that is available to the general public. **Arkansas** and **Rhode Island** do not include the exception for publicly available information.

Notification is to be made as expediently as possible or without unreasonable delay, after the company discovers or is notified of the breach. **California** provides three methods of notification — written, electronic or "substitute," which is a generally publicized notice.

Notices should be clear about the nature of the threat to the individuals whose information was compromised and what steps they can take to protect themselves against identity theft. The **California** Office of Privacy Protection recommends that notices include, among other things, the following:

- a general description of what happened;

- the type of personal information that was involved;

- what steps have been taken to prevent further unauthorized acquisition of personal information;

- the types of assistance to be provided to individuals, such as a toll-free contact telephone number for additional information and assistance;

- information on what individuals can do to protect themselves from identity theft, including contact information for the three credit reporting agencies; and

- information on where individuals can obtain additional information on protection against identity theft, such as the Federal Trade Commission's Identity Theft Web site — http://www.consumer.gov/idtheft.

The **California** Office of Privacy Protection also recommends using clear, simple language that avoids jargon. Both California and the Federal Trade Commission recommend that employers consult with their local law-enforcement department before issuing notices so that the notification does not hamper a criminal investigation. Several states, including **Hawaii, Louisiana, Maine, New Hampshire, New Jersey, New York** and **North Carolina** require that notice about a security breach be made to specific state authorities.

Because of the seriousness of a security breach that involves personal employee information, employers should make a plan for responding if such a breach does occur part of their information security program. The plan should address investigating security breaches, securing information if a breach occurs and taking appropriate steps to respond, which would include notifying employees and assisting them as much as possible.

Use of Social Security Numbers

Social Security numbers are a prime way for criminals to steal another person's identity. Employers use those numbers for a variety of legitimate purposes. There currently is no federal legislation relating to the use of Social Security numbers, but at least 21 states have adopted laws concerning their use, although those laws generally apply to commercial entities that use the numbers as account identifiers.

Most of the state laws restrict the display of Social Security numbers or a use that could provide others with access to them, such as an Internet pass code. However, some states, for example **Michigan**, require employers to eliminate Social Security numbers on such things as identification badges and to have a privacy policy guaranteeing the confidentiality of the numbers. **Maryland** prohibits certain employers from printing or causing to be printed employees' Social Security numbers on wage payment checks, on an attachment to a wage payment check, on a notice of direct deposit of an employee's wages or on a notice of credit of an employee's wage to a debit card or a credit card account.

Seeing a trend, many employers have adopted an alternative number for employee identification and try to limit the use of Social Security numbers in their workforce data.

Requests by Government Agencies, Attorneys and Others

The right of government agencies and plaintiffs' attorneys to view an employee's personnel file generally depends on the jurisdiction, whether charges or lawsuits already have been filed against the company and the stage of any such proceedings.

The Equal Employment Opportunity Commission, for example, as a federal agency enforcing Title VII of the 1964 Civil Rights Act and related statutes, has the power to issue investigatory subpoenas to force employers to comply with its requests for access to those documents — including personnel files — relevant to the discrimination charges it is in the process of investigating. Private attorneys also have the right, once a lawsuit is filed, to compel the disclosure of personnel files, at least relevant portions of those files, through discovery devices such as interrogatories and document requests, requests made during the course of witness depositions, and other means of discovery.

(*Note:* In some states such as **New York**, there is no right of discovery for unemployment insurance proceedings and there is no right for a claimant or his or her attorney to see the personnel file.)

Some state laws require the disclosure of personnel information to state agencies, while others vest such agencies with the authority to require certain disclosures by employers.

In **New Mexico**, under a 1997 statute (N.M.S.A. §50-13-1 *et seq.*) passed to enforce child support laws, employers are required to provide the name, address and Social Security number of each newly hired or rehired employee and the name, address and tax identification number of the employer to the state's Human Services Department.

In **North Carolina**, the state Department of Labor has broad authority to enter any public institution or private place of employment to interview employees and/or to gather facts to determine compliance with wage and hour laws. In addition, it may issue subpoenas to require the attendance and testimony of witnesses and the production of evidence under oath during the course of investigations pursuant to the Retaliatory Employment Discrimination Act or the Occupational Safety and Health Act.

Other states such as **Vermont** prohibit the disclosure of an employee's personnel file, even in the course of a lawsuit, unless the employee first is given notice of the disclosure request and an opportunity to object. Personnel records, according to the Vermont law, include any written or electronic record relating to an employee as well as any medical records in the possession of the employer.

Union Requests

In any state, a union representing the company's employees has a federal right, under the National Labor Relations Act, to information and documentation that is relevant to its administration of the collective bargaining agreement. This standard has been construed liberally, so that personnel files, particularly of employees who are grieving disciplinary actions, generally must be shown to a union requesting access to them.

Helpful Hints in Responding to Government Inquiries

The larger issue for employers in most states is not what the law requires, but how to handle government requests for information and documentation regardless of those requirements. Knowing when to rely on a legal right to resist disclosure, when to insist on protective measures and when to cooperate, even when the law might provide a basis for resistance, may make an enormous difference in the outcome of the government's investigation and in the amount of legal fees expended to get that result.

Consider the following guidelines:

1. Take a Step Back

A common expression for this is, "Try to see the forest for the trees." Before reacting to a government request for information, consider what is at stake. Will resistance by the company make more of this investigation than it is? Is the government concerned with mountains, or just molehills? If molehills, will resistance by the company create the mountains?

For example, a request by the state labor department for records relating to a former employee's claim that he is owed $300 in back wages may be limited to that claim. Resistance by the company to the government's request for information, or an overly dramatic show of concern by the company, may raise a red flag with the government investigator and result in a much broader information request or even, in some extreme cases, a payroll practices audit. The result: the $300 claim may become a $300,000 claim or, even if the claim itself remains small, the legal fees may overshadow it.

2. Take the High Road

Assume the best intentions on the part of the investigator, unless there is real reason to believe he or she has a hidden agenda. Treat the investigator with respect and assure him or her of the company's intention to cooperate with the government in its investigation.

Remember, there almost always will be time to take a tough stand down the road, but once the lines are drawn, it may be difficult to regain any spirit of cooperation.

3. Engage in Discovery

Too many employers fail to ask important questions of government investigators, particularly at the early stages of investigations. An employer should not simply rely on the written, often vague and conclusory claims contained in a complaint or charge. A friendly discussion with an investigator can result in a much fuller understanding of the precise allegations made against the company and the government's intent in conducting the investigation. In some cases, an investigator who truly believes the company is eager to cooperate and has nothing to hide might even let the company know of ways to streamline the investigation and bring it to a quicker conclusion.

4. Consider a Confidentiality Agreement

Even when the government insists on viewing sensitive personnel documents, it may be willing to agree it will not disclose such documents to others, even to the complainant.

If this is a possibility, the company should consult with legal counsel to ensure that any such agreement is in writing and contains adequate protections from disclosure. The agreement generally would address, for example, the return of the documents and any copies to the employer as well as steps to prevent their disclosure under state and federal freedom of information laws, when possible.

5. Know When To Call for Help

Employers sometimes get into trouble when they wait too long to seek out the advice of a professional in dealing with a government inquiry. While it may, under some circumstances, be to the company's benefit to avoid having its attorney "up front" in its dealings with the government, decisions about whether or when to involve an attorney or other expert should be made by legal counsel. The government investigator is likely to be more experienced than the company's representative in conducting an audit. Moreover, the company may be too close to the facts of the case to make objective decisions about the extent to which it will cooperate with the government.

Business Concerns, or Just Because the Law Says You Can, Should You?

Employers in states that do not mandate disclosure of the personnel file to employees still might be wise to consider permitting employee access at least to certain records in the file.

There are workplace documents, typically kept in the personnel file, the employer will want to rely on in making employment decisions, such as performance evaluations and employee disciplinary notices. When faced with claims of discrimination in connection with a termination, for instance, the company may need to demonstrate that the employee knew what was expected of him or her and failed to meet those expectations.

Typically, the employee's knowledge of his or her obligations in the workplace is established by the fact that the employee was shown his or her evaluations or issued warnings. An employer whose policy is to deny employees the right to see such documentation may be hard-pressed to prove to a judge, a jury or a government agency that the employee knew what he or she needed to do to remain employed.

An employer that decides to permit personnel file access even when it legally need not do so should consider the issuance of a written policy that spells out the circumstances under which inspections are allowed and any limitations on the inspection process or the documents subject to review by the employee.

Consider the following sample policy:

Sample Policy

Employee Access to Personnel Records

The Company endeavors to treat information about employees with the utmost sensitivity to its confidential nature. Accordingly, while we understand the desire of employees from time to time to view the information contained in their personnel files, the Company has implemented this policy to ensure any such information is provided only to those with a need to know it.

Employees are permitted to inspect and copy, at their own expense, certain employment records relating to them, provided they submit a written request to do so at least 30 days prior to the inspection.

Records subject to inspection include performance evaluations, discipline, compensation and benefits information, and any Company notices regarding employee rights under the laws of the workplace or Company policies.

The inspection must take place in the presence of a management representative and in an area of the Company designated by the Human Resources Department. An employee is not permitted to be accompanied by his or her attorney or other agent or representative during the inspection without the advance written approval of the Company.

Medical Records

18

Several federal laws apply to employers' handling of employee medical information. Because they tend to focus on a specific employer function (for example, medical leave or health benefits administration), they combine to form a potentially confusing patchwork — to say nothing of the myriad state laws that can apply. However, one common thread is the need to keep medical records separate from general personnel files.

Perhaps the most broadly applicable law is the Americans With Disabilities Act (ADA). While the ADA's primary application to employers involves the "reasonable accommodation" of employees with qualifying disabilities, the act's confidentiality provisions apply to all employees' records.

The Family and Medical Leave Act (FMLA) includes privacy protections for employees who seek FMLA leave. An employer may insist that the applicant substantiate the claimed medical condition, but must follow a carefully delimited process in doing so.

Personal health information related to an employer's group health plan is subject to the elaborate privacy and security requirements of the Health Insurance Portability and Accountability Act (HIPAA). Technically, HIPAA applies only to *health plans*, not employers themselves (except those in the health care field), but HIPAA's privacy and security rules effectively extend the law's reach to plan sponsors (which employers often are) by requiring plan document amendments and, in many cases, organizational firewalls.

Public employers also are subject to constitutional limits on their use and disclosure of employees' medical information. The U.S. Supreme Court has ruled that the U.S. Constitution's implicit right to privacy covers medical records, and appellate courts have upheld this right in the employment context (see Fig. 18-1). Like many constitutional rights, however, this right is not absolute and is subject to a balancing of competing interests.

Fig. 18-1
Constitutional Right to Privacy

When state or federal government action is involved, the "constitutionally protected privacy interest in avoiding disclosure of personal matters clearly encompasses medical information and its confidentiality" (*Norman-Bloodsaw v. Lawrence Berkeley Laboratory*, 135 F.3d 1260 (9th Cir. 1998); see also *Doe v. Attorney General of the United States*, 941 F.2d 780 (9th Cir. 1991) and *Doe v. City of New York*, 15 F.3d 264 (2d Cir. 1994)).

The Lawrence Lab, a research institution jointly operated by state and federal agencies, tested individuals for syphilis, sickle cell trait and pregnancy during mandatory employment entrance examinations and sometimes on subsequent occasions, all without the individuals' knowledge. Reversing the district court's dismissal of laboratory employees' privacy right claims, the appeals court stated that "[o]ne can think of few subject areas more personal and more likely to implicate privacy interests than that of one's health or genetic makeup."

The ADA has strict federal confidentiality requirements for medical records. Information from all medical examinations and inquiries must be kept apart from general personnel files as a separate, confidential medical record. (The Equal Employment Opportunity Commission (EEOC) suggests keeping the information in a separate locked cabinet.) These records can be made available only under limited conditions, including to:

- supervisors and managers who need to know about work restrictions and accommodations;

- first aid and safety personnel if a disability might require emergency treatment or if specific procedures are needed to evacuate the employee in cases of emergency;

- government officials investigating compliance with federal laws;

- relevant information to state workers' compensation officers or second injury funds; and

- insurance companies when required to provide health or life insurance.

The EEOC suggests that employers follow the ADA's medical records restrictions for medical information related to the FMLA as well.

Tests for the illegal use of drugs are not medical examinations under the ADA and are not subject to the same confidentiality restrictions. Medical records related to alcohol use generally are protected under the ADA because alcoholics are considered individuals with disabilities under the law.

Even with these restrictions, the employer must keep medical records somewhere, and managing them is a potential minefield of liability. Apart from the requirements of the law, there are few workplace issues that can evoke the emotion that the unauthorized disclosure of an individual's medical information can.

As a result, applicants, employees and former employees are bringing claims relating to disclosure with increasing frequency, whether premised on alleged invasions of privacy or on state or federal statutes governing the confidentiality of medical records.

What Are Medical Records?

During the course of the employment relationship, employers may receive a wide variety of health-related documents and information regarding its employees. These may include the results of pre-employment physicals, drug and alcohol testing, workplace injury reports, documents related to medical insurance and workers' compensation claims, notes from physicians and other health care providers regarding the reasons for absences or work restrictions, FMLA medical certifications, information relating to ADA reasonable accommodation requests, and more.

Which of these documents are actually considered medical records and which are subject to restrictions from disclosure generally depends on the law — whether federal or state — that contains the restrictions at issue. Under the Occupational Safety and Health Act (29 C.F.R. §1910.1020(c)(6)(i)), for example, medical records include any document regarding an employee's health status made or maintained by a physician, nurse or health care professional. Included in the definition are medical histories, medical examination results and opinions, diagnoses, progress notes and recommendations, first aid records, descriptions of treatments and prescriptions and employee medical complaints.

Routinely discarded physical specimens, health insurance claims records, records created solely for litigation and records concerning voluntary employee assistance programs, if separately maintained, are not included in the definition of employee medical records. However, claims and other information regarding payment for health care are among the "protected health information" subject to HIPAA's privacy requirements.

Some state laws also define medical records (see State Laws below). In **Ohio** (O.R.C. §4113.23), for example, the definition includes any medical report arising from a physical examination by a health care professional and hospital or laboratory test results from tests required as a condition of employment or as a result of a work injury or illness.

HIPAA

Employer group health plans are subject to HIPAA's privacy, security and other "administrative simplification" requirements. Health plans and other "covered entities" must comply with rules issued by the U.S. Department of Health and Human Services (HHS). "Contrary" state laws are preempted unless they are "more stringent." (Key terms are defined in Fig. 18-2).

The privacy rules (45 C.F.R. §164.500 *et seq.*), issued by HHS in 2000 and amended in 2002, restrict health plans' and providers' use and disclosure of beneficiaries' and patients' health information (including claims and other payment-related records). Basically, this "protected health information" may not be used and disclosed without the individual's signed authorization except for specific purposes described by the rules, such as treatment, payment and "health care operations."

The privacy rules' application to employers is complex because HHS lacks jurisdiction over employers *per se*. In practice, employers must comply in their role as plan administrators or — to the extent they outsource administration — obtain contractual assurances of compliance, on the plan's behalf, from their service providers (and other business associates). Most plan sponsors also must amend the plan documents to require HIPAA compliance and prohibit protected health information use for employment purposes.

An underlying principle of the rules is that protected health information used and disclosed in the normal course of business should be limited to the "minimum necessary." Group health plans must develop and update "policies and procedures" for applying this and other privacy standards to their specific health information uses and disclosures. The rules also give individuals the right to access their health information, along with several other procedural rights regarding its content. Many health information disclosures must be accounted for on request.

HIPAA's administrative requirements include appointing a privacy official, issuing a privacy notice and establishing an internal privacy complaint process. The privacy official's central functions include auditing and training; these measures should be ongoing and should be adapted, when necessary, to reflect benefit changes, emerging problems and employee turnover. Fully insured group health plans that receive no protected health information (except summary health information and enrollment data) are exempt from many administrative requirements.

Health plans and providers were required to comply with the privacy rules by April 2003, except for "small health plans," which had until April 2004. A small health plan is defined as "a health plan with annual receipts of $5 million or less." In calculating "receipts," fully insured group health plans should use total premiums and self-insured plans should use the amount paid for claims. Self-administered plans with fewer than 50 participants are exempted altogether.

Security

Along with privacy, group health plans must comply with HIPAA's security rules (45 C.F.R. §164.300 *et seq.*). Issued in 2003, these rules impose administrative, physical and technical standards and "implementation specifications" for safeguarding electronic protected health information. Hard-copy and spoken health information is not subject to the security rules, but is subject to a general safeguards requirement of the privacy rules.

In general, the rules are not very prescriptive but they place a premium on risk analysis, management and documentation. Certain steps are required of all plans with electronic health information, including the appointment of a security official. Security compliance was required by April 2005, or 2006 for small health plans (those with annual receipts of $5 million or less).

Enforcement

HHS' Office for Civil Rights (OCR) enforces the privacy rules and the Centers for Medicare and Medicaid Services enforces the security, electronic transactions and identifier rules. HIPAA's criminal prohibitions on wrongful disclosures and misuse of identifiers are enforced by the U.S. Department of Justice.

Group health plans and other HIPAA-covered entities that violate HIPAA's privacy or security rules are subject to civil and criminal penalties. HHS civil enforcement is generally complaint-based and voluntary compliance-oriented. OCR, which enforces the privacy rules, has received more than 20,000 privacy complaints but has been slow to impose penalties.

Rules governing civil enforcement, issued in February 2006, address how HHS identifies violations, determines the number of violations and calculates civil monetary penalties for such violations, and how covered entities may establish affirmative defenses to the imposition of penalties. However, HHS retains broad discretion to decide both the number of HIPAA violations and the amount of the civil penalty.

In addition to its civil enforcement role, HHS has referred hundreds of potential HIPAA criminal cases to the Justice Department, which has taken the position that not only can covered entities be prosecuted for HIPAA violations, but others can be prosecuted for conspiracy or "aiding and abetting." Several individuals have been convicted on HIPAA charges, albeit for egregious conduct — such as identity theft — that could have been prosecuted under other laws.

HIPAA does not give individuals a "private right of action" to sue for privacy violations. However, employers may still be sued under state law and ERISA, and a growing number of lawsuits cite HIPAA as a standard of care for civil liability purposes.

Fig. 18-2
HIPAA Privacy Terms

Business associate. An outside entity, such as a third-party administrator, that helps a covered entity with a function involving the use or disclosure of individuals' health information.

Covered entity. A health plan, health care provider or health care clearinghouse.

Health care operations. A covered entity's administrative and business functions such as underwriting, audits and fraud detection, and mergers and acquisitions. In the employer context this includes only group health plan-related activities.

Health plan. Includes employer group health plans, whether self-funded or fully insured, and health insurers. Does not include workers' compensation or disability income insurance.

Payment. Includes eligibility and coverage determination along with most claims administration functions.

Protected health information. Health information kept or transmitted by a covered entity regarding an identified individual's condition, treatment or related payment.

State Laws

A number of states have laws that specifically address the confidentiality and disclosure of medical records. Some prohibit employers from disclosing employee medical records to third parties without the employee's written consent. Still others limit the mandate of confidentiality to the results of drug and alcohol testing.

The medical records laws chart in Fig. 18-3 summarizes many of the state laws regarding the treatment of medical records. Of course, all details of the laws themselves should be reviewed and discussed with legal counsel before any decision is made regarding disclosure.

Fig. 18-3 **State Medical Records Laws**	
Arkansas	Drug test results are confidential. (Ark. Code Ann. §11-14-109.)
California	The California Confidentiality of Medical Information Act (Cal. Civil Code §56.20) protects employee medical records from disclosure; requires employers to institute procedures to ensure confidentiality of medical information and to safeguard such information from its unauthorized use and disclosure. With few exceptions (e.g., when there is a valid subpoena, the employee has placed his or her medical condition at issue during a proceeding, or for purposes of administering an employee benefit plan), employers are prohibited from using or disclosing medical information without the employee's prior written authorization in a form prescribed by the statute.
Colorado	Criminal penalties are provided for the unauthorized acquisition and/or disclosure of medical records or information (C.R.S. §18-4-412). Proper authorization may come in the form of written authorization by the employee, a court order, or as otherwise recognized by law such as when medical information is needed to process claims, comply with medical audits or consult with a physician.
	Criminal penalties are provided for the unauthorized disclosure of HIV test results (C.R.S. §10-3-1104.5).
	Information derived from genetic testing is privileged and confidential and generally requires written consent for disclosure.
Connecticut	HIV test results are confidential. Their release can provide the basis for liability whether intentional or willful (Conn. Gen. Stat. §19a-581 *et seq.*).
	An employer may not release health or medical condition information without express authorization from the employee (Conn. Gen. Stat. §31-128f).
Florida	If the employer adopts a drug-free workplace program, the results of applicant and employee drug tests are confidential with limited exceptions (Fla. Stat. §443.1715(3)).
	The results of DNA analysis or genetic testing are confidential as the exclusive property of the person tested (Fla. Stat. §760.40).
Georgia	Employee medical records are confidential; disclosure is permitted only when authorized by law (O.C.G.A. §24-9-43).
	The intentional disclosure of confidential AIDS information is prohibited (O.C.G.A. §24-9-47(b)(1)). The Georgia Department of Human Resources must be privy to confirmed positive HIV tests (O.C.G.A. §24-9-7(h)).

Fig. 18-3
State Medical Records Laws

Hawaii	The Privacy of Health Care Information Act, effective July 1, 2000, broadly protects the rights of employees to privacy with respect to their personal health information. In general, employers must comply with specific notice requirements, cannot use or disclose "protected health information" unless authorized to do so by the employee. Employers may subpoena medical records from the employee's physician only if the subpoena is accompanied by a court order or written authorization by the employee.

With limited exceptions, employees generally have the right to inspect and copy on written request, medical information that concerns them and is maintained by the employer. The company need not permit such an inspection when disclosure of the information could reasonably be expected to endanger the life or safety of the individual who is the subject of the record; the information was provided under a promise of confidentiality; the information relates to proceedings of peer review committees, or hospital or clinic quality assurance committees protected from disclosure by Hawaii law; or the information was collected for or during a clinical trial monitored by an institutional review board, the trial is not complete, and the researcher reasonably believes that access would harm the conduct of the trial.

Employers must post or provide employees with a written notice outlining its confidentiality practices and employee rights regarding protected health information (Haw. Rev. Stat. Chap. 323C). |
| **Illinois** | The results of genetic and AIDS tests are confidential (410 I.L.C.S. 513; 410 I.L.C.S. 305). |
| **Louisiana** | When an employee submits to a medical examination at the employer's request, he or she is entitled to a copy of any written report within 30 days after making a written demand for it (La. Rev. Stat. Ann. §23:1125).

Current and former employees, or their designated representatives, must be given access to records of employee exposure to potentially toxic materials or harmful physical agents (La. Rev. Stat. Ann. §23:1016). |
Massachusetts	Disclosure of confidential medical information without the consent of the employee has been held to violate the Massachusetts Privacy Act (*Doe v. Plymouth,* 825 F. Supp. 1102 (D. Mass. 1993)).
Mississippi	Information obtained by the employer from an employee's drug or alcohol test may not be released to anyone, except the employer's medical, supervisory or other personnel who have a "need to know," absent a waiver from the employee, the need to introduce the information at an arbitration or administrative or judicial proceeding, or a risk to the public health or safety (Miss. Code Ann. §71-5-15(3)).
Nebraska	Information obtained regarding a private or public sector employee's medical condition or history must be maintained in separate confidential medical records files and treated as confidential. The information may be shared with supervisors who have a need to know of any restrictions, first aid and safety personnel, government employees investigating compliance with the state's Fair Employment Practices Act, and in accordance with the state's workers' compensation laws (Neb. Rev. Stat. §48-1107.2(9)).

	Fig. 18-3 **State Medical Records Laws**
New Hampshire	The disclosure of the identity of any employee tested for HIV is prohibited and all records relating to HIV must be kept confidential (N.H. R.S.A. §141-F). Violations can result in criminal penalties and fines of up to $5,000.
New Mexico	All health information relating to and identifying specific individuals as patients is strictly confidential (N.M.S.A. §14-6-1).
New York	HIV-related information concerning an employee generally can be released by an employer only with the employee's written consent or release specifying that the release covers HIV information and indicating to whom the disclosure is authorized, the reason for disclosure and the time frame within which the release will remain effective (N.Y. Pub. Health Law §2780 *et seq.*). In general, employee health records should not be released or disclosed without the employee's authorization, unless otherwise authorized by law.
Ohio	An employer is required to provide to the employee, on written request, a copy of the employee's medical reports (information arising out of any employment-related medical examinations or testing or arising out of any injury or disease related to the employee's employment) (O.R.C. §4113.23).
Oregon	An employee has the right to access his or her medical and exposure records maintained by the employer and may consent to the inspection of such records by his or her designated representative (O.A.R. 437-02-0015).
Rhode Island	An employer must keep all employee medical records confidential, unless the employee signs a release form specifically permitting their disclosure (R.I. Gen. Laws §5-37.3-4(a) (1999)). An employer must develop procedures by which confidential medical records are secured and access to them limited so that unauthorized parties may not uncover the information. The employer may allow access only to those medical records by supervisors on a need-to-know basis. Employers that retain medical records must provide a written statement to employees stressing the necessity of protecting the security of such information and detailing the potential penalties for its unauthorized release. Every employee must acknowledge receipt of this statement by signing a copy of the policy provided by the employer.
South Carolina	Substance abuse test results are confidential. Employers should release such information only under a valid court order, subpoena or other command in a civil or administrative proceeding or pursuant to a valid consent form (S.C. Ann. Code §41-1-15).
Tennessee	Employers who have implemented a drug-free workplace program must keep certain drug and alcohol test records confidential (Tenn. Code Ann. §50-9-109). Tennessee's workers' compensation law requires that any hospital in which an employee has been hospitalized for a workplace injury must, within 30 days of the employee's admission, release its medical records to both the employee and the employer on either's request (Tenn. Code Ann. §50-6-204).

Fig. 18-3 State Medical Records Laws	
Texas	Medical records are confidential. Strict prohibitions exist against employer disclosure of AIDS or HIV information about an employee (Tex. Health & Safety Code Ann. §81.102.103).
	Generally, employee medical information obtained by an employer to determine reasonable accommodations under the ADA or to verify a claimed serious health condition under the FMLA may not be disclosed to others except when the disclosure is consistent with the authorized purposes for which the information was obtained (Tex. Health & Safety Code Ann. §611.004).
Wisconsin	Employees are permitted to inspect their medical records maintained by the employer. The employer may require a written request by the employee. If the employer believes that releasing the records to the employee would be detrimental to the employee's health, it may release the records to the employee's physician (Wis. Stat. §103.13).
	The disclosure of HIV test results is prohibited; intentional disclosure may result in fines and even imprisonment when it results in physical or psychological harm to the employee (Wis. Stat. §252.15).

California

The California Confidentiality of Medical Information Act (CMIA) is one of the most comprehensive state statutes regarding the confidentiality of medical information. In addition to prohibiting disclosure of employee medical information without the employee's consent, the CMIA requires that employers establish specific procedures for handling medical files and security systems restricting access to those files. Under the CMIA, medical records generally may be released only:

- if compelled by a subpoena from a court or government agency;
- if the medical information is relevant in a legal proceeding in which the employee has made his or her medical history or condition an issue; or
- to administer an employee benefit plan, for workers' compensation claims or to determine eligibility for paid or unpaid leave from work.

Hawaii

Hawaii's Privacy of Health Care Information Act, which became effective July 1, 2000, may prove troublesome for employers seeking to make workplace decisions regarding disabled employees or employees claiming serious health conditions (Haw. Rev. Stat. §323C). In general, absent authorization from the employee, employers may not use or disclose "protected health information" — broadly defined to include almost any medical information related to an employee — except for purposes consistent with the reasons for which the information was collected. While the law has not yet been construed by the courts, its language suggests that an employer would be prohibited from using information contained in workers' compensation documents, for example, to make decisions concerning whether an employee is capable of performing his or her job, with or without a reasonable accommodation, and lawfully can be terminated under the ADA. Knowing violations of the act may subject employers to penalties of up to $25,000 for each violation and as much as $100,000 for a "general business practice" inconsistent with the act's requirements.

The Hawaii act requires that employers post or provide employees with written notice of their rights under the law (Haw. Rev. Stat. §323C-13(b)). The notice must contain the following language, placed prominently at the beginning:

> IMPORTANT: THIS NOTICE DEALS WITH THE SHARING OF INFORMATION FROM YOUR MEDICAL RECORDS. PLEASE READ IT CAREFULLY. This notice describes your confidentiality rights as they relate to the information from your medical records and explains the circumstances under which information from your medical records may be shared with others. This information in this notice also applies to others covered under your health plan such as your spouse or children. If you do not understand the terms of this notice, please ask for further explanation.

Employee Assistance Programs

Some employers, though generally larger ones, offer Employee Assistance Programs (EAPs) to help employees overcome workplace problems, including those related to drug and alcohol abuse. Often, an employee agrees to participate in such a program — generally run by private organizations with licensed therapists and other health care providers — in exchange for a "last-chance agreement" with the employer to salvage the employee's job should he or she satisfactorily complete the program.

The employer generally is kept apprised of an employee's progress through reports from the program, though the details contained in those reports may vary depending on state law, employee consent and the arrangements made between the employer and the program. Employers in many states — including **Florida, Idaho, North Dakota** and **Washington** — have an obligation to keep communications and records relating to these programs confidential.

APPENDIX I:

State and EEOC Guidance on Pre-employment and Disability Inquiries

The EEOC and states have published guidelines for employers on questions that may or may not be asked in pre-employment inquiries to protect the privacy of individuals with disabilities. Appendix I contains three examples: the state of **New York's** guidelines for pre-employment inquiries (page 165); the EEOC's ADA Enforcement Guidance: Pre-employment Disability-Related Questions and Medical Examinations (page 167); and, the EEOC's Job Application and Pre-employment Questions (page 182).

Guidelines for Pre-employment Inquiries

Like most states, **New York** has a list of questions that cannot be asked on application forms or during pre-employment interviews. New York's Human Rights Law prohibits discrimination on the basis of race, creed, color, national origin, gender, age, disability, marital status or arrest records. Federal law does not protect the latter two, although most states do. Federal law does, however, prohibit discrimination on the basis of citizenship status unless citizenship is an essential requirement of the job on the basis of another law or regulation.

These guidelines provide actual examples of questions that New York's human rights agency has ruled to be either lawful or unlawful. Not only should interviewers take care to comply with the guidelines, they should not write any comments on employment applications that relate to the prohibited areas of inquiry.

Subject	Lawful Inquiries	Unlawful Inquiries
Name	Applicant's full name. Have you ever worked for this company under a different name? Is any additional information relative to a different name necessary to check work records? If yes, explain.	Original name or maiden name.
Address or Duration of Residence	Current address. How long have you been a resident of this state or city?	
Birthplace		Birthplace of applicant. Birthplace of applicant's parents, spouse or other relatives. Requirements that applicant submit birth certificate, naturalization or baptism record.
Age	Are you 18 or older? This question may be asked only for the purpose of determining whether applicants are of legal age for employment.	
Religion		Inquiry into an applicant's religious denomination, religious affiliation, church parish, pastor, or religious holiday observances.
Race, Color		Complexion or skin color.

Subject	Lawful Inquiries	Unlawful Inquiries
Photograph Height		Any requirement for a photograph prior to hire. Inquiry regarding applicant's height.
Weight		Inquiry regarding applicant's weight.
Marital Status	Is your spouse employed by this employer?	Requirement that an applicant provide any in formation regarding marital status or children.
Gender		Mr., Miss or Mrs. or an inquiry regarding gender. Inquiry as to the ability to reproduce or advocacy of any form of birth control. Requirement that women be given pelvic examinations.
Disability		Inquiries regarding an individual's physical or mental condition that are not directly related to the requirements of a specific job and that are used as a factor in making employment decisions in a way that is contrary to the provisions or purposes of the law.
Citizenship	Can you legally work in the United States?	Are you a U.S. citizen? Do you intend to become a citizen? Of what country are you a citizen? Requirement to produce Social Security card, passport or naturalization papers prior to hiring. Questions about parents', spouse's or other close relatives' place of birth or citizenship status.

Subject	Lawful Inquiries	Unlawful Inquiries
National Origin	Inquiry into languages spoken unless an essential job function.	Inquiry into applicant's lineage, ancestry, national origin, descent, parentage or nationality or that of the applicant's parents or spouse.
Education	Inquiry into academic, vocational or professional education and public and private schools attended.	Inquiry into how applicant acquired ability to read, write or speak a foreign language. Dates of education are questionable because of correlation with age.
Experience	Inquiry into work experience. Inquiry into countries applicant has visited.	
Arrests	Have you ever been convicted of a crime? Are there any felony charges pending against you?	Inquiry regarding arrests that did not result in conviction. (Except for law enforcement agencies.)
Relatives	Names of applicant's reltives already employed by this company.	Address of any relatives.
Notice in Case of Emergency		Names and addresses of emergency contacts can be obtained after hiring.
Organizations	Inquiries into professional organization memberships. (These might indicate race or gender. Caution is advised.)	List all clubs, societies and lodges to which you belong.

U.S. Equal Employment Opportunity Commission
ADA Enforcement Guidance: Pre-employment Disability-Related Questions and Medical Examinations

Introduction

Under the Americans With Disabilities Act of 1990 (the ADA),[1] an employer may ask disability-related questions and require medical examinations of an applicant only after the applicant has been given a conditional job offer. This enforcement guidance explains these ADA provisions.[2]

Background

In the past, some employment applications and interviews requested information about an applicant's physical and/or mental condition. This information was often used to exclude applicants with disabilities before their ability to perform the job was even evaluated.

For example, applicants may have been asked about their medical conditions at the same time that they were engaging in other parts of the application process such as completing a written job application or having references checked. If an applicant was then rejected, s/he did not necessarily know whether s/he was rejected because of disability, or because of insufficient skills or experience or a bad report from a reference.

As a result, Congress established a process within the ADA to isolate an employer's consideration of an applicant's nonmedical qualifications from any consideration of the applicant's medical condition.

The Statutory and Regulatory Framework

Under the law, an employer may not ask disability-related questions and may not conduct medical examinations until after it makes a conditional job offer to the applicant.[3] This helps ensure that an applicant's possible hidden disability (including a prior history of a disability) is not considered before the employer evaluates an applicant's non-medical qualifications. An employer may not ask disability-related questions or require a medical examination pre-offer even if it intends to look at the answers or results only at the post-offer stage.

Although employers may not ask disability-related questions or require medical examinations at the pre-offer stage, they may do a wide variety of things to evaluate whether an applicant is qualified for the job, including the following:

- Employers may ask about an applicant's ability to perform specific job functions. For example, an employer may state the physical requirements of a job (such as the ability to lift a certain amount of weight, or the ability to climb ladders), and ask if an applicant can satisfy these requirements.

- Employers may ask about an applicant's nonmedical qualifications and skills, such as the applicant's education, work history, and required certifications and licenses.

- Employers may ask applicants to describe or demonstrate how they would perform job tasks.

Once a conditional job offer is made, the employer may ask disability-related questions and require medical examinations as long as this is done for all entering employees in that job category. If the employer rejects the applicant after a disability-related question or medical examination, investigators will closely scrutinize whether the rejection was based on the results of that question or examination.

If the question or examination screens out an individual because of a disability, the employer must demonstrate that the reason for the rejection is "job-related and consistent with business necessity."[4]

In addition, if the individual is screened out for safety reasons, the employer must demonstrate that the individual poses a "direct threat." This means that the individual poses a significant risk of substantial harm to him/herself or others, and that the risk cannot be reduced below the direct threat level through reasonable accommodation.[5]

Medical information must be kept confidential.6 The ADA contains narrow exceptions for disclosing specific, limited information to supervisors and managers, first aid and safety personnel, and government officials investigating compliance with the ADA. Employers may also disclose medical information to state workers' compensation offices, state second injury funds, or workers' compensation insurance carriers in accordance with state workers' compensation laws7 and may use the medical information for insurance purposes.8

The Pre-offer Stage

What Is a Disability-Related Question?

Definition: "Disability-Related Question" means a question that is likely to elicit information about a disability.

At the pre-offer stage, an employer cannot ask questions that are likely to elicit information about a disability. This includes directly asking whether an applicant has a particular disability. It also means that an employer cannot ask questions that are closely related to disability.[9]

On the other hand, if there are many possible answers to a question and only some of those answers would contain disability-related information, that question is not "disability-related."[10]

Below are some commonly asked questions about this area of the law.

May an employer ask whether an applicant can perform the job?

Yes. An employer may ask whether applicants can perform any or all job functions, including whether applicants can perform job functions "with or without reasonable accommodation."[11]

May an employer ask applicants to describe or demonstrate how they would perform the job (including any needed reasonable accommodations)?

Yes. An employer may ask applicants to describe how they would perform any or all job functions, as long as all applicants in the job category are asked to do this.

Employers should remember that, if an applicant says that s/he will need a reasonable accommodation to do a job demonstration, the employer must either:

- provide a reasonable accommodation that does not create an undue hardship; or
- allow the applicant to simply describe how s/he would perform the job function.

May an employer ask a particular applicant to describe or demonstrate how s/he would perform the job, if other applicants are not asked to do this?

When an employer could reasonably believe that an applicant will not be able to perform a job function because of a known disability, the employer may ask that particular applicant to describe or demonstrate how s/he would perform the function. An applicant's disability would be a "known disability" either because it is obvious (for example, the applicant uses a wheelchair), or because the applicant has voluntarily disclosed that s/he has a hidden disability.

May an employer ask applicants whether they will need reasonable accommodation for the hiring process?

Yes. An employer may tell applicants what the hiring process involves (for example, an interview, timed written test or job demonstration), and may ask applicants whether they will need a reasonable accommodation for this process.

May an employer ask an applicant for documentation of his/her disability when the applicant requests reasonable accommodation for the hiring process?

Yes. If the need for accommodation is not obvious, an employer may ask an applicant for reasonable documentation about his/her disability if the applicant requests reasonable accommodation for the hiring process (such as a request for the employer to reformat an examination, or a request for an accommodation in connection with a job demonstration). The employer is entitled to know that the applicant has a covered disability and that s/he needs an accommodation.

So, the applicant may be required to provide documentation from an appropriate professional, such as a doctor or a rehabilitation counselor, concerning the applicant's disability and functional limitations.

May an employer ask applicants whether they will need reasonable accommodation to perform the functions of the job?

In general, an employer may not ask questions on an application or in an interview about whether an applicant will need reasonable accommodation for a job. This is because these questions are likely to elicit whether the applicant has a disability (generally, only people who have disabilities will need reasonable accommodations).

Example: An employment application may not ask, "Do you need reasonable accommodation to perform this job?"

Example: An employment application may not ask, "Can you do these functions with ____ without ____ reasonable accommodation? (Check one)."

Example: An applicant with no known disability is being interviewed for a job. He has not asked for any reasonable accommodation, either for the application process or for the job. The employer may not ask him, "Will you need reasonable accommodation to perform this job?"

However, when an employer could reasonably believe that an applicant will need reasonable accommodation to perform the functions of the job, the employer may ask that applicant certain limited questions. Specifically, the employer may ask whether s/he needs reasonable accommodation and what type of reasonable accommodation would be needed to perform the functions of the job.[12] The employer could ask these questions if:

- the employer reasonably believes the applicant will need reasonable accommodation because of an obvious disability;

- the employer reasonably believes the applicant will need reasonable accommodation because of a hidden disability that the applicant has voluntarily disclosed to the employer; or

- an applicant has voluntarily disclosed to the employer that s/he needs reasonable accommodation to perform the job.

Example: An individual with diabetes applying for a receptionist position voluntarily discloses that she will need periodic breaks to take medication. The employer may ask the applicant questions about the reasonable accommodation such as how often she will need breaks, and how long the breaks must be. Of course, the employer may not ask any questions about the underlying physical condition.

Example: An applicant with a severe visual impairment applies for a job involving computer work. The employer may ask whether he will need reasonable accommodation to perform the functions of the job. If the applicant answers "no," the employer may not ask additional questions about reasonable accommodation (although, of course, the employer could ask the applicant to describe or demonstrate performance). If the applicant says that he will need accommodation, the employer may ask questions about the type of required accommodation such as, "What will you need?" If the applicant says he needs software that increases the size of text on the computer screen, the employer may ask questions such as, "Who makes that software?" "Do you need a particular brand?" "Is that software compatible with our computers?" However, the employer may not ask questions about the applicant's underlying condition. In addition, the employer may not ask reasonable accommodation questions that are unrelated to job functions such as, "Will you need reasonable accommodation to get to the cafeteria?"

An employer may only ask about reasonable accommodation that is needed now or in the near future. An applicant is not required to disclose reasonable accommodations that may be needed in the more distant future.

May an employer ask whether an applicant can meet the employer's attendance requirements?

Yes. An employer may state its attendance requirements and ask whether an applicant can meet them. An employer also may ask about an applicant's prior attendance record (for example, how many days the applicant was absent from his/her last job). These questions are not likely to elicit information about a disability because there may be many reasons unrelated to disability why someone cannot meet attendance requirements or was frequently absent from a previous job (for example, an applicant may have had day-care problems).

An employer also may ask questions designed to detect whether an applicant abused his/her leave because these questions are not likely to elicit information about a disability.

Example: An employer may ask an applicant, "How many Mondays or Fridays were you absent last year on leave other than approved vacation leave?"

However, at the pre-offer stage, an employer may not ask how many days an applicant was sick, because these questions relate directly to the severity of an individual's impairments. Therefore, these questions are likely to elicit information about a disability.

May an employer ask applicants about their certifications and licenses?

Yes. An employer may ask an applicant at the pre-offer stage whether s/he has certifications or licenses required for any job duties. An employer also may ask an applicant whether s/he intends to get a particular job-related certification or license, or why s/he does not have the certification or license. These questions are not likely to elicit information about an applicant's disability because there may be a number of reasons unrelated to disability why someone does not have — or does not intend to get — a certification/license.

May an employer ask applicants about their arrest or conviction records?

Yes. Questions about an applicant's arrest or conviction records are not likely to elicit information about disability because there are many reasons unrelated to disability why someone may have an arrest/conviction record.[13]

May an employer ask questions about an applicant's impairments?

Yes, if the particular question is not likely to elicit information about whether the applicant has a disability. It is important to remember that not all impairments will be disabilities; an impairment is a disability only if it substantially limits a major life activity. So, an employer may ask an applicant with a broken leg how she broke her leg. Since a broken leg normally is a temporary condition which does not rise to the level of a disability, this question is not likely to disclose whether the applicant has a disability. But, such questions as "Do you expect the leg to heal normally?" or "Do you break bones easily?" would be disability-related. Certainly, an employer may not ask a broad question about impairments that is likely to elicit information about disability, such as, "What impairments do you have?"

May an employer ask whether applicants can perform major life activities such as standing, lifting, walking, etc.?

Questions about whether an applicant can perform major life activities are almost always disability-related because they are likely to elicit information about a disability. For example, if an applicant cannot stand or walk, it is likely to be a result of a disability. So, these questions are prohibited at the pre-offer stage unless they are specifically about the ability to perform job functions.

May an employer ask applicants about their workers' compensation history?

No. An employer may not ask applicants about job-related injuries or workers' compensation history. These questions relate directly to the severity of an applicant's impairments. Therefore, these questions are likely to elicit information about disability.

May an employer ask applicants about their current illegal use of drugs?

Yes. An employer may ask applicants about current illegal use of drugs[14] because an individual who currently illegally uses drugs is not protected under the ADA when the employer acts on the basis of the drug use.[15]

May an employer ask applicants about their lawful drug use?

No, if the question is likely to elicit information about disability. Employers should know that many questions about current or prior lawful drug use are likely to elicit information about a disability, and are therefore impermissible at the pre-offer stage. For example, questions like, "What medications are you currently taking?" or "Have you ever taken AZT?" certainly elicit information about whether an applicant has a disability.

However, some innocuous questions about lawful drug use are not likely to elicit information about disability.

Example: During her interview, an applicant volunteers to the interviewer that she is coughing and wheezing because her allergies are acting up as a result of pollen in the air. The interviewer, who also has allergies, tells the applicant that he finds "Lemebreathe" (an over-the-counter antihistamine) to be effective, and asks the applicant if she has tried it. There are many reasons why someone might have tried "Lemebreathe" which have nothing to do with disability. Therefore, this question is not likely to elicit information about a disability.

May an employer ask applicants about their lawful drug use if the employer is administering a test for illegal use of drugs?

Yes, if an applicant tests positive for illegal drug use. In that case, the employer may validate the test results by asking about lawful drug use or possible explanations for the positive result other than the illegal use of drugs.

Example: If an applicant tests positive for use of a controlled substance, the employer may lawfully ask questions such as, "What medications have you taken that might have resulted in this positive test result? Are you taking this medication under a lawful prescription?"

May an employer ask applicants about their prior illegal drug use?

Yes, provided that the particular question is not likely to elicit information about a disability. It is important to remember that past addiction to illegal drugs or controlled substances is a covered disability under the ADA (as long as the person is not a current illegal drug user), but past casual use is not a covered disability. Therefore, the question is fine as long as it does not go to past drug addiction.

Example: An employer may ask, "Have you ever used illegal drugs?" "When is the last time you used illegal drugs?" or "Have you used illegal drugs in the last six months?" These questions are not likely to tell the employer anything about whether the applicant was addicted to drugs.

However, questions that ask how much the applicant used drugs in the past are likely to elicit information about whether the applicant was a past drug addict. These questions are therefore impermissible at the pre-offer stage.

Example: At the pre-offer stage, an employer may not ask an applicant questions such as, "How often did you use illegal drugs in the past?" "Have you ever been addicted to drugs?" "Have you ever been treated for drug addiction?" or "Have you ever been treated for drug abuse?"

May an employer ask applicants about their drinking habits?

Yes, unless the particular question is likely to elicit information about alcoholism, which is a disability. An employer may ask an applicant whether s/he drinks alcohol, or whether s/he has been arrested for driving under the influence because these questions do not reveal whether someone has alcoholism. However, questions asking how much alcohol an applicant drinks or whether s/he has participated in an alcohol rehabilitation program are likely to elicit information about whether the applicant has alcoholism.

May an employer ask applicants to "self-identify" as individuals with disabilities for purposes of the employer's affirmative action program?

Yes. An employer may invite applicants to voluntarily self-identify for purposes of the employer's affirmative action program if:

- the employer is undertaking affirmative action because of a federal, state, or local law (including a veterans' preference law) that requires affirmative action for individuals with disabilities (that is, the law requires some action to be taken on behalf of such individuals); or

- the employer is voluntarily using the information to benefit individuals with disabilities.

Employers should remember that state or local laws sometimes permit or encourage affirmative action. In those cases, an employer may invite voluntary self-identification only if the employer uses the information to benefit individuals with disabilities.

Are there any special steps an employer should take if it asks applicants to "self-identify" for purposes of the employer's affirmative action program?

Yes. If an employer invites applicants to voluntarily self-identify in connection with providing affirmative action, the employer must do the following:

- state clearly on any written questionnaire, or state clearly orally (if no written questionnaire is used), that the information requested is used solely in connection with its affirmative action obligations or efforts; and

- state clearly that the information is being requested on a voluntary basis, that it will be kept confidential in accordance with the ADA, that refusal to provide it will not subject the applicant to any adverse treatment, and that it will be used only in accordance with the ADA.

In order to ensure that the self-identification information is kept confidential, the information must be on a form that is kept separate from the application.

May an employer ask third parties questions it could not ask the applicant directly?

No. An employer may not ask a third party (such as a service that provides information about workers' compensation claims, a state agency, or an applicant's friends, family, or former employers) any questions that it could not directly ask the applicant.

What Is a Medical Examination?

Definition: A "medical examination" is a procedure or test that seeks information about an individual's physical or mental impairments or health.

At the pre-offer stage, an employer cannot require examinations that seek information about physical or mental impairments or health. It is not always easy to determine whether something is a medical examination. The following factors are helpful in determining whether a procedure or test is medical:

- Is it administered by a health care professional or someone trained by a health care professional?

- Are the results interpreted by a health care professional or someone trained by a health care professional?

- Is it designed to reveal an impairment or physical or mental health?

- Is the employer trying to determine the applicant's physical or mental health or impairments?

- Is it invasive (for example, does it require the drawing of blood, urine or breath)?

- Does it measure an applicant's performance of a task, or does it measure the applicant's physiological responses to performing the task?

- Is it normally given in a medical setting (for example, a health care professional's office)?

- Is medical equipment used?

In many cases, a combination of factors will be relevant in figuring out whether a procedure or test is a medical examination. In some cases, one factor may be enough to determine that a procedure or test is medical.

> Example: An employer requires applicants to lift a 30 pound box and carry it 20 feet. This is not a medical examination; it is just a test of whether the applicant can perform the task. But, if the employer takes the applicant's blood pressure or heart rate after the lifting and carrying, the test would be a medical examination because it is measuring the applicant's physiological response to lifting and carrying, as opposed to the applicant's ability to lift and carry.

> Example: A psychological test is designed to reveal mental illness, but a particular employer says it does not give the test to disclose mental illness (for example, the employer says it uses the test to disclose just tastes and habits). But, the test also is interpreted by a psychologist, and is routinely used in a clinical setting to provide evidence that would lead to a diagnosis of a mental disorder or impairment (for example, whether an applicant has paranoid tendencies, or is depressed). Under these facts, this test is a medical examination.

Below are some commonly asked questions about the ADA's restrictions on pre-offer medical examinations.

May an employer require applicants to take physical agility tests?

Yes. A physical agility test, in which an applicant demonstrates the ability to perform actual or simulated job tasks, is not a medical examination under the ADA.[16]

Example: A police department tests police officer applicants' ability to run through an obstacle course designed to simulate a suspect chase in an urban setting. This is not a medical examination.

May an employer require applicants to take physical fitness tests?

Yes. A physical fitness test, in which an applicant's performance of physical tasks — such as running or lifting — is measured, is not a medical examination.[17]

However, if an employer measures an applicant's physiological or biological responses to performance, the test would be medical.

Example: A messenger service tests applicant's ability to run one mile in 15 minutes. At the end of the run, the employer takes the applicant's blood pressure and heart rate. Measuring the applicant's physiological response makes this a medical examination.

May an employer ask an applicant to provide medical certification that s/he can safely perform a physical agility or physical fitness test?

Yes. Although an employer cannot ask disability-related questions, it may give the applicant a description of the agility or fitness test and ask the applicant to have a private physician simply state whether s/he can safely perform the test.

May an employer ask an applicant to assume liability for injuries incurred in performing a physical agility or physical fitness test?

Yes. An employer may ask an applicant to assume responsibility and release the employer of liability for injuries incurred in performing a physical agility or fitness test.

May an employer give psychological examinations to applicants?

Yes, unless the particular examination is medical. This determination would be based on some of the factors listed above such as the purpose of the test and the intent of the employer in giving the test. Psychological examinations are medical if they provide evidence that would lead to identifying a mental disorder or impairment (for example, those listed in the American Psychiatric Association's most recent Diagnostic and Statistical Manual of Mental Disorders (DSM)).

Example: An employer gives applicants the RUOK Test (hypothetical), an examination which reflects whether applicants have characteristics that lead to identifying whether the individual has excessive anxiety, depression and certain compulsive disorders (DSM-listed conditions). This test is medical.

On the other hand, if a test is designed and used to measure only things such as honesty, tastes, and habits, it is not medical.

Example: An employer gives the IFIB Personality Test (hypothetical), an examination designed and used to reflect only whether an applicant is likely to lie. This test, as used by the employer, is not a medical examination.

May an employer give polygraph examinations to applicants?

Although most employers are prohibited by federal and state laws from giving polygraph examinations, some employers are not prohibited from giving these examinations. Under the ADA, polygraph examinations are not medical examinations.[18] Many times, however, polygraph examinations contain disability-related questions such as questions about what lawful medications the applicant is taking. Employers cannot ask disability-related questions as part of a pre-offer examination, even if the examination is not itself "medical."

May an employer give vision tests to applicants?

Yes, unless the particular test is medical. Evaluating someone's ability to read labels or distinguish objects as part of a demonstration of the person's ability to do the job is not a medical examination. However, an ophthalmologist's or optometrist's analysis of someone's vision is medical. Similarly, requiring an individual to read an eye chart would be a medical examination.

May an employer give applicants tests to determine illegal use of controlled substances?

Yes. The ADA specifically states that, for purposes of the ADA, tests to determine the current illegal use of controlled substances are not considered medical examinations.

May an employer give alcohol tests to applicants?

No. Tests to determine whether and/or how much alcohol an individual has consumed are medical, and there is no statutory exemption.

The Post-offer Stage

After giving a job offer to an applicant, an employer may ask disability-related questions and perform medical examinations. The job offer may be conditioned on the results of post-offer disability-related questions or medical examinations.

At the "post-offer" stage, an employer may ask about an individual's workers' compensation history, prior sick leave usage, illnesses/diseases/impairments, and general physical and mental health. Disability-related questions and medical examinations at the post-offer stage do not have to be related to the job.[19]

If an employer asks post-offer disability-related questions, or requires post-offer medical examinations, it must make sure that it follows certain procedures:

- all entering employees in the same job category must be subjected to the examination/inquiry, regardless of disability;[20] and

- medical information obtained must be kept confidential.[21]

Below are some commonly asked questions about the post-offer stage.

What is considered a real job offer?

Since an employer can ask disability-related questions and require medical examinations after a job offer, it is important that the job offer be real. A job offer is real if the employer has evaluated all relevant nonmedical information which it reasonably could have obtained and analyzed prior to giving the offer. Of course, there are times when an employer cannot reasonably obtain and evaluate all nonmedical information at the pre-offer stage. If an employer can show that is the case, the offer would still be considered a real offer.

Example: It may be too costly for a law enforcement employer wishing to administer a polygraph examination to administer a pre-offer examination asking nondisability-related questions, and a post-offer examination asking disability-related questions. In this case, the employer may be able to demonstrate that it could not reasonably obtain and evaluate the non-medical polygraph information at the pre-offer stage.

Example: An applicant might state that his current employer should not be asked for a reference check until the potential employer makes a conditional job offer. In this case, the potential employer could not reasonably obtain and evaluate the nonmedical information from the reference at the pre-offer stage.

Do offers have to be limited to current vacancies?

No. An employer may give offers to fill current vacancies or reasonably anticipated openings.

May an employer give offers that exceed the number of vacancies or reasonably anticipated openings?

Yes. The offers will still be considered real if the employer can demonstrate that it needs to give more offers in order to actually fill vacancies or reasonably anticipated openings. For example, an employer may demonstrate that a certain percentage of the offerees will likely be disqualified or will withdraw from the pool.

Example: A police department may be able to demonstrate that it needs to make offers to 50 applicants for 25 available positions because about half of the offers will likely be revoked based on post-offer medical tests and/or security checks, and because some applicants may voluntarily withdraw from consideration.

Of course, an employer must comply with the ADA when taking people out of the pool to fill actual vacancies. The employer must notify an individual (orally or in writing) if his/her placement into an actual vacancy is in any way adversely affected by the results of a post-offer medical examination or disability-related question.

If an individual alleges that disability has affected his/her placement into an actual vacancy, the EEOC will carefully scrutinize whether disability was a reason for any adverse action. If disability was a reason, the EEOC will determine whether the action was job-related and consistent with business necessity.

After an employer has obtained basic medical information from all individuals who have been given conditional offers in a job category, may it ask specific individuals for more medical information?

Yes, if the follow-up examinations or questions are medically related to the previously obtained medical information.[22]

Example: At the post-offer stage, an employer asks new hires whether they have had back injuries, and learns that some of the individuals have had such injuries. The employer may give medical examinations designed to diagnose back impairments to persons who stated that they had prior back injuries, as long as these examinations are medically related to those injuries.

At the post-offer stage, may an employer ask all individuals whether they need reasonable accommodation to perform the job?

Yes.

If, at the post-offer stage, someone requests reasonable accommodation to perform the job, may the employer ask him/her for documentation of his/her disability?

Yes. If someone requests reasonable accommodation so s/he will be able to perform a job and the need for the accommodation is not obvious, the employer may require reasonable documentation of the individual's entitlement to reasonable accommodation. So, the employer may require documentation showing that the individual has a covered disability, and stating his/her functional limitations.

Example: An entering employee states that she will need a 15-minute break every two hours to eat a snack in order to maintain her blood sugar level. The employer may ask her to provide documentation from her doctor showing that: (1) she has an impairment that substantially limits a major life activity; and (2) she actually needs the requested breaks because of the impairment.

Confidentiality

An employer must keep any medical information on applicants or employees confidential, with the following limited exceptions:

- supervisors and managers may be told about necessary restrictions on the work or duties of the employee and about necessary accommodations;
- first aid and safety personnel may be told if the disability might require emergency treatment;
- government officials investigating compliance with the ADA must be given relevant information on request;[23]

- employers may give information to state workers' compensation offices, state second injury funds or workers' compensation insurance carriers in accordance with state workers' compensation laws;[24] and

- employers may use the information for insurance purposes.[25]

Below are some commonly asked questions about the ADA's confidentiality requirements.

May medical information be given to decisionmakers involved in the hiring process?

Yes. Medical information may be given to — and used by — appropriate decision-makers involved in the hiring process so they can make employment decisions consistent with the ADA. In addition, the employer may use the information to determine reasonable accommodations for the individual. For example, the employer may share the information with a third party such as a health care professional to determine whether a reasonable accommodation is possible for a particular individual. The information certainly must be kept confidential.

Of course, the employer may only share the medical information with individuals involved in the hiring process (or in implementing an affirmative action program) who need to know the information. For example, in some cases, a number of people may be involved in evaluating an applicant. Some individuals may simply be responsible for evaluating an applicant's references; these individuals may have no need to know an applicant's medical condition and therefore should not have access to the medical information.

Can an individual voluntarily disclose his/her own medical information to persons beyond those to whom an employer can disclose such information?

Yes, as long as it's really voluntary. The employer cannot request, persuade, coerce, or otherwise pressure the individual to get him/her to disclose medical information.

Does the employer's confidentiality obligation extend to medical information that an individual voluntarily tells the employer?

Yes. For example, if an applicant voluntarily discloses bipolar disorder and the need for reasonable accommodation, the employer may not disclose the condition or the applicant's need for accommodation to the applicant's references.

Can medical information be kept in an employee's regular personnel file?

No. Medical information must be collected and maintained on separate forms and in separate medical files.[26] An employer should not place any medical-related material in an employee's nonmedical personnel files. If an employer wants to put a document in a personnel file, and that document happens to contain some medical information, the employer must simply remove the medical information from the document before putting it in the personnel file.

Does the confidentiality obligation end when the person is no longer an applicant or employee?

No, an employer must keep medical information confidential even if someone is no longer an applicant (for example, s/he was not hired) or is no longer an employee.

Is an employer required to remove from its personnel files medical information obtained before the ADA's effective date?

No.

Footnotes to ADA Enforcement Guidance: Pre-employment Disability-Related Questions and Medical Examinations

[1]Codified as amended at 42 U.S.C. §12101-§12117, §12201-12213 (Supp. V 1994).

[2]The analysis in this guidance also applies to federal sector complaints of nonaffirmative action employment discrimination arising under Section 501 of the Rehabilitation Act of 1973. 29 U.S.C.A. §791(g) (West Supp. 1994). In addition, the analysis applies to complaints of nonaffirmative action employment discrimination arising under Section 503 and employment discrimination under Section 504 of the Rehabilitation Act. 29 U.S.C.A. §793(d), §794(d) (West Supp. 1994).

[3]42 U.S.C. §12112(d)(2); 29 C.F.R. §1630.13(a), §1630.14(a)(b).

[4]42 U.S.C. §12112(b); 29 C.F.R. §1630.10, §1630.14(b)(3).

[5]42 U.S.C. §12113(b); See 29 C.F.R. Part 1630 App. §1630.2(r).

[6]29 C.F.R. §1630.14(b)(1)(i-iii).

[7]See 42 U.S.C. §12201(b); 29 C.F.R. Part 1630 App. §1630.14(b).

[8]See 42 U.S.C. §12201(c); 29 C.F.R. Part 1630 App. §1630.14(b). For example, an employer may submit medical information to the company's health insurance carrier if the information is needed to administer a health insurance plan in accordance with §501(c) of the ADA.

[9]Of course, an employer can always ask about an applicant's ability to perform the job.

[10]Sometimes, applicants disclose disability-related information in responding to an otherwise lawful pre-offer question. Although the employer has not asked an unlawful question, it still cannot refuse to hire an applicant based on disability unless the reason is "job-related and consistent with business necessity."

[11]However, an employer cannot ask a question in a manner that requires the individual to disclose the need for reasonable accommodation. For example, as described later in this guidance, an employer may not ask, "Can you do these functions with ____ without ____ reasonable accommodation? (Check one.)."

[12]It should be noted that an employer might lawfully ask questions about the need for reasonable accommodation on the job and then fail to hire the applicant. The rejected applicant may then claim that the refusal to hire was based on the need for accommodation. Under these facts, the EEOC will consider the employer's pre-offer questions as evidence that the employer knew about the need for reasonable accommodation, and will carefully scrutinize whether the need to provide accommodation was a reason for rejecting the applicant.

[13]However, investigators should be aware that Title VII of the Civil Rights Act of 1964, as amended, applies to such questions and that nothing in this Enforcement Guidance relieves an employer of its obligations to comply with Title VII. The commission has previously provided guidance for investigators to follow concerning an employer's use of arrest/conviction records. See Policy Guidance No. N-915-061 (9/7/90) ("Policy Guidance on the Consideration of Arrest Records in Employment Decisions Under Title VII of the Civil Rights Act of 1964," as amended, 42 U.S.C. §2000e et seq. (1982)); EEOC Compliance Manual, Vol. II, Appendices 604-A ("Conviction Records") and 604-B ("Conviction Records — Statistics").

[14]"Drug" means a controlled substance, as defined in schedules I through IV of Section 202 of the Controlled Substances Act (21 U.S.C. §812). 29 C.F.R. §1630.3(a)(1).

[15]42 U.S.C. §12114(a); 29 C.F.R. §1630.3(a).

[16]Of course, an employer cannot use a test in violation of other federal civil rights statutes. For example, if a test has an adverse impact under Title VII of the Civil Rights Act of 1964, as amended, 42 U.S.C. §2000e et seq., it must be shown to be job-related and consistent with business necessity.

[17]Although physical agility tests and physical fitness tests are not "medical" examinations, these tests are still subject to other parts of the ADA. For example, if a physical fitness test which requires applicants to run one mile in 10 minutes screens out an applicant on the basis of disability, the employer must be prepared to demonstrate that the test is "job-related and consistent with business necessity."

[18]A polygraph examination purportedly measures whether a person believes s/he is telling the truth in response to a particular injury. The examination does not measure health or impairments. Rather, it just measures relative changes in physiological responses of the test taker.

[19]But, if an individual is screened out because of disability, the employer must show that the exclusionary criterion is job-related and consistent with business necessity. 42 U.S.C. §12112(b); 29 C.F.R. §1630.10, §1630.14(b)(3).

[20]42 U.S.C. §12112(d)(3); 29 C.F.R. §1630.14(b)(1),(2).

[21]Id.

[22]Once again, if an examination or inquiry screens out someone because of disability, the exclusionary criteria must be "job-related and consistent with business necessity." Where safety considerations are the reason, the individual can only be screened out because s/he poses a "direct threat."

[23]29 C.F.R. §1630.14(b)(1)(i-iii).

[24]See 42 U.S.C. §12201(b); 29 C.F.R. Part 1630, App. §1630.14(b).

[25]See 42 U.S.C. §12201(c); 29 C.F.R. Part 1630.14(b). For example, an employer must submit medical information to the company's health insurance carrier if the information is needed to administer a health insurance plan in accordance with §501(c) of the ADA.

[26]A notation that an individual has taken sick leave or had a doctor's appointment is not confidential medical information. Of course, documentation of the individual's diagnosis or symptoms would be medical information.

EEOC Job Application and Pre-employment Questions

According to the EEOC, the following are examples of questions that may not be asked on a job application or during an interview.

- Have you ever had or been treated for any of the following conditions or diseases?

- Have you been treated in the past three years for any conditions or diseases and, if so, what were they?

- Have you ever been hospitalized? If so, for what condition?

- Have you ever been treated by a psychiatrist or psychologist? If so, for what condition?

- Have you ever been treated for any mental condition?

- Is there any health-related reason you may not be able to perform the job for which you are applying?

- Have you had a major illness in the last five years?

- How many days were you absent from work because of illness last year?

- Do you have any physical defects that preclude you from performing certain kinds of work? If yes, describe such defects and specific work limitations.

- Do you have any disabilities or impairments that may affect your performance in the position for which you are applying?

- Are you taking prescribed drugs?

- Have you ever been treated for drug addiction or alcoholism?

- Have you ever filed for workers' compensation insurance?

APPENDIX II:
Federal Fair Credit Reporting Act Forms

Appendix II features sample forms created by the Worklaw Network based on the federal Fair Credit Reporting Act to assist employers in obtaining background credit checks of prospective employees and authorizing the release of applicants' consumer reports. Appendix II also includes sample pre-adverse and adverse letters and a summary of federal consumer rights under the Fair Credit Reporting Act.

The final form in Appendix II is a summary of rights under the California Investigative Consumer Reporting Agencies Act, supplied by the law firm of Orrick Herrington & Sutcliffe.

Sample Certification for User of Consumer Report

Company Name _____

Address _____

City _____

State _____ Zip Code _____

In compliance with the Fair Credit Reporting Act (FCRA), as amended,

_____ (name of user, i.e.,

employer) hereby certifies to _____

(name of consumer reporting agency) that it has complied or will comply with the following provisions:

We have:

1. Made a written, clear and conspicuous disclosure to the applicant or current employee, in a document consisting solely of that document, that a consumer report may be obtained for employment purposes; and

2. Obtained written authorization from the applicant or current employee before ordering any consumer reports regarding that individual.

We will:

3. Advise the applicant, or current employee, if applicable, that before any adverse action is taken with regard to that individual, which is based in whole or in part on a consumer report, that we will provide to the individual a copy of the consumer report and a description in writing of the rights the individual has with regard to the report as prescribed by the Federal Trade Commission. (Summary of Your Rights); and

4. Not use the information provided in the consumer report to violate any applicable federal or state equal employment opportunity law or regulation.

The undersigned agrees to abide by all of the above referenced provisions as provided by the FCRA, as amended.

Name (printed) _____

Signature _____ Date _____

Sample Notification and Authorization
for Release of Consumer Report

In connection with my application for employment, and/or employment with this company, I understand and am hereby notified by this document that [insert name of company] is authorized to request a consumer report from a consumer reporting agency for evaluation of me for employment (i.e., employment, promotion, reassignment, or retention as an employee). I understand that these consumer reports may contain information from public records, including written, oral, or other communications bearing on my credit worthiness, credit standing, credit capacity, character, general reputation, personal characteristics, or mode of living, which may or may not be used as a factor for employment purposes. I further understand that inquiries may include, but are not limited to, criminal convictions, motor vehicle records, education and previous employment verification.

In addition, I understand that you may request information from various federal, state, and other agencies which maintain records concerning my past activities and history.

I authorize without reservation any party or agency contacted by this employer to furnish the above-mentioned information.

I further authorize ongoing procurement of the above-mentioned reports at any time, either during the time my application for employment is being considered or throughout the duration of my employment in the event I am hired.

Name (printed): _____

Signature: _____ Date: _____

Sample Pre-adverse Action Letter

Dear Applicant [or Current Employee]:

As you know, during your application process with the Company [or review process for promotion, etc.], you signed an authorization for release of your consumer report to the Company. Based on your authorization, the Company requested and received your consumer report. The Company is currently reviewing your consumer report to determine whether you qualify for employment with the Company [promotion within the Company] based on its employment [promotion] criteria.

The Company may decide not to hire [promote] you based in whole or in part on your consumer report. Because the Company may make a decision about hiring [promoting] you based in whole or in part on your consumer report, the Company is providing you with this pre-adverse action notice as required by the Fair Credit Reporting Act, as amended (FCRA). Enclosed with this letter are two documents for your review and information: (1) A copy of your consumer report that was requested and reviewed by the Company; and (2) A Summary of Your Rights Under the FCRA.

The consumer report that the Company requested and received about you was not prepared by the Company. If you have any questions or concerns regarding your consumer report, please contact the company that provided your consumer report at the telephone numbers listed in the Summary of Your Rights Under the FCRA. If you have any employment [promotion] related questions or concerns, please do not hesitate to contact us.

We sincerely thank you for your interest in working [the promotion] for the Company. The Company will contact you as soon as a decision is made regarding your interest in employment with [promotion within] the Company.

Sincerely,

_____

[Employer's Representative]

A Summary of Your Rights Under the
Fair Credit Reporting Act (FCRA)

The federal Fair Credit Reporting Act (FCRA) is designed to promote accuracy, fairness and privacy of information used in the process of granting credit by consumer reporting agencies (CRAs). This information is supplied by public record sources, credit grantors and others to the CRAs. The CRAs organize and store the information for distribution to credit grantors, employers and insurers who are making credit, employment and insurance decisions about you. The FCRA gives suppliers and users of credit information, and CRAs, specific responsibilities in connection with their respective roles in the credit granting and reporting process. The FCRA also gives you specific rights in dealing with these entities, as outlined below. You can find the complete text of the FCRA, 15 U.S.C. 1681 et seq., as amended, at the Federal Trade Commission's web site (http://www.ftc.gov/credit) or write to: Consumer Response Center, Room 130-A, Federal Trade Commission, 600 Pennsylvania Ave., NW, Washington, DC 20580. You may have additional rights under state law. You may contact a state or local consumer protection agency or a state attorney general to learn those rights.

1. **You must be told if information in your file was a factor considered by a third party who took unfavorable actions toward you.** Anyone who uses information from a CRA to take action against you — such as denying an application for credit, insurance, or employment — must tell you, and give you the name, address and phone number of the CRA that provided the consumer report. Keep in mind that the third party, not the CRA, took the unfavorable action toward you and that the CRA will not be able to provide you with the reason for the unfavorable action.

2. **You can find out what is in your file.** Upon your request, a CRA must give you the information in your file, and a list of everyone who has recently requested it. There is no charge for the report if a person has taken action against you because of information supplied by the CRA, if you request the report within sixty (60) days of receiving notification that the information in your file was used by a third party unfavorably. You are also entitled to one free report if: (1) you are the victim of identity theft and place a fraud alert in your file; (2) your file contains inaccurate information as a result of fraud; (3) you are unemployed and plan to seek employment within 60 days; or (4) you are on public assistance. In addition, all consumers are entitled to one free disclosure every 12 months upon request from each nationwide credit bureau and from nationwide specialty consumer reporting agencies. See www.ftc.gov/credit for additional information.

3. **You can dispute inaccurate information with the CRA.** If you tell a CRA that your file contains inaccurate information, the CRA must reinvestigate the items (usually within thirty (30) days) by presenting to its information source all relevant evidence you submit, unless your dispute is frivolous. The source must review your evidence and report its findings to the CRA. (The source also must advise national CRAs, to which it has provided the data, of any error.) The CRA must give you a written report of the investigation, and a copy of your report, if the investigation results in any change. If the CRA's investigation does not resolve the dispute, you may add a brief statement to your file. The CRA must normally include a summary of your statement in future reports. If an item is deleted or a dispute statement is filed, you may

ask that anyone who has recently received your report be notified of the change.

4. **Inaccurate information must be corrected or deleted.** A CRA must remove or correct inaccurate or unverified information from its files, usually within thirty (30) days after you dispute it. However, the CRA is not required to remove accurate data from your file unless it is outdated (as described below), or cannot be verified. If your dispute results in any change to your report, the CRA cannot reinsert into your file a disputed item unless the information source verifies its accuracy and completeness. In addition, the CRA must give you a written notice telling you that it has reinserted the item. The notice must include the name, address and phone number of the information source. The CRA may continue to report information it has verified as accurate.

5. **You can dispute inaccurate information with source of the information.** If you tell anyone — such as a creditor who reports to the CRA — that you dispute an item, they may not then report the information to a CRA without including a notice of your dispute. In addition, once you have notified the source of the error in writing, they may not continue to report it if it is in fact an error.

6. **Outdated information may not be reported.** In most cases, a CRA may not report negative information that is more than seven (7) years old; ten (10) years for bankruptcies.

7. **Access to your file is limited.** A CRA may provide information about you only to people with a need recognized by the FCRA, usually to consider an application you have submitted with a creditor, insurer, employer, landlord or other business, or to consider you for an unsolicited offer of credit.

8. **Your consent is required for reports that are provided to employers, or reports that contain medical information.** A CRA may not give out information about you to your employer, or prospective employer, without your written consent. A CRA may not report medical information about you to creditors, insurers or employers without your permission.

9. **You may choose to exclude your name from CRA lists for unsolicited credit and insurance offers.** Creditors and insurers may use file information as the basis for sending you unsolicited offers of credit or insurance. Such offers must include a toll-free phone number for you to call if you want your name and address removed from future lists. If you call, you must be kept off the lists for two years. If you request and complete the CRA form provided for this purpose, you can have your name and address removed indefinitely.

10. **You may seek damages from violators.** If a CRA, a user or (in some cases) a provider of CRA data, violates the FCRA, you may sue them in state or federal court.

11. **Identity theft victims and active duty military personnel have additional rights.** For more information, see www.ftc.gov/credit.

The FCRA gives several different federal agencies authority to enforce the FCRA. For questions or concerns regarding CRAs, creditors and others not listed, please contact any of the below listed entities.

For Questions or Concerns Regarding:	Please Contact:
CRAs, creditors and others not listed below	Federal Trade Commission Bureau of Consumer Protection Washington, DC 20560 202-326-3224
National banks, federal branch agencies of foreign banks (word "National" or initials "N.A." appear in or after bank's name	Office of the Comptroller of the Currency Compliance Management — Mail Stop 6-6 Washington, DC 20219 800-613-6743
Federal Reserve System member banks (except national banks and federal branches/agencies of foreign banks)	Federal Reserve Board Division of Consumer & Community Affairs Washington, DC 20551 202-452-3693
Savings associations and federally chartered savings banks (word "Federal" or initials "F.S.I.B." appear in federal institution's name)	Office of Thrift Supervision Consumer Programs Washington, DC 20552 800-842-8929
Federal credit union (words "Federal Credit Union" appear in institution's name)	National Credit Union Administration 1775 Duke St. Alexandria, VA 22314 703-518-6360
Banks that are state chartered, or are not Federal Reserve System members	Federal Deposit Insurance Corporation Div. of Compliance & Community Affairs Washington, DC 20429 800-934-FDIC
Air, surface or rail common carriers regulated by former Civil Aeronautics Board and Interstate Commerce Commission	Department of Transportation Office of Financial Management Washington, DC 20590 202-366-1306
Activities subject to the Packers and Stockyards Act, 1921	Department of Agriculture Office of Deputy Administrator — GIPSA Washington, DC 20250 202-720-7051

Sample Adverse Action Letter

Date: _____

Dear Applicant:

We regret to inform you that based on our hiring criteria [or promotion criteria, etc.], we are unable to consider you further for an employment opportunity with our organization. This decision was made at least in part from the information we obtained from _____ [name of company conducting background check]. _____ [name of company conducting background check] did not make this decision to _____ [type of action taken] and is unable to provide you with the specific reasons why the action was taken.

You have the right to dispute the accuracy or completeness of information contained in your consumer report by contacting the consumer reporting agency or if the report is a credit report, contacting the credit bureau that furnished the report.

You also have the right to obtain an additional free copy of the credit report from the credit bureau upon request within sixty [60] days of receiving this letter.

For credit report, contact the bureau that supplied the report: [You must include the name, address and telephone number of the consumer reporting agency, including an 800 number if applicable, that furnished the report to the person].

Contact for any report except a consumer credit report: [You must include the name, address and telephone number of agency that supplied consumer credit report].

Any dispute regarding the information in your report must be resolved with the agency above.

Again, we appreciate your interest in employment with our organization [or similar language depending on the circumstances].

Sincerely,

_____

(Employer's Representative)

Sample Notification and Authorization
for Release of Investigative Consumer Report

In connection with my application for employment, and/or employment with this company, I understand and am hereby notified by this document that [insert name of company] is authorized to request an investigative consumer report from a consumer reporting agency for evaluation of me for employment (i.e., employment, promotion, reassignment or retention as an employee). I understand that an investigative consumer report may contain information from public records, including written, oral, or other communications bearing on my credit worthiness, credit standing, credit capacity, character, general reputation, personal characteristics or mode of living, which may be obtained through personal interviews with neighbors, friends or associates of me and may or may not be used as a factor for employment purposes. I understand that I have a right to make a written request to the Company for additional information concerning the nature and scope of the investigation requested and a written summary of my rights under the Fair Credit Reporting Act, as amended.

In addition, I understand that you may request information from various federal, state, and other agencies which maintain records concerning my past activities and history.

I authorize without reservation any party or agency contacted by this employer to furnish the above-mentioned information.

I further authorize ongoing procurement of the above-mentioned reports at any time, either during the time my application for employment is being considered or throughout the duration of my employment in the event I am hired.

Name (printed): _____

Signature: _____ Date: _____

A Summary of Your Rights Under the California Investigative Consumer Reporting Agencies Act

For California Applicants Only

You also have the following rights under the California Investigative Consumer Reporting Agencies Act in connection with inspecting an investigative consumer report maintained on you by the CRA:

• At your request and upon presenting proper identification, the CRA must allow you, during normal business hours and upon reasonable notice, to visually inspect all files maintained regarding you (except that sources of information, other than public records and records from data bases available for sale, acquired solely for use in preparing an investigative consumer report and actually used for no other purpose, need not be disclosed except under discovery procedures in any civil action brought under the Investigative Consumer Reporting Agencies Act, Civil Code section 1786 *et seq.*).

• The CRA must disclose to you the recipients of any Investigative Consumer Report furnished for employment or any other purposes within the three-year period preceding the request.

• Files maintained on you shall be available for your inspection as follows:

1. You may inspect your file(s) in person if you appear and furnish proper identification. Proper identification includes documents such as a valid driver's license, social security account number, military identification card, and credit cards. A copy of your files shall also be available to you for a fee not to exceed the actual costs of duplication services provided.

2. You may obtain a copy of your file by certified mail if you make a written request with proper identification for copies to be sent to a specified addressee. A CRA complying with a request for a certified mailing is not liable for disclosure to third parties caused by mishandling of mail after the mailing leaves the CRA.

3. A summary of all information contained in your files that you have a right to receive shall be provided by telephone, if you have made a written request, with proper identification for telephone disclosure, and the toll charge, if any, for the telephone call is prepaid by or charged directly to you.

4. The CRA must provide trained personnel to explain to you any information that you have a right to receive.

5. The CRA must provide a written explanation of any coded information contained in files maintained on you. This written explanation must be distributed whenever a file is provided to you for visual inspection as discussed above.

6. You have a right to be accompanied by one other person of your choosing, who shall furnish reasonable identification when inspecting your file. A CRA may require you to furnish a written statement granting permission to the CRA to discuss your file in another person's presence.

Court Case Index

— B —

Ballaron v. Equitable Shipyards, Inc., 38

Barrows v. City of Glencoe, 108

Bedker v. Domino's Pizza, Inc., 93

Bohack v. City of Reno, 119

Boler v. (California) Superior Court, 59

Boost Co. v. Faurce, 102

Bushby v. Truswal Systems Corp., 62

— C —

Cameco, Inc. v. Gedicke, 102

Carroll v. Talman Federal Savings and Loan Assoc., 92

Carswell v. Peachford Hospital, 92

City of Sherman v. Henry, 79

Cotran v. Rollins Hudig Hall Intern'l, Inc., 57

Crosier v. United Parcel Service (UPS), 78

— D —

De Cintio v. Westchester City Med. Ctr., 99

Doe v. Attorney General of the United States, 154 Fig. 18–1

Doe v. City of New York, 154 Fig. 18–1

Doe v. Plymouth, 159 Fig. 18-3

— E —

EEOC v. Rath Packing Co., 95

E.I. du Pont & Co. (NLRB), 115

— F —

Farmer v. City of Fort Lauderdale, 38

Fish v. Adams, 102

Fitzpatrick v. Duquesne Light Co., 95

Ford Motor Co. v. Robert Lane d/b/a Warner Publications, 117

— G —

Gore v. Healthex, Inc., 30

Griswold v. Fresenius USA, Inc., 111

Groves Truck & Trailer (NLRB), 113

— H —

Haddock v. City of New York, 47

Harris Corp. (NLRB), 113

(Hawaii) State v. Lo, 64

Hopkins v. Price Waterhouse, 92

— I —

In Re: Amendments to Rule of Judicial Administration, 116

IRIS-USA (NLRB), 116

— J —

Johnson v. Board of Commnrs. of the Port of New Orleans, 78

Johnson v. Pike Corporation, 19

— K —

K-Mart Corp. Store No. 7441 v. Trotti, 109

— M —

Martinez v. City of Grants, 102

Media General Operations, Inc. d/b/a Richmond Times-Dispatch v. NLRB, 113

McGuinness v. Federal Express, 93

McLaren v. Microsoft Corp., 109

Michigan Dept. of Civil Rights v. Sparrow Hospital, 92

— N —

New Orleans, Johnson v. Board of Commnrs. of the Port of, 78

(New York) State v. Wal-Mart Stores, 79

NLRB v. Weingarten, 65

Norman-Bloodsaw v. Berkeley Laboratory, 154 Fig. 18–1

— O —

O'Connor v. Ortega, 2, 108

— P —

Pasch v. Katz Media Corp., 79

People v. Freedman, 64

Planchet v. New Hamphsire Hospital, 93

Postal Service (NLRB), 113

Pratt & Whitney (NLRB), 113, 115, 116

— R —

Randi v. Muroc Joint Unified School District, 31

Restuccia v. Burk Tech., 110

Rudas v. Nationwide Mutual Ins. Co., 111

Russel v. United Parcel Service (UPS), 77

— S —

Sanders v. American Broadcasting Co., 64

Shapiro v. Health Ins. Plan of Greater New York, 49

Sherman (City of) v. Henry, 79

Sioux City Police Officers Assoc. v. City of Sioux City, 96

Smith v. Wal-Mart Stores, 78

Smyth v. Pillsbury Company, 109

State v. Lo, 64

State v. Wal-Mart Stores, 79

Steve Jackson Games, Inc. v. United States Secret Service, 118

— T —

Texas State Employees Union v. Texas Department of Mental Health, 79

Thompson v. Sanborn's Motor Express, Inc., 97

Timekeeping Systems, Inc. (NLRB), 113

— U —

United States v. Angevine, 108

United States v. Long, 109

United States v. Simons, 121

Untied States v. Zigler, 108

— V —

Vegas-Rodriguez v. Puerto Rico Tel. Co., 64

— W —

Watkins v. L.M. Berry Co., 62

Weingarten rights regarding searches of personal employee space, 65

— Y —

Young v. McKelvey, 79

— Z —

Zubulake v. USS Warburg, 112

Index

— A —

Access by employees to personnel files, 142–144

ADA. *See* Americans With Disabilities Act of 1990

Age Discrimination in Employment Act of 1967 (ADEA), 5, 17, 41

Age, pre-employment inquiries regarding, 17, 18

AIDS/HIV testing, 33

Alabama

    background check requirements, 26

    dating policies, 89

    employment references, 30, 31

    employment-at-will state, 56

    lie detectors/polygraph tests, 38

    loyalty duty/public statements, 101

    marital status discrimination, 98

    nepotism/favoritism, 99

    personnel files, employee access to, 143

    private sector employee privacy rights, 47

    privileged statements, 50

    telephone calls, monitoring, 62

Alaska

    dating policies, 89

    employment-at-will state, 56

    marital status discrimination, 98

    negligent retention, 47

personnel files, employee access to, 143, 144

private sector employee privacy rights, 47

privileged statements, 50

video monitoring, 64

Alcohol use and abuse, 33–35, 162

Americans With Disabilities Act of 1990 (ADA), 6

EEOC enforcement guidance, Appendix I

genetic testing, 36

honesty and personality tests, 41

medical records, 146, 153–154

personnel files, 138, 139, 141, 146

pre-employment inquiries, 17, 19

screening, 32–33

substance abuse, 34

Appearance and grooming, 91–94

Application forms, 15–16

Arizona

dating policies, 89

employment-at-will state, 56

marital status discrimination, 98

personnel files

employee access to, 143

security breaches, notification of, 146

Arkansas

compelled self-publication, 49

criminal records, background checks as to, 24

dating policies, 89

employment references, 30, 31

employment-at-will state, 56

loyalty duty/public statements, 101

marital status discrimination, 95, 98

medical records and information, 158

nepotism/favoritism, 95

personnel files

employee access to, 143

security breaches, notification of, 146

private sector employee privacy rights, 47

privileged statements, 50

Arrest record

    background checks, 23–25

    pre-employment inquiries regarding, 18

At-will employment, 54–55, 72

Attorney-client privilege, 140

— **B** —

Background checks, 23–29

    credit record, 26–29

    criminal records, 23–25

    state laws regarding, 24–28

Bankruptcy Act, 26

Bankruptcy Code, 46

Behavior of employees, on-duty and off-duty, 75–76

    dating and fraternization, 77–81, 99

    loyalty, duty of, 101–103

    nepotism/favoritism, 95–99

    office equipment and supplies, personal use of, 90

    personal appearance, 91–94

    public statements by employees, 101–103

    smoking rights, policies, and restrictions, 83–87

    telephone use, 89–90

Blogging, 123–124

Bulletin boards, electronic, 116

— **C** —

California

    computer and e-mail monitoring and use, 119, 124

    constitutional privacy rights, 46

    credit reports, 27

    dating policies, 78, 80

    employment references, 31

    garnishment, termination for, 19

    genetic testing, 36

    marital status discrimination, 98

    medical examinations and inquiries, 33

    medical records and information, 158, 161

    negligent retention, 48

personal appearance policies, 93

personnel files

employee access to, 143, 144

security breaches, notification of, 146–147

private sector employee privacy rights, 47

privileged statements, 50

sexual privacy, heightened protection for, 59

telephone calls, monitoring, 62

video monitoring, 64

wrongful discharge actions, recognition of, 56, 67–68

Charts, tables, and figures. *See* List of figures

Checklists

interviews, 20–21

investigations, 69–74

policies, adopting, 3

sexual harassment investigations, 73–74

Children, pre-employment inquiries regarding, 18

Chronology as investigative technique, 72–73

Citizenship

personnel files, exclusion from, 140

pre-employment inquiries regarding, 19

Civil Rights Act of 1964. *See* Title VII of Civil Rights Act of 1964

Collective bargaining

computer and e-mail use, 112–116

personnel files, 138, 148

searches of personal employee space, 64, 65

Colorado

computer and e-mail monitoring and use, 120, 124

credit reports, 27

criminal records, background checks as to, 24

dating policies, 78, 80

loyalty duty/public statements, 101

marital status discrimination, 96, 98

medical records and information, 158

nepotism/favoritism, 96

personnel files

employee access to, 143

security breaches, notification of, 146

privileged statements, 50

smoking rights, policies, and restrictions, 84

telephone calls, monitoring, 62

wrongful discharge actions, recognition of, 56, 58

Common law

defamation, 48–54, 72

negligent retention, 47–48, 72

privacy rights, 46–47

Compelled self-publication, 49

Computer and e-mail monitoring and use, 105, 107–108

blogging, 123–124

bulletin boards, electronic, 116

casual approach to electronic communications, 110

confidential information, 117–118

copyright infringement, 117–118

cybersmearing, 123–124

defamation suits, 116–117

definition of e-mail as conversation or documentation, 115–116

deletion of messages, misconceptions regarding, 111, 112

discrimination, 111

employee privacy vs. employer property issues, 107–108

federal cases, 108–109, 118–119

federal laws, 118–119

harassment, 111

instant messaging, 125

invasion of privacy, 121–122

PATRIOT Act, 65–67

policies

contents, 127–128

sample policies, 128–134

tips for creating, 125

written policy, need for, 127

preservation of electronically stored information (ESI), 112

protected concerted activity, 112–116

reasons for employers to monitor, 110–111

restrictions and limitations on, 118–122

sample policies, 127–134

searches of hard drives, 113–114

state laws, 109–110, 119–121, 124

trade secrets, 117–118

union solicitations and business, 112–116

Confidential business information, 117–118

Connecticut

AIDS/HIV testing, 33

computer and e-mail monitoring and use, 120, 124

dating policies, 80

drug and alcohol testing, 35

employment references, 30

employment-at-will state, 56

genetic testing, 36

marital status discrimination, 98

medical records and information, 158

personnel files

employee access to, 143, 144

security breaches, notification of, 146

privileged statements, 51

smoking rights, policies, and restrictions, 85

telephone calls, monitoring, 62

Consent of parties to monitoring of telephone conversation, 62

Constitution

due process rights, 43

First Amendment rights, 124

Fourth Amendment, 2, 34, 45

medical records, right to privacy regarding, 153, 154

privacy rights, 2, 45, 153, 154

Consumer Reporting Agency (CRA), 23, 27–29

Consumer reports. *See* Credit record

Controlling employee behavior. *See* Behavior of employees, on-duty and off-duty

Conversations, monitoring

e-mail as conversation or documentation, 115–116

oral conversations, recording, 64

telephone conversations, recording, 61–63

Conviction record

background checks, 23–25

pre-employment inquiries regarding, 18

Copyright infringement, 117–118

CRA (Consumer Reporting Agency), 23, 27–29

Credit record

    background checks, 26–29

    Bankruptcy Act, 26

    Fair and Accurate Credit Transactions Act (FACT Act), 5, 29

    Fair Credit Reporting Act (FCRA), 5, 27–29, 46

    pre-employment inquiries regarding, 19

    State laws on credit reports, 27

Criminal record

    background checks, 23–25

    pre-employment inquiries regarding, 18

Cybersmearing, 123–124

—— **D** ——

Date of birth, pre-employment inquiries regarding, 18

Dating and fraternization, 77–81, 99

Defamation, 48–54, 72

    compelled self-publication, 49

    computer and e-mail monitoring and use, 116–117

    elements of, 48

    false light invasion of privacy, 49

    privileged statements, 49–54

Delaware

    background check requirements, 26

    dating policies, 80

    employment-at-will state, 56

    genetic testing, 36

    marital status discrimination, 98

    negligent retention, 47

    personnel files

        employee access to, 143, 144

        exclusion of documents from, 140

        security breaches, notification of, 146

    telephone calls, monitoring, 62

Department of Health and Human Services (HHS), 155–157

Disability. *See* also Americans With Disabilities Act of 1990

    medical examinations and inquiries, 32–33

    pre-employment inquiries regarding, 19

Disclosure of employee records, 135

    Medical records. *See* Medical records and information

    Personnel files. *See* Personnel files

Discrimination

    Age Discrimination in Employment Act of 1967 (ADEA), 5, 17, 41

    computer and e-mail monitoring and use, 111

    disability. *See* Americans With Disabilities Act of 1990

    Familial status discrimination, Michigan's prohibition of, 18

    Kansas Act Against Discrimination, 17

    marital status discrimination

        nepotism/favoritism policies, 95–99

        pre-employment inquiries, 20

    National origin discrimination. *See* National origin discrimination

    personal appearance policies viewed as, 91–94

    race discrimination, 91–94

    religious discrimination, 92

    sex discrimination, 91–94. *See* also Sexual harassment

Disparate impact of honesty and personality tests, 41

Distribution of union literature via e-mail or Internet, 112–116

District of Columbia

    dating policies, 80

    employment-at-will state, 56

    marital status discrimination, 98

    medical examinations and inquiries, 33

    personal appearance, discrimination based on, 20

    personnel files, employee access to, 143

    smoking rights, policies, and restrictions, 83, 85

    telephone calls, monitoring, 62

Drug abuse, 33–35, 162

Drug-Free Workplace Act of 1988, 5

Due process, 43

—— **E** ——

E-mail. *See* Computer and e-mail monitoring and use

EAPs (employee assistance programs), 162

ECPA (Electronic Communications Privacy Act of 1986), 118–119

EEOC. *See* Equal Employment Opportunity Commission (EEOC)

Electronic Communications Privacy Act of 1986 (ECPA), 118–119

Electronic workplace. *See* Computer and e-mail monitoring and use

Electronically stored information (ESI), preservation of, 112

Employee assistance programs (EAPs), 162

Employee behavior, controlling. *See* Behavior of employees, on-duty and off-duty

Employee Polygraph Protection Act of 1988 (EPPA), 5 37, 46

Employee records, 135

    Medical records. *See* Medical records and information

    Personnel files. *See* Personnel files

Employment eligibility, verification of, 19, 140

Employment law generally, privacy concerns raised by, 1–2

Employment references, 29–32

Employment-at-will, 54–55, 72

English-only rules, 20

EPPA (Employee Polygraph Protection Act of 1988), 5, 37, 46

Equal Employment Opportunity Commission (EEOC)

    ADA enforcement guidance, Appendix I

    favoritism, 99

    genetic testing, 36

    medical records, guidelines on disclosing, 154

    personal appearance, 91–92

    personnel file information, access to, 148

    pre-employment inquiries, guidance on, Appendix I

pre-employment inquiry guidelines, 15–16

Equal employment opportunity statement on application form, 16

ESI (electronically stored information), preservation of, 112

Executive Orders 11246 and 11141, 17

— **F** —

Fair and Accurate Credit Transactions Act (FACT Act), 5, 29

Fair Credit Reporting Act (FCRA), 5, 27–29, 46, Appendix II

Fair Labor Standards Act (FLSA), 138, 141

False light invasion of privacy, 49

Familial status, pre-employment inquiries regarding, 18

Family and Medical Leave Act (FMLA), 6

    medical records, 153, 154

    personnel files, 138, 139, 141

Favoritism, 95–99

FCRA (Fair Credit Reporting Act), 5, 27–29, 46, Appendix II

Federal laws, 5–7, *See also* specific statutes

    computer and e-mail monitoring restrictions, 108–109, 118–119

    medical records and information, 153–157, 155–157

    personnel files, 138

        contents, 139–140

        government access to files, 148–150

        retention requirements, 141

    telephone conversations, recording, 61–62

Figures, tables, and charts. *See* List of figures

First Amendment rights, 124

Florida

    AIDS/HIV testing, 33

    background check requirements, 26

    computer and e-mail monitoring and use, 120

    criminal records, background checks as to, 24

    dating policies, 80

    employment-at-will state, 56

    false light invasion of privacy, 49

    genetic testing, 36

    lie detectors/polygraph tests, 28

    loyalty duty/public statements, 102

    marital status discrimination, 98

    medical records and information, 158

    personnel files

        employee access to, 143

        security breaches, notification of, 146

    private sector employee privacy rights, 47

    privileged statements, 51

    telephone calls, monitoring, 62

FLSA (Fair Labor Standards Act), 138, 141

FMLA. *See* Family and Medical Leave Act

Forms

    application forms, 15–16

    Fair Credit Reporting Act (FRCA) forms, Appendix II

    I-9 forms, exclusion from personnel files, 140

Fourth Amendment rights, 2, 34, 46

Fraternization and dating, 77–81, 99

Free speech rights, 124

— G —

Garnishment, pre-employment inquiries regarding, 19

Genetic testing, 35–36

Georgia

    background check requirements, 26

    computer and e-mail monitoring and use, 119–120, 120

    criminal records, background checks as to, 24

    dating policies, 80

    employment-at-will state, 56

    marital status discrimination, 98

    medical records and information, 158

    personal appearance policies, 92

    personnel files

        employee access to, 143

        security breaches, notification of, 146

    privileged statements, 51

    telephone calls, monitoring, 62

Government

    federal laws. *See* Federal laws, and specific statutes

    personnel files, requests for information from, 148–150

    state laws. *See* State laws, and individual states

Grooming and appearance, 91–94

— H —

Hair, rules regarding, 91–94

Harassment

    computer and e-mail monitoring for, 111

    sexual. *See* Sexual harassment

Hawaii

    criminal records, background checks as to, 24

    dating policies, 80

    employment-at-will state, 56

    marital status discrimination, 98

    medical records and information, 159, 161–162

    personnel files

        employee access to, 143

        security breaches, notification of, 146, 147

    private sector employee privacy rights, 47

privileged statements, 51

smoking rights, policies, and restrictions, 83

telephone calls, monitoring, 62

video monitoring, 64

Health and Human Services Department (HHS), 155–157

Health care records. *See* Medical records and information

Health inquiries. *See* Medical examinations and inquiries

Health Insurance Portability and Accountability Act (HIPAA), 6

investigations, 46

medical records, 153, 155–157

personnel records, 138, 139, 146

privacy terms used by, 157

Height and weight requirements, 20

HHS (Department of Health and Human Services), 155–157

HIPAA. *See* Health Insurance Portability and Accountability Act

Hiring practices. *See* Recruitment and hiring practices

HIV/AIDS testing, 33

Homeland Security Act, 6, 57

Honesty tests, 40–41

—— **I** ——

I-9 forms, 140

Idaho

criminal records, background checks as to, 24

dating policies, 80

drug and alcohol testing, 35

employment references, 30

employment-at-will state, 56

lie detectors/polygraph tests, 38

marital status discrimination, 98

personnel files

employee access to, 143

security breaches, notification of, 146

privileged statements, 51

telephone calls, monitoring, 62

Identity theft, 145–148

Illinois

AIDS/HIV testing, 33

background check requirements, 25

dating policies, 80

employment-at-will state, 56

genetic testing, 36

lie detectors/polygraph tests, 38

marital status discrimination, 98

medical examinations and inquiries, 33

medical records and information, 159

personnel files

employee access to, 143, 144

exclusion of documents from, 140–141

security breaches, notification of, 146

private sector employee privacy rights, 47

privileged statements, 51

telephone calls, monitoring, 62

IM (instant messaging), 125

Immigrant status

personnel files, exclusion from, 140

pre-employment inquiries regarding, 19

Immigration Reform and Control Act (IRCA), 6, 17, 19

Indiana

dating policies, 80

employment-at-will state, 56

marital status discrimination, 98

personnel files, employee access to, 143

security of personnel files, notification of breaches of, 146

Instant messaging (IM), 125

Internet. *See* Computer and e-mail monitoring and use

Interviews, investigative, 70–71

Interviews, job applicants, 16–21

checklist, 20–21

pre-employment inquiries to avoid in, 18–20

Invasion of privacy

computer and e-mail monitoring and use, 121–122

false light invasion of privacy, 49

investigations, 72

Investigations, 43

accused person, importance of interviewing, 70–71

checklist, 69–74

chronology, use of, 72–73

common law rights, 46–54

due process, 43

interviews, conducting, 70–71

invasion of privacy, 72

liability issues, 45–59, 72

loose lips litigation, avoiding, 71–72

open mind, importance of, 69–70

searches of personal employee space, 64–65

sexual harassment, 48, 58–59, 73–74

surveillance and monitoring practices, 61–67

suspension pending, 73

who, what, where, when, and why; nailing down, 71

Iowa

compelled self-publication, 49

dating policies, 80

employment-at-will state, 56

false light invasion of privacy, 49

genetic testing, 36

marital status discrimination, 96, 98

nepotism/favoritism, 96

personnel files, employee access to, 143

private sector employee privacy rights, 47

telephone calls, monitoring, 62

IRCA (Immigration Reform and Control Act), 6, 17, 19

—— **J** ——

Job application forms, 15–16

Job Interviews. *See* Interviews, job applicants

Just cause to terminate, 54–55

—— **K** ——

Kansas

Act Against Discrimination, 17

credit reports, 27

criminal records, background checks as to, 24, 25

dating policies, 80

employment references, 30

employment-at-will state, 56

genetic testing, 36

marital status discrimination, 96, 98

medical examinations and inquiries, 33

nepotism/favoritism, 96

personnel files

 employee access to, 143

 security breaches, notification of, 146

Kentucky

dating policies, 80

employment-at-will state, 56

marital status discrimination, 98

negligent retention, 47

personal appearance policies, 93

personnel files, employee access to, 143

privileged statements, 51

smoking rights, policies, and restrictions, 85

telephone calls, monitoring, 62

Knowledge-testing quiz, 9–12

— L —

Labor unions

computer and e-mail use, 112–116

personnel files, 138, 148

searches of personal employee space, 64, 65

Language

Inappropriate e-mail language in context of protected concerted activity, 112–116

proficiency requirements and English-only rules, 20

Lie detectors, 37–40

Employee Polygraph Protection Act of 1988 (EPPA), 5, 37, 46

state laws, 38–40

Long-hair rules, 91–92, 93

Loose lips litigation, 71–72

Louisiana

background check requirements, 26

dating policies, 78, 80

drug and alcohol testing, 34

employment-at-will state, 56

genetic testing, 36

lie detectors/polygraph tests, 38

loyalty duty/public statements, 102

marital status discrimination, 96, 98

medical records and information, 159

nepotism/favoritism, 96

personnel files

employee access to, 143

security breaches, notification of, 146, 147

private sector employee privacy rights, 47

privileged statements, 51

smoking rights, policies, and restrictions, 85

telephone calls, monitoring, 62

Loyalty, duty of, 101–103

—— **M** ——

Mail Tampering Act, 46

Mail, opening, 64

Maine

credit reports, 27

dating policies, 80

drug and alcohol testing, 35

employment references, 31

employment-at-will state, 56

lie detectors/polygraph tests, 38

marital status discrimination, 98

personnel files

employee access to, 143, 144

security breaches, notification of, 146, 147

private sector employee privacy rights, 47

privileged statements, 52

smoking rights, policies, and restrictions, 83, 85

telephone calls, monitoring, 62

Marital status discrimination

nepotism/favoritism policies, 95–99

pre-employment inquiries, 20

state laws, 95–99

Maryland

    background check requirements, 26

    criminal records, background checks as to, 25

    dating policies, 80

    employment-at-will state, 56

    lie detectors/polygraph tests, 38–39

    marital status discrimination, 98

    medical examinations and inquiries, 33

    personal appearance policies, 93

    personnel files

        employee access to, 143

        Social Security numbers, use of, 147

    private sector employee privacy rights, 47

    privileged statements, 52

    smoking rights, policies, and restrictions, 83

    Social Security numbers, use of, 147

    telephone calls, monitoring, 62

Massachusetts

    computer and e-mail monitoring cases, 110

    criminal records, background checks as to, 25

    dating policies, 80

    employment-at-will state, 56

    marital status discrimination, 98

    medical examinations and inquiries, 33

    medical records and information, 159

    personnel files, employee access to, 143, 144

    private sector employee privacy rights, 47

    privileged statements, 52

    telephone calls, monitoring, 62

    video monitoring, 64

Medical examinations and inquiries, 32–36

    AIDS/HIV testing, 33

    alcohol use and abuse, 33–35

    disability, 32–33

    drug abuse, 33–35

    genetic testing, 35–36

    personality test considered as medical examination, 41

    pre-employment inquiries, 19

state laws, 32–36

substance abuse, 33–35

Medical records and information, 153–162

Constitutional right to privacy regarding, 153, 154

defined, 155

employee assistance programs (EAPs), 162

federal laws, 153–157, 155–157

personnel files, excluded from, 139–140

state laws, 157–162

Michigan

AIDS/HIV testing, 33

dating policies, 80

employment references, 31

employment-at-will state, 56

false light invasion of privacy, 49

familial status discrimination, prohibition of, 18

height and weight, pre-employment inquiries regarding, 20

marital status discrimination, 98

personal appearance policies, 93

personnel files

employee access to, 143, 144

exclusion of documents from, 141

Social Security numbers, use of, 147

private sector employee privacy rights, 47

privileged statements, 52

Social Security numbers, use of, 147

telephone calls, monitoring, 62

Miller Brewing Company sexual harassment case stemming from Seinfeld episode, 58–59

Mini-privacy acts, state, 46

Minnesota

computer and e-mail monitoring and use, 113

dating policies, 80

employment-at-will state, 56

marital status discrimination, 98

personnel files

employee access to, 143, 144

exclusion of documents from, 141

security breaches, notification of, 146

Mississippi

    background check requirements, 26

    dating policies, 80

    loyalty duty/public statements, 102

    marital status discrimination, 96, 98

    medical records and information, 159

    nepotism/favoritism, 96

    personnel files, employee access to, 143

    private sector employee privacy rights, 47

    privileged statements, 52

    smoking rights, policies, and restrictions, 85

    telephone calls, monitoring, 63

Missouri

    credit reports, 27

    criminal records, background checks as to, 25

    dating policies, 80

    employment-at-will state, 56

    genetic testing, 36

    marital status discrimination, 98

    personnel files, employee access to, 143

    privileged statements, 52

    smoking rights, policies, and restrictions, 83–84

    telephone calls, monitoring, 62

Monitoring and surveillance practices, 61–67. *See also* Computer and e-mail monitoring and use

Montana

    dating policies, 80

    drug and alcohol testing, 35

    marital status discrimination, 96, 98

    negligent retention, 47

    nepotism/favoritism, 96

    personnel files

        employee access to, 143

        security breaches, notification of, 146

    private sector employee privacy rights, 47

    privileged statements, 52

    smoking rights, policies, and restrictions, 85

    telephone calls, monitoring, 62

    wrongful discharge actions, recognition of, 56, 58

—— N ——

National Labor Relations Act (NLRA), 5–6

    computer and e-mail monitoring and use, 112–113

    investigations, 46

    loyalty duty/public statements, 102

    personnel records, 148

    screening, 34

National origin discrimination

    language proficiency questions regarded as, 20

    personal appearance policies as, 91–94

    personnel files, information excluded from, 140

    pre-employment inquiries regarding citizenship or country of birth, 19

Nebraska

    computer and e-mail monitoring and use, 120–121

    dating policies, 80

    drug and alcohol testing, 35

    employment-at-will state, 56

    false light invasion of privacy, 49

    genetic testing, 36

    lie detectors/polygraph tests, 39

    marital status discrimination, 96, 98

    medical examinations and inquiries, 33

    medical records and information, 159

    nepotism/favoritism, 96

    personnel files

        employee access to, 143

        security breaches, notification of, 146

    private sector employee privacy rights, 47

    telephone calls, monitoring, 62

Negligent retention, 47–48, 72

Nepotism, 95–99

Nevada

    background check requirements, 26

    dating policies, 80

    employment references, 31

    employment-at-will state, 56

    genetic testing, 36

    marital status discrimination, 96, 98

nepotism/favoritism, 96

personnel files

    employee access to, 143, 144

    security breaches, notification of, 146

    private sector employee privacy rights, 47

    smoking rights, policies, and restrictions, 85

    telephone calls, monitoring, 62

New Hampshire

dating policies, 80

employment-at-will state, 56

genetic testing, 36

marital status discrimination, 96, 98

medical records and information, 159

nepotism/favoritism, 96

personal appearance policies, 93

personnel files

    employee access to, 143

    security breaches, notification of, 146, 147

private sector employee privacy rights, 47

privileged statements, 52

smoking rights, policies, and restrictions, 85

telephone calls, monitoring, 62

video monitoring, 64

New Jersey

criminal records, background checks as to, 25

dating policies, 80

drug and alcohol testing, 35

employment-at-will state, 56

genetic testing, 36

lie detectors/polygraph tests, 39

loyalty duty/public statements, 102

marital status discrimination, 97, 98

nepotism/favoritism, 97

personnel files

    employee access to, 143

    security breaches, notification of, 146, 147

privileged statements, 52

smoking rights, policies, and restrictions, 83

telephone calls, monitoring, 63

video monitoring, 63

New Mexico

background check requirements, 26

credit reports, 27

dating policies, 80

employment-at-will state, 56

genetic testing, 36

loyalty duty/public statements, 102

marital status discrimination, 98

medical records and information, 160

personnel files

employee access to, 143

state government access to, 148

telephone calls, monitoring, 63

New York

computer and e-mail monitoring and use, 124

credit reports, 27

criminal records, background checks as to, 25

dating policies, 78–79, 80

employment-at-will state, 54, 56

genetic testing, 36

lie detectors/polygraph tests, 39

loyalty duty/public statements, 102

mail, opening, 64

marital status discrimination, 97, 98

medical records and information, 160

nepotism/favoritism, 97

personal appearance policies, 93

personnel files

employee access to, 142, 143

security breaches, notification of, 146, 147

state government access to, 148

privileged statements, 52

searches of personal employee space, 65

smoking rights, policies, and restrictions, 83, 84, 85

telephone calls, monitoring, 62

unpaid wages claims, 142

video monitoring, 63

NLRA. *See* National Labor Relations Act

No fraternization policies, 77–81, 99

North Carolina

    dating policies, 80

    employment-at-will state, 56

    genetic testing, 36

    marital status discrimination, 98

    personnel files

        employee access to, 143

        security breaches, notification of, 146, 147

        state government access to, 148

    private sector employee privacy rights, 47

    privileged statements, 53

    smoking rights, policies, and restrictions, 85

    telephone calls, monitoring, 62

North Dakota

    dating policies, 80

    employment-at-will state, 56

    marital status discrimination, 98

    personnel files

        employee access to, 143

        security breaches, notification of, 146

    smoking rights, policies, and restrictions, 83, 85

—— O ——

Occupational Safety and Health Administration (OSHA) and OSH Act, 140, 141

Off-duty employee behavior, controlling. *See* Behavior of employees, on-duty and off-duty

Office equipment and supplies, personal use of, 90

Ohio

    AIDS/HIV testing, 33

    background check requirements, 26

    computer and e-mail monitoring and use, 121

    criminal records, background checks as to, 24

    dating policies, 77, 80

    employment-at-will state, 56

    false light invasion of privacy, 49

    marital status discrimination, 98

medical records and information, 160

negligent retention, 48

personnel files, employee access to, 143

private sector employee privacy rights, 47

privileged statements, 53

security of personnel files, notification of breaches of, 146

telephone calls, monitoring, 62

Oklahoma

dating policies, 80

employment-at-will state, 56

genetic testing, 36

marital status discrimination, 97, 98

negligent retention, 47

nepotism/favoritism, 97

personnel files

employee access to, 143

security breaches, notification of, 146

smoking rights, policies, and restrictions, 85

telephone calls, monitoring, 63

Omnibus Crime Control and Safe Streets Act, 6, 46, 61

On-duty employee behavior, controlling. *See* Behavior of employees, on-duty and off-duty

Oregon

conversations at work, monitoring, 63

criminal records, background checks as to, 24

dating policies, 80

employment-at-will state, 56

genetic testing, 36

marital status discrimination, 97, 98

medical records and information, 160

nepotism/favoritism, 97

personnel files, employee access to, 143, 144

privileged statements, 53

smoking rights, policies, and restrictions, 85

telephone calls, monitoring, 62

OSHA (Occupational Safety and Health Administration) and OSH Act, 140, 141

—— P ——

PATRIOT Act (Uniting and Strengthening America by Providing Appropriate Tools
Required to Intercept and Obstruct Terrorism Act), 6, 43, 65–67

Pennsylvania

    computer and e-mail monitoring cases, 109–110

    dating policies, 80

    employment-at-will state, 56

    lie detectors/polygraph tests, 39

    marital status discrimination, 98

    personnel files

        employee access to, 143, 144

        security breaches, notification of, 146

    telephone calls, monitoring, 62

Personality tests, 40–41

Personnel files, 137–151

    access by employees to, 142–144

    contents, 139–141

    defined, 138

    employees' access to, 142–144

    excluded documents, 139–141

    federal laws, 138

        contents, 139–140

        government access to files, 148–150

        retention requirements, 141

    former employees' access to, 144–145

    government requests for information, 148–150

    I-9 forms, exclusion of, 140

    identity theft, 145–148

    medical records excluded from, 139–140

    national origin and immigration documentation, exclusion of, 140

    notification of security breaches, 146–147

    OSHA records, exclusion of, 140

    privileged information, exclusion of, 140

    retention of records, 141–142

    Social Security numbers, use of, 147–148

    state laws

        employee access, 142–144

        exclusions allowed by, 140–141

government access to files, 148

retention requirements, 141–142

unofficial, 139

Policies

checklist for adopting, 3

computer and e-mail monitoring and use. *See* under Computer and e-mail monitoring and use

need for, 2–3

sample policies. *See* Sample policies

Polygraph tests, 37–40

Employee Polygraph Protection Act of 1988 (EPPA), 5, 37, 46

state laws, 38–40

Post Office, U.S.

Mail Tampering Act, 46

opening U.S. mail, 64

Pre-employment inquiries, 15–21

application forms, 15–16

checklist, 20–21

disability-related questions, 19

EEOC and state guidance on, 15–16, Appendix I

interviews, 16–21

subjects to avoid, 18–20

Pregnancy, pre-employment inquiries regarding, 18

Preservation of electronically stored information (ESI), 112

Privacy Act of 1974, 46

Private sector employee privacy rights, state laws recognizing, 47

Privileged statements, 49–54, 140

Property interest of employers in computer systems, 107–108

Provider exception to telephone call monitoring, 62

Public policy violations, 55

Public statements by employees, 101–103

—— **Q** ——

Quiz on employment law knowledge, 9–12

—— **R** ——

Race discrimination, personal appearance policies as, 91–94

Records, employee, 135

Medical records. *See* Medical records and information

Personnel files. *See* Personnel files

Recruitment and hiring practices, 13

application forms, 15–16

checklist, 20–21

Interviews, 16–21

pre-employment inquiries, 15–21

screening candidates, 23–41

References, 29–32

Rehabilitation Act of 1973, 17

Religious discrimination, personal appearance policies as, 92

Retention of employees, negligent, 47–48, 72

Retention of personnel records, 141–142

Rhode Island

dating policies, 80

drug and alcohol testing, 35

employment references, 31

employment-at-will state, 56

genetic testing, 36

honesty tests, 40

marital status discrimination, 98

medical records and information, 160

personnel files

employee access to, 143, 144

security breaches, notification of, 146

private sector employee privacy rights, 47

privileged statements, 53

smoking rights, policies, and restrictions, 85

telephone calls, monitoring, 62

Right to work, verification of, 19

Romantic relationships between employees, 77–81, 99

— **S** —

Sample policies

computer and e-mail monitoring and use, 128–134

dating/no-fraternization, 81

office equipment and supplies, personal use of, 90

personal appearance policies, 94

personnel files, employee access to, 150–151

telephone use, 90

Saturday work hours, pre-employment inquiries regarding, 18

Screening, 23–41

background checks, 23–29

employment references, 29–32

honesty tests, 40–41

lie detectors, 37–40

medical examinations and inquiries, 32–36

personality tests, 40–41

polygraph tests, 37–40

Searches of personal employee space, 64–65, 113–114

Security

HIPAA requirements, 156

personnel files, notification of breaches of, 146–147

Seinfeld, sexual harassment case stemming from, 58–59

Self-publication, compelled, 49

Sex discrimination, personal appearance policies as, 91–94

Sexual harassment

accuser and accused, privacy concerns of, 58–59

checklist for investigating, 73–74

computer and e-mail monitoring for, 111

dating/fraternization policies, 77–81, 99

favoritism as form of, 99

negligent retention, 48

Seinfeld, Miller Brewing Company case stemming from, 58–59

Sexual relationships between employees, 77–81, 99

Smoking rights, policies, and restrictions, 83–87

Social Security numbers, 147–148

Solicitation via e-mail or Internet, 112–116

South Carolina

computer and e-mail monitoring, 121

dating policies, 79, 80

employment-at-will state, 56

invasion of privacy, 121

marital status discrimination, 98

medical records and information, 160

negligent retention, 47

personnel files, employee access to, 143

private sector employee privacy rights, 47

privileged statements, 53

smoking rights, policies, and restrictions, 86

telephone calls, monitoring, 63

South Dakota

dating policies, 80

employment-at-will state, 56

marital status discrimination, 98

personnel files, employee access to, 143

Spamming as form of harassment, 111

Speech, freedom of, 124

State laws. *See also* individual states

AIDS/HIV testing, 33

alcohol use and abuse, 34–35

at-will employment, 54–55

compelled self-publication, 49

computer and e-mail monitoring and use, 109–110, 119–121, 124

credit reports, 27

criminal background information, 23–25

dating policies, 78–81

defamation, 48–54

drug abuse, 34–35

employment references, 30–30–31

employment-at-will, 54–55

false light invasion of privacy, 49

genetic testing, 36

lie detectors, 38–40

loyalty, duty of, 101–102

marital status discrimination, 95–99

medical examinations and inquiries, 32–36

medical records and information, 157–162

mini-privacy acts, 46

negligent retention, 47–48

nepotism/favoritism, 95–99

personal appearance policies, 92–94

personnel files. *See* under Personnel files

polygraph tests, 38–40

pre-employment inquiries, guidance on, Appendix I

privacy rights, 2, 45, 46

privileged statements, 49–54

public statements by employees, 101–102

searches of personal employee space, 64–65

smoking rights, policies, and restrictions, 83–87

substance abuse, 34–35

telephone conversations, recording, 62–63

video monitoring, 63–64

wrongful discharge actions, recognition of, 55–58

Substance abuse, 5, 33–35, 162

Sunday work hours, pre-employment inquiries regarding, 18

Surveillance and monitoring practices, 61–67. *See also* Computer and e-mail monitoring and use

Suspension pending investigation, 73

— **T** —

Tables, charts, and figures. See List of figures

Telephones

employee use policies, 89–90

monitoring and recording conversations, 61–63

Tennessee

background check requirements, 26

dating policies, 80

employment references, 31

employment-at-will state, 56

lie detectors/polygraph tests, 39–40

loyalty duty/public statements, 102

marital status discrimination, 97, 98

medical records and information, 160

nepotism/favoritism, 97

personnel files

employee access to, 143

security breaches, notification of, 146

private sector employee privacy rights, 47

privileged statements, 53

smoking rights, policies, and restrictions, 86

telephone calls, monitoring, 62

Termination of employment, 54–58

Test on employment law knowledge, 9–12

Texas

    background check requirements, 26

    compelled self-publication, 49

    computer and e-mail monitoring cases, 109

    dating policies, 79, 80

    employment-at-will state, 56

    genetic testing, 36

    marital status discrimination, 98

    medical records and information, 161

    personnel files

        employee access to, 143

        security breaches, notification of, 146

    private sector employee privacy rights, 47

    privileged statements, 53

    telephone calls, monitoring, 63

Title VII of Civil Rights Act of 1964, 5, 7

    appearance and grooming, 91, 92

    nepotism/favoritism, 95, 99

    personnel files, 148

    pre-employment inquiries, 17

    screening, 34, 41

Trade secrets, 117–118

—— **U** ——

U.S. Post Office

    Mail Tampering Act, 46

    opening mail, 64

Unions

    computer and e-mail use, 112–116

    personnel files, 138

    searches of personal employee space, 64, 65

Uniting and Strengthening America by Providing Appropriate Tools Required to Intercept and Obstruct Terrorism Act (USA PATRIOT Act), 6, 43, 65–67

Utah

    dating policies, 80

    employment references, 31

employment-at-will state, 56

lie detectors/polygraph tests, 40

marital status discrimination, 98

personnel files

    employee access to, 143

    security breaches, notification of, 146

privileged statements, 53

telephone calls, monitoring, 62, 63

video monitoring, 64

— V —

Verification of eligibility for employment, 19

Vermont

    AIDS/HIV testing, 33

    compelled self-publication, 49

    dating policies, 80

    employment-at-will state, 56

    genetic testing, 36

    lie detectors/polygraph tests, 40

    marital status discrimination, 98

    negligent retention, 47

    personnel files

        employee access to, 143

        security breaches, notification of, 146

        state government access to, 148

    private sector employee privacy rights, 47

    telephone calls, monitoring, 63

Video monitoring, 63–64

Virginia

    background check requirements, 26

    computer and e-mail monitoring cases, 111

    dating policies, 80

    employment references, 31

    employment-at-will state, 56

    marital status discrimination, 98

    personnel files, employee access to, 143

    privileged statements, 53

    smoking rights, policies, and restrictions, 86

— **W** —

Washington

    AIDS/HIV testing, 33

    dating policies, 80

    employment references, 31

    employment-at-will state, 56

    lie detectors/polygraph tests, 40

    marital status discrimination, 97, 98

    nepotism/favoritism, 97

    personnel files, employee access to, 143, 144

    privileged statements, 54

    smoking rights, policies, and restrictions, 84

    telephone calls, monitoring, 62

Weekend hours, pre-employment inquiries regarding, 18

Weight and height requirements, 20

Weingarten rights, 65

West Virginia

    dating policies, 80

    employment-at-will state, 56

    marital status discrimination, 98

    personnel files, employee access to, 143

Wiretapping law, federal, 61–62

Wisconsin

    AIDS/HIV testing, 33

    computer and e-mail monitoring and use, 121

    criminal records, background checks as to, 25

    dating policies, 80

    employment-at-will state, 56

    genetic testing, 36

    invasion of privacy, 121

    lie detectors/polygraph tests, 40

    mail, opening, 64

    marital status discrimination, 97, 98

    medical records and information, 161

    nepotism/favoritism, 97

    personal appearance policies, 94

    personnel files, employee access to, 143, 144

    private sector employee privacy rights, 47

      privileged statements, 54

      smoking rights, policies, and restrictions, 86

      telephone calls, monitoring, 62

Workplace appearance, 91–94

Workplace investigations. *See* Investigations

Workplace records, 135

      Medical records. *See* Medical records and information

      Personnel files. *See* Personnel files

Wrongful discharge actions, 54–58, 72

Wyoming

      computer and e-mail monitoring and use, 121

      dating policies, 80

      employment-at-will state, 56

      marital status discrimination, 98

      personnel files, employee access to, 143

      privileged statements, 54

      smoking rights, policies, and restrictions, 86

      telephone calls, monitoring, 62

Practical, Time-Tested Guidance For HR and Benefits Professionals —

ADA Compliance Guide
Helps employers understand, step-by-step, what they can and cannot do in their practices under the sweeping Americans with Disabilities Act.

Thompson's Employee Handbook Builder
Create an expert employee handbook... completely online... in about an hour... and at a fraction of what an attorney or consultant charges.

Family and Medical Leave Handbook
Comprehensive guidance on the FMLA to help employers manage employee leave, reduce costs and minimize workplace disruption.

Fair Labor Standards Handbook for States, Local Governments and Schools
Offers public employers timely news, cost-effective guidance and expert analysis of federal wage and hour requirements under the FLSA.

Thompson's HR Employment Forms
Gathers over 300 HR forms, covering everything from hiring to retirement, in one easy to use resource- also includes a CD with electronic versions of every form in the book so that you can customize the forms to meet your specific needs.

Employer's Guide to Military Leave Compliance
Explains employers' responsibilities under the Uniformed Services Employment and Reemployment Rights Act (USERRA), including the December 2005 final regulations.

Employer's Guide to the Fair Labor Standards Act
Helps employers determine which employees are covered by the FLSA, compute overtime compensation, understand what constitutes hours worked and properly maintain employee records.

Employer's Guide to the Health Insurance Portability and Accountability Act
Explains HIPAA's portability provisions, including pre-existing condition exclusions, creditable coverage, special enrollment provisions, certificates of coverage, and more.

The Leave and Disability Coordination Handbook
Helps employers coordinate employee leave under the ADA, FMLA and state workers' compensation laws.

Public Employer's Guide to FLSA Employee Classification
Shows public employers how to properly classify employees, understand the executive, administrative, professional and other exemptions, and find remedies for a misclassification.

FLSA Employee Exemption Handbook
Enables private-sector employers to properly classify employees under the FLSA and other relevant federal laws.

Guide to Consumer-Directed Health Care
Shows employers how to save money and improve health through a combination of account-based and health and wellness programs, including the experience of early adopters.

HR Question and Answer Book
While most of the other question and answer books deal with generic hiring and firing issues, Thompson's *HR Question and Answer Book* covers the entire employment relationship with over 200 real questions. Not only does it answer your questions quickly and thoroughly, it provides you with the tools to move forward in the right direction.

Workplace Accommodations Under the ADA
Helps employers to understand their obligations under the Americans with Disabilities Act and provides practical solutions to effectively handle accommodation requests from individuals with disabilities.

Investigating Sexual Harassment: A Practical Guide to Resolving Complaints
Provides advice for employers on thoroughly investigating and resolving sexual harassment complaints under the evolving body of sexual harassment law.

HR Guide to Business Continuity Planning
Walks you through the planning process by providing strategies and expert guidance on how to implement your plan correctly and minimize the risks associated with an unexpected interruption.

Labor and Employment Law: The Employer's Compliance Guide
Uniquely organized around the employee life-cycle, the *Guide* provides instant access to key text and accurate answers on employment laws and regulations.

Understanding and Preventing Workplace Retaliation
Describes the many forms retaliation can take and provides practical advice for safeguarding against incidents.

Domestic Partner Benefits: An Employer's Guide
With an implementation strategy, model documents and much more, this resource is designed to guide you through the process of establishing and running a domestic partner program.

To start your RISK-FREE trial subscription:
- call toll-free: 1-800-677-3789
- order online at: www.thompson.com

 THOMPSON

HR0707